THE QUEEN OF INDIAN POP

ADVANCE PRAISE FOR THE BOOK

'I've enjoyed a long and abiding friendship with Usha Uthup, and this book shares the gifts of her friendship with the world—her tenacity, charm, wit and compassion are woven through its pages. Vikas Kumar Jha's compelling narrative and immersive storytelling confirm what I have long known: Usha's legacy is more than her extraordinary musical talent. It is also the grace, fearlessness and wisdom with which she lives her life'—Shashi Tharoor, member of Parliament

'Usha Uthup is a timeless treasure. I am unequivocally her biggest fan since my teenage years. I am fortunate to be counted as a dear friend. This biography is a piece of history that will always remind us of Usha's majestic persona'—Kiran Mazumdar-Shaw, founder and chairperson, Biocon

'Usha is Calcutta and Calcutta is Usha. But unlike my home city, even though she triggers nostalgia for those swinging times, she isn't suspended in that formaldehyde. She has continued to reinvent herself, making herself as relevant to Generations X and Y as she is to their parents and grandparents. One thing remains unchanged. When she's belting out those numbers in her smoky voice, you'd better keep that extinguisher handy, because she never fails to set the stage on fire. Personally, I've known her ever since I wrote about her in the *Junior Statesman*. The article was titled "Pop Goes the Iyer" . . . Over the years, our acquaintance has deepened into friendship and beyond. Usha is among the warmest, most genuine, most generous people I know. If you think I'm showing off about being so close to her, come to one of her shows, and you will hear her hollering out to me if I'm in the audience. Love you, Usha, "kaw" bindi, silver bangles, brocade sneakers and all'—Bachi Karkaria, journalist and columnist

'I first heard Usha at the Talk of the Town. She was unique and not just a singer with a mic. So different in many ways. I would say she had the "Usha stamp" all over her! She truly is the queen of Indian pop music'—Waheeda Rehman, actor

'It is a joy to watch Usha sing. She makes us sing along. She is all life, colour and gaiety . . . Coming from a traditional south Indian family, she broke the stigma of singing at nightclubs or doing Western music, while always maintaining her Indianness: her colourful sarees, jewellery and the bindi. Not to forget, she and I share a relationship with the police uniform!'—Kiran Bedi, twenty-fourth lieutenant governor of Puducherry and former IPS officer

'Field marshals, industrialists, royalty, film stars and singers, too, have sat as her audience, absorbing every single musical note, lyric, joke and heartfelt anecdote when she performed. I sat as a ten-year-old at the base of the stage, watching performer and audience together. And I learnt much of what I know today, right there. Her words to this ten-year-old still ring in my ears: "Sing Elvis, Sinatra, Reeves or Ray Charles . . . But make the song yours! Always be an original." Thank you, Usha. There is no other like you'—Boman Irani, actor

THE QUEEN OF INDIAN POP

THE AUTHORIZED BIOGRAPHY OF

USHA UTHUP

VIKAS KUMAR JHA

TRANSLATED BY **SRISHTI JHA**

EBURY
PRESS

An imprint of Penguin Random House

EBURY PRESS

USA | Canada | UK | Ireland | Australia
New Zealand | India | South Africa | China | Singapore

Ebury Press is part of the Penguin Random House group of companies
whose addresses can be found at global.penguinrandomhouse.com

Published by Penguin Random House India Pvt. Ltd
4th Floor, Capital Tower 1, MG Road,
Gurugram 122 002, Haryana, India

First published in Ebury Press by Penguin Random House India 2022

ISBN 9780670095872

Typeset in Adobe Caslon Pro by Manipal Technologies Limited, Manipal
Printed at Replika Press Pvt. Ltd, India

www.penguin.co.in

This is a legitimate digitally printed version of the book and therefore might not
have certain extra finishing on the cover.

Contents

Preface

Call of Joy

To narrate the story of the queen of Indian pop music, it is essential for me to remember the late Anjan Das. In the *Ramcharitmanas*, Tulsidas wrote, 'Again, with a sincere heart, I greet the unkind, who are hostile without purpose even to those who are friendly, to whom others' loss is like a personal gain, who seek joy in others' desolation and wail over their prosperity.'

Anjan Das, a resident of Bhowanipore in Kolkata, was Usha Uthup's Studio Vibration's man Friday. Whenever someone was unavailable for any studio work, Anjas Das filled in for them. The jack of all trades. Since my teenage years, I have been an ardent fan of Usha Uthup's fascinating and free-spirited songs, and when I decided to become a journalist, it was the obvious urge to do a detailed interview with her. But unfortunately, I was confronted by her man Friday each time I called requesting a meeting. He reminded me of Bali's son Angada, who challenged everyone in Ravana's court to move his leg, and no one actually could.

In his unrelenting tone, which was backed by a broken mixture of Hindi and Bangla, he used to say, 'Not possible! Didi is very busy.' This went on for about two and a half decades or so. Almost every trip to Kolkata was a failed attempt, as Anjas Das would have the same response, and just to make my trip worthwhile, I would interview some other eminent personality and return.

During that phase, I had the privilege of interviewing many larger-than-life personalities, like the legendary actor Utpal Dutt's wife, Shobha Sen, who, in her heyday, was one of the most reputed actresses in Bangla cinema; the Bengali actress Debashree Roy; famous Bengali writers Shyamal Gangopadhyay, Sunil Gangopadhyay and Shirshendu Mukhopadhyay, among others. But each time, I would return with this unfulfilled feeling, of not being able to meet one of my most favourite singers. I started to believe that Anjan Das was the Angada in my life who would never let me meet her. Ever.

But I was also stubborn. A few years ago, I again visited Kolkata, tried the landline number yet again and asked, 'Is that Anjan Das speaking?'

A voice on the other side said, 'No, he went up.'

Intrigued, I asked, 'Upstairs? Top floor?'

'No, Dada not upstairs! He went to the final floor.'

So, finally, my Angada had left the world. I didn't know what to say. After a brief pause, I said that I had been trying to get in touch with Usha Uthup for many years now, but Anjan Dada always refused saying Didi was busy. The man on the other side said that he was passing my call to Studio Vibrations' manager, Nabeen Ghosh, and that I should talk to him about this. Nabeen Ghosh warmly told me, 'I am giving you her number. Talk to her directly.'

I finally got her number. But despite that, it took me almost two years to meet her. Though she wanted to, we were unable to do so, due to some serious family emergency she was facing. Finally, in the year 2018, we met. No book had been written on Usha Uthup. So I thought why write her biography. She liked my proposal. Having bid adieu to a three-decade-long career in journalism, I was entirely dedicated to novel-writing. But after meeting her, I decided to write her biography. Now, when I look back, I realize that the late Anjan Das did me a huge favour by holding back that meeting for years. Had I succeeded in meeting her all those years ago, I would have been satisfied with a profile interview of hers. But God had planned it differently. He wanted me to do a book on her. The almighty had deployed Anjan Das, aka Angada, to postpone the meeting to that day. Hence this biography!

However, let me clarify that I haven't written this biography on the lines of 'Devi Shahastranaam', the Goddess's narrative. There is always this danger in biography-writing as one tends to fall prey to a certain fascination and indulges in over-celebrating the subject. I restricted myself and cautiously shied away from portraying her as this elevated figure adorned with exquisite flowers and scented pollens. Through Usha Uthup's story, I tried to narrate a simple Indian woman's story—a woman who has done, and continues to do, many extraordinary things. Actually, Usha Uthup's story is the story of a woman who is far ahead of her time. And this is not only the story of her life. This is the story of a progressive Tamil family that operates on the principle of Vasudhaiva Kutumbakam (the world is one big family). Usha Uthup's maternal and paternal sides of the family have lived this idea. Her multicultural family has members from different communities and cultures from across the world.

While writing this book, I encountered many questions, like 'What is so interesting in this biography?' I told many such curious friends that whatever I have to share in terms of her illustrious music career is known to many. But what is of primary interest in this book is the story of her family, her close friends, her peers, who formed the Usha we know today. In that sense, this is a biographical novel. An intimate tale of a progressive Tamil family.

From the very beginning, Usha was an adored child. Her eldest sister, Indira, lovingly called her 'Ush'. For her husband, Jani Uthup, she is 'Sutu'. She is 'Bukka Masi' to her nieces and nephews, and 'Umbukka' to her grandchildren. Her loved ones call her 'Didi'. A universal Didi. That is why she often says, with that characteristic smile, 'There are many who are known for their "dadagiri", but I am the only one who does "didigiri".' She is the fearless one. All the love that she has received from her family, and from her fans from across the world, is due to the fact that she is naturally a joyous person. Her good cheer is sprinkled with a fragrance, like a flower that blooms afresh with the morning ray of, sun as her name suggests.

It is the youthful self still is alive in me that encouraged and pushed me to write her biography. It was the '70s, the disco era, the days of my youth, full of life. Watching films with friends and setting out with them on many adventures were part of our daily routine. The sorrow-laden characters in the films weren't our favourites. The favourites were the stylish Dev Anand, who sported a classic puff of hair, complemented with a bright scarf around his neck; the enigmatic and energetic Shammi Kapoor, who bowled us over in his film *Junglee*; and the evergreen superhuman Dara Singh, who frantically battled the villains. Sad films had no place in our lives.

And yet, back in those days, the majority of the audiences had a weak spot for films that induced tears and sadness. They could relate to such films, which were reflective of the realities of life. They felt real. When my maternal grandmother accompanied my mother to a movie theatre, she would return and say to me, 'It was a nice film. We cried a lot.' It was her parameter for judging a film: the flood of emotions that a film could trigger. This trend of tear-jerkers continued and was much loved by many. And it wasn't limited to Hindi films. Even regional cinema was operating on the same theme.

In the '90s I visited Bhuvneshwar to do a report on the state of Oriya films. When I reached the famous Kalinga Studio, there was a shoot going on. The film was *Chaka Akhi Sabu Dekhuchi Duniya*. The meaning of the title was beautiful: Lord Jagannath (Chaka), through his eyes, watches over the world. The film was being directed by Raju Mishra, one of the famous Oriya directors. During the lunch break, our conversation began.

'To make Hindi films work, a hybrid of spicy sensationalism is incorporated to please and entertain the audiences. What is the recipe to make an Oriya film work? Or is it the same for you as well?' I asked.

Without even batting an eyelid, Raju Mishra said, 'Roll. Put tears. Roll. Put tears.'

'I didn't get you. What tears?' I asked, a bit startled.

'Try to understand it. In terms of food habits, women like salty and spicy things—food that leads to tears. Men like to eat sweet things. Women who like crying are our target audience. If you are able to bring the female crowd to the theatre, nothing can stop your film from becoming a hit. This is the only formula. If a housewife wants to watch a film, there is no way her husband is going to refuse to take her. If she is going, the children are going to accompany her. Inviting a woman to cry for a few hours brings an entire family to the theatre. And the film is a super hit,' Raju Mishra explained the process with the utmost seriousness. But I couldn't stop my laughter at this fascinating theory.

When I remember that episode even now, I feel that tears are a reality of life. They appear at every step of life. We come into this world crying and we leave with those same overwhelming tears. But can we not try discovering some islands of joy in life's sea of tears? This is why Usha Uthup's music resonates with me: she tenaciously looks for such islands of happiness. Even though Usha's life is surrounded by the salty seawater, she keeps seeking lush green islands of hope. 'What is in our eyes? The bright islands of joy that lighten our lives,' she says.

Usha has always been surrounded by the sea. She was born in Bombay, now Mumbai. Her maternal home is in Madras, now Chennai. Her in-laws live in Kerala. And she is now a resident of Calcutta, now Kolkata. All these parts of India are surrounded by the sea.

In the process of writing her biography, during one of my early visits to Kolkata, I met her gang of friends at one of her favourite cafés, Wise Owl. That was when the topic came up, of the sea always encircling her life. As the conversation deepened, one of her close friends turned towards me and said, 'There is a famous poet, José Chaves. Listen to one of his poems! Usha Di's entire personality is weaved into those words.' We were engrossed immediately, and with the utmost excitement she began to recite:

> For her
> the ocean was more than a dream,
> it was a place she needed to visit
> to find herself.
> And when she returned to the city,
> you could see the sun in her eyes,
> the wind in her hair,
> and taste the infinite salt on her lips.

The poem left everyone overwhelmed. There was silence for a while. With this poem, the evening at Wise Owl became an unforgettable one.

One of the initial challenges of writing this book for me was how to narrate the story of this musical life and where to even begin! I almost knew nothing about that life surrounded by the sea. I am from Bihar, and there is no trace of the sea in entire north India. To understand Usha Uthup's life, it was crucial for me to understand the emotion and the symbolic idea of the sea that merges into the ocean in the end and seeks fulfilment. Usha Uthup's music represents exactly that sort of merging, when the sea meets the ocean and becomes one. Complete. Content. Worldly. That is why Usha's songs are loved by the international queen of pop music Madonna. And not only Madonna, many celebrated singers in the West admire Usha's voice and singing. The magic of this charming and textured voice has entranced many across the world.

Usha has also found acclaim for the way she has embraced Indian traditions and cultural patterns in the most unique way, inspiring many women across the country. She showed the world that one can have the most modern and progressive approach towards life while being rooted and respectful towards traditions. With her beautiful Kanjivaram sarees, vermilion on her forehead, tinkling bangles and ornamental bindis, Usha, in the five decades of her illustrious music career, has conveyed that embracing progressive values is much more important than taking up modernity in a physical, materialistic way. Trying to appear modern in terms of beauty and fashion, people often fail at becoming mentally progressive, ahead in terms of their vision. They get bogged down in appearances.

Through her music, Usha has also tried to convey to Indian women that their fate is not just burdened with tears and that they, too, have a right to laughter. Her song 'Aage Badho' (Walk Ahead), in support of women's empowerment, has been sung in fifteen Indian languages.

And lastly, an interesting episode! When I told a friend of mine, who lives in Delhi, that I am writing Usha Uthup's biography, his wife couldn't contain her joy. 'Her personality is compelling!' she said. 'Such clean lyrics. No double-meaning songs. Whenever she is performing in Delhi, I never miss it.'

Hearing that, my friend chuckled and said about his wife, 'Once, she read in one of Usha Uthup's interviews that she irons her own sarees. Inspired by that, she bought an ironing table and kept it in the house.' As he said this, he pointed at the teakwood ironing table placed in a corner.

Polishing shoes, stitching clothes and ironing sarees are all part of Usha's day-to-day life. There is a lot more in this 'Usha Charita'.

I often tell her, 'You are triple "U". Not only Usha Uthup. You are Usha "Ullas" Uthup. Usha "Joy" Uthup.' The call of joy.

Enough character establishment. Now, let me tell you her story.

January 2022   Vikas Kumar Jha
Patna

1

The Kite-Flying Girl

It was a moment of wondrous amusement. The lady doctor at Dr Patrao Nursing Home was amazed beyond belief. The strikingly tall and slender Meenambal Sami reached the nursing home on Lamington Road in South Bombay trying to camouflage the pain in her eyes, her lips in a tight line, and there was no time to ask her any questions.

It was a pleasant autumn afternoon in the beginning of November. The doctor immediately ordered the nurses to take her to the delivery room. One of the nurses recognizing Meenambal said, 'She lives in Meher Villa, right across the road. She's the wife of Someshwar Sami, the police officer.'

After the delivery when Meenambal regained a little strength, she gazed at the newborn baby next to her. The nurse smiled and told her, 'You have had a beautiful baby girl. She is very naughty. She was kicking desperately to come out. She didn't even give us any time to call anyone.' Meenamabal's lips turned upwards into an overwhelmed, exhausted mother's smile.

A few hours later, on Meenambal's request, the nursing home's vehicle dropped her back to Meher Villa across the road. While seeing her off, the lady doctor, with utmost adoration, said to Meenambal, 'I have heard a lot about your husband's valour, but today I got to see how brave his wife is as well.'

It was the evening of 8 November 1947. Vaidyanath Someshwar Sami was speechless when he reached home. He almost couldn't believe how brave Meenambal had been with the delivery this time. When she was pregnant for the first time, as per tradition, she went to her parent's house in Pune. At that time, Meenambal's father, Hallasya K. Nadhan, was an engineer with the Public Development Department. Meenambal's first child, Indira, aka Indru, was born there. Their second daughter, Uma, was born in Bombay. After Indira and Uma, two brothers, Shyamsundar and Tyaagraj, were also born in Bombay. For her fifth child's delivery, Meenambal was comfortably in Bombay. She didn't go to her parents this time.

Lying in bed, Meenambal looked at her newborn daughter, virtually caressing her with her eyes. The little girl lying next to her would cry at times and then suddenly blossom with laughter. As the days passed, Meenambal noticed that when the little girl smiled, dimples appeared on her cheeks. When Meenambal's mother, Dharmambal aka Madras Patti Ma, saw the baby girl for the first time, she took the child in her arms and said, 'She is Usha. Her smile is like a beautiful morning.'

All the magic then was in Usha's dimples. Over time, her family members realized that she was different. At home or at school, Usha had the image of a carefree tomboyish girl who was always busy with toy spindles and flying kites. She played cricket, badminton, hu-tu-tu, gilli–danda, seven tiles and police–thief, among others. And when she was bored of playing, she would be found lying with her head on a pillow, reading comic books under the dense branches of the guava tree in the Meher Villa courtyard.

She would also play with dolls accompanied by her friends, Umrana and Shameen, and that was the least of her eccentricities.

She took great joy in stitching clothes for a doll's wedding. Once, Meenambal was upset when she found that Usha had made bridal clothes for a doll out of her year-old green lehenga that she got for Diwali.

All the household expenses, including the children's education, had to be managed within Usha's father's limited salary. Apart from school uniforms, the kids got new clothes only during festivals. Even though she had adventurous boyish traits, Usha also possessed girlish qualities. By the age of ten, she learnt to sew on the tailoring machine. Usha's father (Appa) jokingly used to tell his wife, 'Minnie, she will become a tailor!'

Usha was also good at polishing shoes and her father used to say, 'If Usha doesn't become a tailor, she will definitely become a skilled cobbler.' Appa's life lessons for his children were mostly inspired by the small, simple day-to-day occurrences. For instance, the value of hard work in life. Whenever Usha needed a little more money for a school picnic or to buy a small gift for her classmate's birthday, she used to begin shining Appa's shoes in the morning. Appa understood. That is how Appa taught the importance of hard work to his children.

When he was sipping his morning tea or reading the newspaper, Usha would stand near the door and greet him chirpily, 'Hi Appa!' Appa with a smile would ask, 'How much Usha?' Then he would point towards the nearby drawer that had coins. Usha grabbed as much as she could in her tiny fist. Many years later, when at times Appa visited Usha's room, standing at the door, he would say, 'Hi Usha!', she would smile back, asking, 'How much Appa?' Actually, Appa was more of a friend than a father to his children. Usha, in adoration for her father, would polish the medals on his police uniform until they glinted in the light. From polishing shoes to medals, Usha had learned the art from her maternal uncle, Kripakar Mama, who stayed in Bombay with her parents for a significant amount of time. Usha always kept an eye on Appa's shoes and medals.

Usha admired Appa in his police uniform: tall, strong and fearless. But she was scared of Appa's service revolver. He always kept it out of reach of the kids when he was at home. Usha still cannot bear looking at a revolver. She never even liked buying toy guns for her grandson Riyad. During childhood, no matter how carefree and daring Usha was, the fear of the revolver never left her.

One of Usha's closest friend's father was also a police officer. He also had two sons apart from four daughters. One afternoon, when he came home for lunch, his children were also home from school. In a careless moment, he left his unlocked service revolver on the bedroom table. While he was eating, he heard a loud bang followed by his son's scream. He ran towards his bedroom and saw his nine-year-old son holding the service revolver; his other son was lying dead on the floor, drenched in blood. In sheer childishness, the nine-year-old had aimed at his brother and pulled the trigger. After this unfortunate incident, the police officer was suspended from duty. Later he remarried and moved to England. After that, Usha's friend and her siblings had to battle difficult times.

Her friend's sadness lingered in Usha's heart for a long time, but her childhood was also filled with joyful moments. Usha vaguely remembers Lamington Road's Meher Villa, but the government bungalow in Byculla's Love Lane is clearly etched in her memory. Usha must have been five or six when Appa moved from Meher Villa to this huge European-style bungalow. Built in 1927, the double-storey house had a red roof decorated with tiles that made it look like a swaggering British official wearing a sharp, red hat. There were four bedrooms on the top floor, a giant sitting room downstairs, an equally spacious dining room, a big bedroom and a kitchen. There was also a prayer room—Pujai Ul. In the storage area, Kripakar Mama who used to stay with the family kept his engineering tools, kerosene oil, cycle pump along with many unusual things creating a whole web that occupied the room.

Apart from a garage, there were three small servant quarters and a guard room. At the entry door, the two pillars were etched with the words 'European Bungalow (West)'. Usha has vivid memories of each and every corner of the house and its surroundings. To top it all, there was a magnificent tennis court in the compound.

Right outside the bungalow, near the gate, was a very old almond tree, which is still there. Not only that, but a green canopy of banyan, ashoka, mango, java plum, guava and jackfruit trees among others still keeps the house beautiful and alive. Inside the bungalow, near the gate, there stands a crooked old mango tree that continues to be blessed with an abundance of fruit. Etched with affection in Usha's memory are the bursting ripe jackfruit's tempting fragrance and the dense hanging panoramic banana clusters. The ashoka trees that surrounded the bungalow like a battalion of soldiers, pointing their guns and glaring towards the sky, are still very much there. The 100-year-old peepul tree, which had witnessed little Usha's joyous laughter while she flew kites, has grown much older. The memories of many games and Usha's childish escapades seem to still echo, smiling quietly amid the shadows within the bungalow.

Among all the brothers and sisters, Usha and Tyaagraj aka Babu, were the thickest. There wasn't much age difference between the two. Coincidently, their birthdays also fell in the same month—November. Usha was born on 8 November and Babu on 14 November. Once on Usha's birthday, Babu gifted Usha her favourite ink pot that he had bought from his monthly pocket money that was three rupees. Six days later, Usha bought Babu a kite set from the three rupees that she also got as pocket money.

Shamu aka Shyamsundar, Babu and Usha were crazy about flying kites. The kite's spindle was made by Usha and Babu during the lazy afternoons when everyone was napping. The green soda water bottles were ideal for creating a kite spindle, and Usha and Babu left no stone unturned in arranging those bottles. Usha still remembers the chikoo tree in the compound under which they used to spread newspapers before breaking the soda water bottles. And after breaking the bottles, they collectively picked up the newspapers with broken glass and took them to the concrete area of the house.

They would then cover the broken pieces of glass with paper and crush the pieces to dust with a stone pestle. When the glass was almost powdery, they tip-toed to the kitchen to get refined flour for creating a paste. Once the paste was smoothly thickened, they added the glass powder into it. Their hands could easily get bruised with the glass particles, but neither Usha nor Babu cared. Once the flour and glass dust were mixed properly into a paste, one end of the thread was tied to the jackfruit tree and the other end to the garage gate. The paste was constantly applied on the thread. When the thread soaked in the paste had dried, it was ready to be wrapped around the soda bottle. Such afternoons filled with Usha and Babu's amusing adventures also had another enthusiastic participant—Dadu, their Maharashtrian helper.

When the kite was tied to the spindle, it was Usha's responsibility to run and throw the kite higher and higher towards the sky, and she had a command over the art. It was upon Babu and Shamu to handle the spindle. Dadu always insisted on flying the black kites. However, when the kites, wildly playing with the wind, begun to touch the sky, Babu and Shamu out of excitement used to give the spindle in Usha's hands. The kite-flying competition with the kids from the nearby police lines was quite thrilling. Babu, Shamu, Dadu and Usha, turn by turn, tried their somersault tricks in cutting the opponent's kite. Whenever they lost at the hands of their opponents, Shamu used to twist Usha's ears, blaming her for it. But whenever they had a winning day cutting the kites of the other kids, Usha earned a pat on the back.

The European bungalow's ambience often resounded with the sound of children playing cricket, badminton or a game of kabaddi. There was no dearth of players for a cricket team. In one team, there were Pathan uncle's children, Yusuf Bhai, Asad, Abbas, Shamim and Jamila. The other team had Usha, along with Shamu, Babu, Kripakar Mamu, Dadu, driver Parab and the constable in the house, Kadam. Usha was a good batter but Babu always gave her the runner's duty. But whenever Usha had the opportunity to bat, she used to unleash fours and sixes.

School had its own share of fun. Usha was studying in Convent of Jesus and Mary, on Clare Road in Byculla. She finished her schooling here. The school was not far from the house. One had to just cross a bridge to get to it. But Usha used to leave for school an hour before it started, walking amid trees, enjoying the chirpy surroundings and people, and playing for a while before the day began. Usha's Kripakar Mama was then working with Air India and stayed with her family. He had a bike. On certain occasions, Kripakar Mama dropped Usha to the school. But Usha's youngest sister Maya was quite spoilt by the family and went to school in the car. The happy-go-lucky Usha enjoyed walking to the school, observing all the worldly chaos.

Usha has fond memories of her school sports teacher, Miss Ellen. Generally speaking, sports teachers are strong and robust but Miss Ellen was quite delicate, mesmerizingly beautiful and sweet-spoken. Usha always felt that it was an act of pure injustice towards Miss Ellen that she was made the sports teacher.

The school had a lovely badminton court and a sandpit for long jump. Usha made the most of it when it came to sports. She never missed a game of hu-tu-tu, kho-kho and net ball. A carefree, playful and tomboyish Usha didn't know then that her life would be an unusual and amusing game filled with music and love.

Over time she realized that even though she didn't have what others would call a melodious voice for a girl, she should sing from within her soul with passion and keep singing till the end. And singing from deep within brings the sorrowful world close to you and tickles it to joy. Many years later, Usha came to know with complete realization that her male-like voice might challenge the norms and richness of traditional music, but the truth remains that singing ultimately has more to do with the soul than the voice.

Years later, even many years after her marriage, Usha came to realize how love approaches one like soft stems resting on the waves during a tide and makes the world go around. Time made that little playful girl believe that praying, music and love might be three different words, but their meaning remains the same. Kite-flying champion during childhood, the one who made the spindle with the broken glass dust, Usha also rubbed glass particles abundantly on the threads of her life. Usha began to believe in this philosophy since childhood that the kite will also stay up in the sky, flying firmly only if the spindle is strong.

2

Never Know How Much I Love You

The period from March to May in Chennai is gruelling. A summer of hot dust and sultry humidity coils around the city like a python. The 'gateway to South India' is in a state of unbearable heat for these three months, much like the fire of a yajna, hot enough to cause some to faint. June onward, heavy rainfall, lightning and windy tornadoes create a fascinating ebb and flow to the weather. Amid this atmospheric swing, the heady fragrance of jasmine and rose begin to permeate Chennai's very being.

It was a rainy evening in the middle of June 1967. In the nightclub Nine Gems situated in the basement of three cinema theatres on Mount Road—Emerald, Blue Diamond and Sapphire—a gig was underway. With dense hair down to the waist, deep emotive eyes, twenty-something Usha was belting out a number wearing a green and yellow saree and blouse, ruby-like vermilion/sindoor on the forehead and light-green bangles. She was accompanied by the Jazz Standard Band, singing an English song:

Never know how much I love you
Never know how much I care,

When you touch . . . you give me fever . . .
That's so hard to bear . . .

Twilight was merging into the night. For life, for spring, in her blazing voice, with all turbulences of the soul, in conversation with the sea, she was sprinkling pollen on the coast of hope. As if she were asking: 'Do dreams come true? Does sadness have a fragrance?' Lost in the tones, the tiny jasmine flowers in Usha's long braid were flaring in the nightclub's dim, blue light. Such fragrance to sound, like tuberoses (rajnigandha) blooming in kohl garden beds. Free from within, Usha's all-embracing voice had a sense of reassuring fullness to it. In colours of rhythm, flying on the delicate wings of emotions when Usha was passionately at the peak of her song, an old guest at the nightclub couldn't hold himself back. Overwhelmed, he got up and said, 'Falcon . . .! Such a dominating and assertive voice! Destroyer of the words of a spherical vajra; a phenomenal, welcoming and confident voice! My God! This girl in her rhythm flies like a hawk. The hawk's edgy, strong wings glide in her voice.' Another admirer of jazz said, 'Many years ago, I had heard the famous American jazz singer Peggy Lee sing the 'Fever' song that she was singing right now. Today this girl has defeated Peggy Lee.'

The rain had stopped outside. But the furore inside Nine Gems wasn't coming to an end. Like there was no tomorrow. Can a girl sing in such an unusual, larger-than-life voice? Weaving the tones into the rhythm, how swiftly she spreads joy in the valleys of the heart like the wild wind that collects leaves and flowers and hurls it around intensely in all the ten directions of the universe. The Jazz Standard Band was done for the evening. Usha came and sat next to her family members. The owner of Nine Gems, hotelier Yashwant Vikamsi, was amazed. Vikamsi also had a gorgeous resort in Mahabalipuram. But he spent most of his time at Nine Gems. Absolutely delighted, Yashwant requested Usha if she could, even if for at least a week, sing for the nightclub. In response, Usha playfully looked at her quietly chuckling maternal aunt, Leela Nadhan, who she lovingly called Jippi Ma. That night, she had accompanied her maternal aunt and uncle to the Nine Gems. The band was tuning their instruments when all of them entered the nightclub. Suddenly after a while, Jippi Ma said in a caressing tone, 'Usha! You go and sing! Go, Go!'

Everything happened in a moment. Like a bolt of lightning amid dark clouds, the chords of the Jazz Standard halted for a bit and picked up pace again. Usha began singing. It was a rich, vigorous voice. That rainy evening, in Nine Gems' velvety, enchanting light, India's first female pop singer was being born.

Five decades later, Usha Uthup hasn't forgotten any of it. The romance of that evening and the charming clouds, Nine Gems, Jippi Ma bursting with pride and joy, Yashwant Vikamsi insisting upon having her sing for a week and the beautiful Kanjeevaram saree that she got as her first remuneration.

Many years have passed by celebrating the independence of life and singing songs of the joys of life. Such an unbelievable journey. When addressing a big crowd of listeners, she still says, 'I have been a nightclub singer. That's how I began. Let's go . . . Ready to rock . . .?' As the evening deepens, the restless fans who eagerly wait to listen to her feel as if she is saying, 'Yes, dreams do come true. That the storm and thumping in the sea don't tire the fish.'

'What did you say? Did you like my saree? My bindi and bangles as well?' Holding the mic and wrapping an end of the saree's corner around it, Usha begins and people forget to blink. Doused in the country's cultural traditions, when an Indian woman sings an African–American jazz chord adding her own dash of flavour, it brings a festive vibe to the ambience.

Usha Uthup's entire craft is illuminated with the joy of celebration. A unique, original and affirming style. This perpetual joy and the celebrating soul intrigues and enamours people at the same time. Infinite seashell horns echo when the listeners cheer. As if a big rose-pink circle of bliss is spreading across the earth and the sky. Like clouds suddenly appearing in the sky amid life's unbearable soreness. Then welcoming the embracing of the delightful years. The weary, tired scattered lives across the Singhal bridge to the Malay Archipelago. The throbbing smell of the heat. Amid this, the shower of Usha's songs filled with happiness.

What did you say? There is no joy? Dreams are unconscious? Water is turning into ashes? The sound of the piano is trembling? No, no. Look at it, the clouds of joy are getting dense like the wild grass in the mind's sky. The Kadamba trees are dancing sumptuously on the earth. Mogali flower forests are quivering with desire. The new soft buds are smiling on the Arjuna tree. Pass through this lively lane in the cosmos. Here lies the call of the carnival.

Call of happiness! Boat of joy. Usha 'Ullas' Uthup! A honeyed, impulsive and wavering mix of myth, reality and happiness. 'The only thing better than singing is more singing,' said famous American jazz singer Ella Fitzgerald who in her unique tone sang for more than five decades. The incessant incredible melodious journey of Usha Vaidyanath Someshwar Sami to Usha Uthup is similar to that.

The year 1968 was quite a turbulent and significant year for India and the world. Martin Luther King Jr and Robert F. Kennedy who persistently fought for human rights were killed. The Beatles-inspired film *Yellow Submarine* was made. The first crewed spacecraft Apollo 8 orbited the moon in the same year. Amid all these seminal events, India's first pop singer was shaping up.

After finishing school, a playful, young Usha was married off at the tender age of eighteen. She was pursuing a degree from Bombay's Sir JJ School of Art, which she had joined in 1965. Despite studying in an art school, her sixth sense kept telling her that her future lay in music and not in colours. Usha remembers the year 1968 when the world's most famous gospel singer Mahalia Jackson visited Bombay for a show. She was famous as the 'Queen of Gospel'. Usha loved her songs.

The American Center, Voice of America and the US Information Centre had organized Mahalia's performance. That day, after requesting the organizers, Usha went backstage at the venue where Mahalia Jackson was waiting to go on stage. Usha sang a few lines of Mahalia's famous song 'It Don't Cost Very Much' for her. Mahalia was so elated listening to Usha that she said, 'You will sing the same song with me on the stage right now.' However, the shyly reluctant Usha said, 'I doubt that I will be able to sing given your command over the phonetics.' But Mahalia was adamant. She kept insisting, 'I am sure you will manage. No more discussion. Come with me and sing.' Noticing Usha's charming dimples, she said, 'Those who possess dimples are brought into this world by God for divine accomplishments.'

It was an overwhelmingly rare moment when Mahalia Jackson addressed the audience, 'This is Usha. She is my daughter! She will sing with me today.' That day's performance is an ethereal memory, still vividly alive in Usha's body and soul. Mahalia who touched many souls with her song 'Take My Hand, Precious Lord' that triggered a gush of emotions, pain and sadness was one of the first, among others, who supported and encouraged Usha. By making Usha sing along with herself, Mahalia in a way took Usha ceremoniously under her wing. She had awakened the rainbow hidden within Usha. Earlier, Usha had sung jingles for kids. Her siblings at home, and friends and dear ones outside, used to poke fun at Usha for her unusual, unique voice, which they jocularly said sounded like actor and wrestler Dara Singh's. However, the Mahalia Jackson performance left everyone astounded.

Obviously, Mahalia's recognition of Usha's talent boosted the latter's self-confidence. It meant a lot to the young girl. That's why when Mahalia passed away on 27 January 1972, there was no end to Usha's tears. By then, she had become India's first female pop singer. The year 1968 was the milestone that shaped the present-day Usha. With her indestructible diligence, she mastered her unrivalled voice, giving herself a new direction.

There were many who encouraged her in her journey of five decades. 'Usha, you are always on my mind . . .' Such words of affection settled on her soul and still cheer and liven her up. Back in September 2016, when Mother Teresa was posthumously canonized by Pope Francis at the Vatican City, Usha sang the Canonization Song. Tears trickled down her eyes as she sang, 'You filled their hearts, with love and peace, Oh Mother . . . Mother Teresa! You loved and gave them reason to live, Oh Mother . . . Mother Teresa!' Even now Usha gets intensely nostalgic thinking about her four-decade-long relationship with Mother Teresa.

'Your voice is always in my prayers, Usha,' an emotional Mother Teresa used to tell her with love. Mrs Indira Gandhi wasn't in regular contact but whenever they met, she used to smile and tell Usha, 'Usha! You are fabulous.' Etched deep within Usha's memory are those who were part of her audience and also her well-wishers. These, she recalls, included Nelson Mandela, Mother Teresa, Pope John Paul II, Indira Gandhi, Rajiv Gandhi and former Kenyan president Jomo Kenyata. She also remembers the bemused face of a young handicapped girl who used to beg on the streets and how when the light turned green, she ran to Usha and asked, 'Didi! You didn't put the "क" bindi today?'

Despite being Tamil-speaking, Usha is veritably India's culture capital Kolkata's cultural ambassador. The 'क' (*kaw*, the first consonant of the Bengali alphabet) etched on her big bindi is her flag of pride. Calcutta or Kolkata adorns Usha as much as Usha adorns the city, like the crimson colours that decorate her forehead. That's why whenever the ornamental 'क' bindi went missing from Usha's forehead, Calcutta got worried, 'No "क" bindi today?', they would ask. Usha was one who embraced the life and culture of the city, and it showed in the vermillion on her forehead.

Usha, who believes 'the world is one family', sings in twenty-two languages and has performed in many countries. The 'क' on her bindi represents western music suffused and radiant in vibrant Indian colours. It's in Calcutta's nature to be both provincial and international. Nothing in between. This is reflected in iconic personalities like the great poet Rabindranath Tagore, Mother Teresa and Amartya Sen.

A permanent resident of metropolitan Kolkata, Usha Uthup is also an 'international Didi'. This international Didi always says, 'I communicate with people through my music.' How to communicate via music one can learn from Usha. With this art of hers, she lives in people's hearts and apart from this deep engagement with them, she also expresses her dedicated love and respect for Indian traditions. By opening the horizons of her audiences' inner self with her infectious smile, she extends infinite joy and this is how she has come to be a cult figure.

'What did you say? Do you like my glass bangles? I wear four dozens of them . . . forty-eight glass bangles. If I am wearing a gold or a silver bangle, then I wear thirty-six glass bangles.' She engages with the audiences in an informal and personal manner. Dressed in a traditional saree, adorning vermillion, bangles and *mangalsutra*, she moves to Western music, twirling the threads of love in the hearts of her audience. Sometimes at the end of a song, amid the unending shower of applause, she spots spellbound listeners. She laughs and says to them, 'C'mon, clap your hands. The song is over.' But her fans know that Usha's music and the endless joy it brings is never quite over.

3

Listen to the Pouring Rain

With time many momentous landmarks of the past fade into memory. The city becomes strange for those who have lived in it and loved it. Old Madras and present-day Chennai's residents H.M. Belgamwala and his wife Dr D. Dilnawaz are busy, like restless squirrels, storing their memories.

Belgamwala won't be able to show his son the Spencer Cafe located in a bright red building on Mount Road in Madras, which came alive every evening. Nor will he be able to show him the three iconic cinema theatres on Mount Road—Emerald, Blue Diamond and Sapphire—with their massive basement area and nightclub, Nine Gems, where the evenings were soaked in romantic dim lights, dancing on the waves of joy. Nine Gems and its owner, Yashwant Vikamsi, aren't alive any more, but Belgamwala resides safely in his memories. He smiles at his wife Dilnawaz and says, 'Those were our days of romance. India's famous pop singer Usha Uthup sang her first pop song here at Nine Gems.'

More golden memories of Madras. Fragrant, like tiny jasmine flowers. The rhythm and sounds of Gemini Studio and the Madras Race Club. The exhilarating Sholavaram racetrack, Burma Bazaar, Woodland's famous dosa and filter coffee combo . . . But Nine Gems remained at the top of the list. Usha also fondly remembers that one unforgettable week at Nine Gems and the atmosphere in the basement nightclub. The unique Jazz Standard Band's chords evocatively embraced the briny music born out of love. Although fifty years have passed, those endearing moments still come to life. Like every year, the month of May came in 1968 and towards the end of the month, the summer vacations began.

After repeated invitations from her aunt Mrs Leela Nadhan, instead of going to meet Amma, Appa and her siblings, Usha and her husband Ramaswami Iyer aka Ramu went to Madras that year. After pursuing a three-year degree from Bombay's Sir JJ School of Art, Usha's summer vacation had begun after the exams. Her sisters were busy with their respective families. Even Appa had no holiday amid the chaos in Bombay's bureaucracy. There was no way Amma was going anywhere without Appa. Worrying about his daily meals, Amma used to hold herself back.

So, in the year 1968, Usha made a plan to visit Madras after her exams. Leela Mami's daughter, Meena aka Chikku, and Usha got along very well. Both were childhood friends. This year Usha's Madras visit was full of delight. Usha's childhood was synonymous with holidays in Madras. It was an annual or biannual ritual for the Sami family to go on a vacation out of Bombay. And that destination was Madras.

Usha's father was a senior police officer in Bombay known for his fearlessness and dynamism. For two decades he headed the Investigation Bureau. The criminal gangs of Bombay used to dread his name. They were well aware of the fact that he was an honest police officer and could not be bought by any means. Remembering her father's valour, Usha says that Dawood wouldn't have existed if Appa was alive. During his time, big and small dons were neutralized in encounters. Obviously, such an earnest police officer's source of income was only his salary. Husband, wife and six kids had to be sustained on that income. Social obligations had to be also fulfilled. So, when the children insisted on going on holiday once or twice in a year, a trip to Madras was planned. The Sami family would travel third-class by train.

Vaidyanath Someshwar Sami was a simple, gentle person. His father, an Iyer brahmin of Mysore, belonged to the family of Sir Kumarpuram Sheshadri Iyer who was an influential diwan from 1883 to 1901 in Mysore. Sheshadri Iyer hailed from the Palghat region of the then Malabar district. Because he was the second diwan of Mysore, his family settled there. His mother was from Palakkad, Kerala. Back in the day, the entire region was known as Travancore.

Vaidyanath was the eldest of four brothers. The younger brothers were Sheshu, Chandrashekhar and Devu. They had a sister Sushila who was married into the Kolleval region in Travancore. Usha's grandmother who was called Bombay Patti Ma by the children stayed with the family till her last days. Tides of times were such that a thread of the Sami family's lineage was left in Mysore and Palakkad. Leaving Mysore, the land of his ancestors, for Bombay always remained a sore point for Vaidyanath. Madras, the city where his in-laws lived, compensated for this.

Madras was home to Usha's maternal side of the family. It was Usha's first music school. Usha's maternal grandfather, Hallasya K. Nadhan, was an ardent admirer of Carnatic as well as Western music. By profession, Hallasya was an electrical engineer in the Public Development Department in Pune. He studied engineering at the Victoria Jubilee Technical Institute, Bombay, and was a gold medallist. His father, Ramaswami, and mother, Sitalakshmi, were pious and scholarly. His wife, Usha's maternal grandmother, Dharmambal Nadhan, was a traditional housewife. Nadhan's family home was located in Mylapore, a centrally located neighbourhood in Madras, near Marina Beach. These days, the area is known as Radhakrishnan Salai, previously called Edward Eliot Road. Former president S. Radhakrishnan's house is at the corner of Usha's maternal home, Shanti.

Shanti was always bubbling with music, literature and activity. From fancy dress competitions to quizzes, chess, carom, table tennis as well as cricket and football, all happened there with active participation of the residents. They organized musical theatre from time to time at Shanti. The household was one of its kind as, during the 1930s, they published a personal family magazine, *Nanatma*. All the contributors were family members and relatives. *Nanatma* went out of publication in the 1970s; however, it was revived in 1995–96.

For its uninterrupted publication, the family formed a board of directors. While V.S. Shankar was appointed as president, V. Chandar was made the treasurer and V.S. Chandrashekar and V.S. Sundar secretaries. Vasanti Ram was the editor. While turning the pages of *Nanatma*, one gets a peek into the family's creative abilities and their deep sense of commitment. From Vaidhyanath Someshwar Sami to Usha Uthup, almost every family member has written for the magazine. Undoubtedly, the Shanti house was a picture of joy and that's why Usha and her siblings—Indira, Uma, Tyaagraj aka Babu, and Shyamsundar aka Shamu couldn't contain their happiness on being there. The fun of rollicking around the huge premises, enjoying verakdalai (peanuts) and the restless tides on the Marina Beach were incomparable forms of joy. The two-storied Shanti and its basement was home to many such moments of immense happiness.

The three floors were gleefully lost in different genres of music. One resounded with Western music, the melodies of Bach, Beethoven and Mozart; the other echoed with north Indian classical music featuring iconic names like Ghulam Ali Khan, Pandit Mallikarjun Mansur and Pandit Bhimsen Joshi; the third floor was reserved for south Indian classical with M.S. Subbulakshmi's voice kissing the tears of the heart. Usha's maternal grandmother Dharmambal was an ardent follower of Subbulakshmi. Her mornings began with her song 'Suprabhatam'.

Dharmambal was skilled at playing the violin. The music reached a crescendo when Usha's mother and her maternal aunts and uncles got together. Usha's eldest maternal uncle, the happy-go-lucky Balram Nadhan, was her favourite who passionately played and danced to Western music. The loving memories of Shanti along with a vivid image of Balram Nadhan swaying to music still elates Usha. By watching him, Usha understood the unknown appeal of dance and melodies.

Usha's mother Meenambal was the eldest of the seven siblings. Meenambal was named by her father after the fish-eyed goddess Meenakshi. Her eyes were extraordinarily beautiful. After Meenambal, her brother Balram was born, then Shivmani Nadhan, Kripakar Nadhan, sister Nirmala, brother Ambi Nadhan and the youngest, brother Balkrishna Nadhan. They all had their jobs and independent lives but the deep-rooted love for music was a common thread in the family. Balram Nadhan took after his father and was a brilliant engineer. He carried out a range of inventions in the area of wind machines, for which he made a few trips to the United States to gain patents for them. Wind machines are used in theatres to replicate the sound of the wind. It was Balram Nadhan who provided many film studios in Madras with wind machines and state-of-the-art microphones.

The obsession with mechanics was such that Usha's evergreen bachelor mama, Balram, was always busy inventing something or the other and used to buy scraps of helicopters, bullets and cars used during the wars. He was an expert in making wind machines out of the carved wings of helicopters. But Balram Nadhan's skillset was not limited to wind machines and microphones. With his innovative mind, he also created a blood suction unit for hospitals. To nurture such eccentricities, he chose to stay single all his life. Usha recalls how Balram Mama's factory was a centre of great curiosity for many where helicopter parts, shreds of war bullets and a variety of similar things helped him imagine a series of amusing inventions.

Right next to the garage within the sprawling premises of the house stood his fascinating factory. It housed a range of tools, including a lathe machine. Like a clock, from day to night, he ticked along with these machines. Usha and her siblings thought that one fine day Balram Mama would make a unique helicopter and they would all go for a ride during a summer holiday. They believed that Balram Mama could accomplish the impossible. If he decided, he could take his nieces and nephews to the moon. Balram Nadhan was sweet and wonderful. He was the *jaadu babu* (magician) of the Nadhan family. Usha and her brothers and sisters were ardent admirers of the many talents their uncles possessed, whether it was fixing bulb holders or electric wires across the house. Not only that, from plumbing to repairing all kinds of appliances, no one could do it better than their uncles. They were natural engineers. But Balram Mama was at the top of the heap. He was a mix of Ibn Battuta, Christopher Columbus and Vasco da Gama. Immensely sharp and bright, Balram Nadhan was also quite self-involved and not very generous. Lost in himself, he was so particular that he got blue threads embroidered on the edges of his vests so that they wouldn't get exchanged with the underclothes of his siblings.

He was not interested in unwanted niceties and had the back seat removed from his motorbike so that no one could ride pillion. Later on, when he bought a car, the first thing he did was to remove the back seat. The lift-seeking requests were unbearable for him. If he was in a generous mood, he would get the back seat from the garage and put it back in the car. But such generosity was granted to very few. Usha's Appa lovingly called it 'The Stationary Wagon'! Balram Mama had quirks which he followed all his life. For instance, if he was in a happy mood and someone called on him, he would take few grapes out of the icebox and give it to his visitor like a holy offering.

Despite his devotion to his inventions, Balram Mama was short on savings. However, he distributed money and things the same way as he gave grapes from the icebox. The ice in the icebox was for his brothers and the grapes for his dedicated co-workers at his factory. Similarly, the helicopter and junk bullets went to his brothers and money in his account to his co-workers.

Alongside, he left a considerable amount to a relief organization, Alacrity. These gestures left no one surprised in the house. Everybody laughed and said, 'This is typical Balram Mama.' The spontaneous lesson that Usha learnt from Balram Mama was that one should do everything on their own and not depend on others. Also, give a hundred per cent to whatever one does.

There was a lot to learn and imbibe at Shanti, where even the walls seemed to breathe music reflecting different shades of happiness and sorrow. Be there and listen to the wind and the gentle sound of the dew falling on the silent, fearless night. You realize that life is not just about sorrow and suffering. It has an inner voice which seems to be saying, 'You only live twice.' Once for yourself and once for your dreams. To make the dreams come alive, you would have to listen to the heartbeats that reverberated through the house. Kripakar Mama who occupied the basement of Shanti listened to Bach, Beethoven and Mozart as well as Indian classical. The way the evergreen bachelor and innovator Balram Mama joyously danced was fascinating for Usha and all the siblings. 'Hava nagila . . . Hava nagila . . . Hava nagila . . . Venismeha . . . Uru, Uru ahim . . . Uru ahim be-lev sameah . . . Uru ahim be-lev sameah . . . Uru ahim . . . Uru ahim.' The joy of this Hebrew song was maddening. This and many other songs were Balram Mama's favourites. He recorded music as well, lost in its beauty. Anything he did had his absolute commitment.

Balram Nadhan's younger brother Shivmani aka Ini, the most adored member of Shanti, was also quite peculiar. Usha's Ini Mama, also an engineer, was deeply committed towards his elder brother's work. Immensely compassionate, he was a cheerful person by nature. He marked his arrival at Shanti by honking his motorbike when he was a kilometre away from the house. Shivmani Mama was amusing, especially the way he attracted everyone's attention. There used to be a rocking chair in the porch of Shanti where Usha's nani, Dharmambal, aka Patti Ma, spent her leisurely hours. Whenever Shivmani Mama came from somewhere, he sat on the rocking chair and began to say, 'Oh . . . I am so tired.' Then Patti Ma would come and take care of her son.

Shivmani was a married man. His wife Leela Nadhan was in government service and much respected in Madras as the director of tourism. Short in stature with a milky fair complexion, Leela hailed from a Marathi–Kannadiga Brahmin family. She was truly beautiful and a woman of few words. She never paid any attention to Shivmani's daily ode to tiredness, which continued for a lifetime. Usha remembers those days when she used to visit Madras to perform at Hotel Savera and the fun-filled days with Shivmani Mama and Leela Mami's daughter, Meena aka Chikku. Shivmani Mama mostly accompanied her for her evening performances at the hotel. One day Chikku told Usha, 'Papa's presence creates a lot of pressure upon us. Neither can we laugh wholeheartedly nor talk freely.' Then Usha came up with a fun plan. Next evening when Shivmani Mama came home singing his typical ode to tiredness, Usha said, 'Mamu! You must be really tired, right?'

'Very!' he said.

'I see you get really tired after work at the office.'

'Yes, Usha, I get really exhausted.'

'Then you must take complete rest when you get home from work. You will feel better. Don't come to my show.' Usha pretended she sympathized with him, somehow hiding her laughter. 'After a long day at work, if you come to my show, you will get even more tired.'

Trapped in his own saga of fatigue, Shivmani Nadhan had no other way but to rest at home. Chikku filled with joy and excitement told Usha, 'Wow Usha! What an amazing idea to get rid of Papa!'

Chikku was Shivmani Mama and Leela Mami's elder daughter and the younger one was Yamuna aka Muna. Chikku worked in advertising and her husband Jaidev was also in the same profession. Jaidev was quite jovial and deep. He passed away in 2017 due to cancer. Chikku lives in Bengaluru as does her younger sister. Muna and her husband work in the field of advertising as well. Even now, Usha gets thrilled when she remembers the nonchalant Leela Mami. There was nothing dramatic about her. She despised unnecessary theatrics. She was not at all interfering in any matter. What Usha learnt from her was that one should avoid being a fake at all costs. Leela was a woman with a calm sense of balance. She was adorable as a daughter-in-law, wife, mother and aunt. She had travelled the world and was well versed in literature. Her husband Shivmani loved listening to Frank Sinatra, Peter, Paul and Mary and The Kingston Trio among others. Leela aka Jippi Ma also listened to her husband's favourite songs whenever she found some free time. Each time Chikku and Usha got together, they relived and cherished their childhood memories of Chennai with utmost joy. Now neither Balram Nadhan nor Shivmani is alive. Leela also passed away in November 2017. She was the Mami Usha adored the most.

Meena Jaidev aka Chikku was ten years younger than Usha. Apart from being Usha's maternal cousin, she was also her childhood friend and companion. Since childhood, Chikku had loved birds and animals. She used to bring sick stray dogs and cats to Shanti and took proper care of them.

Birds and animals also know what's best for them. That's why the jumpy restless squirrels that were out of reach for others used to comfortably appear on Chikku's palms at her behest. Usha visited Madras on a regular basis for her shows and was enamoured by Chikku's love for birds and animals. Chikku had a pet cat she named Ratnavali. Once when Usha visited Madras, she learnt that Ratnavali had passed away the day before. Chikku was inconsolable. So Usha wrote a song as an ode to the cat:

> *We talk of all kinds*
> *of non-descript things!*
> *We talk about this and that!*
> *We talk of shallow*
> *meaningless things!*
> *Who thought of the death*
> *of a pretty cat, Ratnavali?*

When Usha sang the song for Chikku, she felt consoled. It was like a collective farewell to Ratnavali. Later on, Usha did many charity shows for the welfare of birds and animals. Usha even told her cousin that she does such charity shows out of love for her. Chikku says, 'In our family, whatever the beginning of a conversation might be, it always concludes with music.'

Shivmani Nadhan worked with Royal Enfield and his younger brother Kripakar was quite a connoisseur of Indian classical and Western music. His wife Prema was a loving person with a remarkable story. She was the perfect representation of the large-hearted family which was much ahead of its times. Prema's mother was a cook at one of Usha's maternal relative's house. After work, she would often come to meet everyone at Shanti.

She had two daughters and their marriage was always a worry for her given her weak finances.

One evening when she visited Shanti, she met Kripakar at the gate. She requested Kripakar to suggest someone suitable for Prema. Out of the blue Kripakar said, 'You ask Prema, if she is willing, I will marry her.' Prema's mother couldn't believe her ears. Also, a fear loomed within. She wondered how Kripakar's parents would react to it. Despite that, she went inside and jokingly repeated Kripakar's words to his parents. Usha's grandmother without delay said, 'If Kripakar has said so, then what is wrong with this idea? Let's do this!' Prema's mother was astounded by Madras Patti Ma's response.

In the same month, amid joyous celebrations, Kripakar and Prema were married. Kripakar's son Ashok was a lot like his father. Giving and loving, just like him. Kripakar who died of cancer was fond of good clothes and proficient in the art of woodwork. This skill survived in the family and taken over by Usha's brothers Shamu and Babu. Kripakar was also well versed in aeromodelling. He used to make aeroplanes out of soft balsa wood. And not only that, he also made wooden tables and chairs, medicine boxes from pinewood and cedarwood as well as picture boxes and small beautiful drawers. Usha's brother Shamu was Kripakar Mama's ardent disciple. There was no other like Kripakar when it came to decorating woodwork.

Usha and her brother Shamu also learnt the art of polishing shoes to perfection from Kripakar Mama who was truly affectionate. Whenever Usha sat down to polish her school shoes, Kripakar Mama would say with a smile, 'Give a girl the right shoes, and she can conquer the world.' Till today, Usha remains very particular about her shoes. She designs them herself and says, 'Your shoes determine the direction of your personality.' She remembers Kripakar Mama each time there is a mention of shoes.

Younger to Kripakar Mama was Nirmala Masi aka Usha's Papu Ma. She had a great love for Indian classical music and Eastern music traditions. She had quite a grip over Carnatic music as well. She was trained in playing the veena. And it was said that when she played it, she resembled Goddess Saraswati. Papu Ma's husband V. Chandar was Parry's managing director and hailed from the illustrious family of the Nobel laureate Sir C.V. Raman. Chandar's sister Shankari was reputed in the area of cancer research. Papu Ma and Chandar had one daughter, Anuradha, who married into a prestigious scholarly family. Anuradha's husband is Nagendra.

Younger to Papu Ma, Ambi Mama travelled extensively to Germany and Russia. He had good command over Russian and German and was a skilled translator which is why he kept in regular correspondence with the Russian and German embassies. Due to Ambi Mama's busy life, it was difficult to meet him very often, but his countless foreign trips provided astonishing stories for Usha and her brothers and sisters.

There were two Ambis in Shanti—Peri Ambi aka Bade Ambi and Chinn Ambi aka Chote Ambi. Peri Ambi Mama, who was mostly away on foreign trips, was a serious and deep man. His name was V.H. Ram. He was married into a well-known family. His wife Basanti true to her name was delightful. Chinn Ambi Mama aka Balkrishna was Usha's youngest maternal uncle who was with Kripakar Mama in Royal Enfield and was addicted to jazz and pop. Chinn Ambi's marriage tale was even more surprising than Kripakar's.

Chinn Ambi's marriage story is linked to Leela Nadhan, aka Jippi Ma. Leela Mami who was in a government job was once transferred to New York. Her daughter Meenu aka Chikku was one year old at that time. Muna who was younger to Chikku was only a few months old. That's why along with husband Shivmani, Chikku and Muna, Leela began preparing to move to New York. But one thought that kept troubling her was how she would be able to take care of two little daughters while working in New York. Even though Shivmani was quitting his job in Madras and was readily moving to New York with her, Leela wondered how her husband would manage two little girls when she was away at work. Everyone knew that getting a maid or help in New York was next to impossible. After much contemplation, they found a girl, Sumati, to look after the kids.

Jippi Ma was from a Marathi–Kannadiga family and coincidently Sumati also hailed from a good Kannadiga family. But her parents were not well-to-do. So Sumati agreed to go as a help to New York where Leela served for three years. But after returning from New York, Leela was sent to Canada. By that time, Chikku and Muna had also grown up. When Leela returned to Madras from Canada, Sumati who had become a part of her family began helping out in household work at Shanti. Short in stature and adorable, Sumati became indispensable to everyone at Shanti.

Sumati took special care of Chinn Ambi aka Balkrishna. Whenever she called out 'Ambi-ee-ee', it seemed like she was singing a song. No one knew what Madras Patti Ma sensed, but one morning she suggested that Sumati be married to Chinn Ambi. Actually, the way Chinn Ambi had been avoiding the topic of marriage, everyone felt that like his eldest brother Balram Nadhan, he would stay a bachelor all his life. Madras Patti Ma never said anything to anyone, but she did worry about it. As Chinn Ambi was the youngest, he was the most adored by Patti Ma.

However, Madras Patti Ma's announcement took everyone by surprise. Even Chinn Ambi and Sumati were taken aback. Later Patti Ma took both their opinions, and the two agreed to get married. Chinn Ambi and Sumati's wedding took place with utmost simplicity and joy. When Usha remembers the Shanti days, she feels that along with the Western and Indian classical music traditions, Shanti also had its own sweet and fundamental life-music that she acquired during her childhood. Each member of the family had their own elemental melody, their own instrument of glee and joy. Overall, the Madras maternal home was a multi-coloured music pad, where Ustad Bade Ghulam Ali Khan, Pandit Omkarnath Thakur, Balkrishna Murli and M.S. Subbulakshmi to Bach, Beethoven, Mozart and Frank Sinatra conversed through music.

Currently at Shanti only Papu Ma, Peri Ambi, and Chinn Ambi along with his wife continue to live. Chinn Ambi is almost blind now. Usha gets overwhelmed when she revisits Shanti's musical and joyous past. Usha heard Frank Sinatra for the first time at her nani's house. The young Usha loved Sinatra's music so much so that she wrote a letter to him one day:

My dear Sinatra,

My name is Usha Sami. I belong to a family that loves music. I sing all of your songs. I dream of the day I would get to meet you.

Usha only knew that Sinatra lived in New York, America. So, she bought some stamps with money she had saved from her allowances and addressed the envelope to 'Frank Sinatra, New York, America'. After dropping that secret letter into the letterbox, Usha waited for days for Sinatra's response.

All of Usha's sisters —Indira, Uma and the youngest Maya—loved music. Indira and Uma during the 1950s made a name for themselves in pop music as the Sami Sisters. Bombay, where Lata Mangeshkar and Asha Bhosle were celebrated in the Hindi film industry, in the realm of pop the Sami Sisters set listeners on fire. Their repertoire included jazz, calypso, melancholic waltz and countless Latin American songs. Uma is not in this world any more but her voice till date has no comparison. Watching her sisters perform, Usha also felt a deep desire to sing. But her voice was quite heavy, almost masculine. That's why during Usha's childhood and teenage years, her family could never even imagine that one day she will create her own wonder world in music.

Even at Convent of Jesus and Mary school, her teachers had come to believe that singing was next to impossible for Usha who was always busy flying kites and playing games more suited for boys. Usha never was the right fit in any of the music societies at school. Her voice with a deep foundation would never work with her classmates who sang at a higher pitch. That is why it was decided that Usha could never be included in any musical group at school. But Mrs Davidson, the school's music teacher, stood out as the only ray of hope who believed that nothing was impossible for the bold and courageous Usha Sami. With this hidden expectation, she delegated Usha to play the tambourine in the school's music group. During the Western music rehearsals at school, triangles, a three-cornered instrument, was played. Usha was involved in that too by Mrs Davidson. In time, she began including Usha in the choir as well. However, Mrs Davidson's colleagues were certain that Usha Sami couldn't be turned into a singer.

Since her school days, Usha used to listen to Radio Ceylon religiously. During those days two brothers, Ameen Sayani and Hamid Sayani, were immensely popular. One of the programmes was *Ovaltine Amateur Hour*, presented by Hamid Sayani. Usha was barely ten when she threw a tantrum at home to participate in the programme and visited the studio with her sister. The programme provided an opportunity for children to sing. Usha began singing the song 'Mockingbird Hill' but forgot some words and began to cry. Hamid Sayani laughed and said, 'Come again next week.' Next week, she practised a different song—'Itsy Bitsy Teenie Weenie Yellow Polka Dot Bikini'. She again forgot a couple of words during the singing, but she had promised herself that come what may, she wouldn't cry like the last time.

Once when Ameen Sayani asked her to sing a Hindi song, Usha was in a dilemma as she mostly knew Marathi and English songs. But since childhood Usha was not the one to easily give up. So, during Ameen Sayani's programme, she picked a poem from one of her school books, 'Titli Rani, Badi Sayani', and sang it melodiously. Till today, Usha believes that in countries like India, a land of mostly villages, the video will never be able to replace the radio. She remembers her favourite programmes on Vividh Bharti: *Jaimala* and *Madhur Geetam*. The latter featured south Indian songs.

After Nelson Mandela came to power in South Africa, Usha visited the country and heard their local radio. Durban had a station called Lotus FM, which played a range of songs for expat Indians. It included Hindi, Tamil, Telugu, Kannada and Bhojpuri songs. Usha was impressed but also disappointed a radio programme with the diversity of Indian languages was missing in India. When the *India Today* group launched its radio station, Red FM, Usha also presented a programme on it called *The Lazy Sunday Afternoon*. It had wide listenership. Though these days radio stations like Radio Mirchi and Radio Mango have a significant audience, Usha feels that the stardom enjoyed by Ameen Sayani and Hamid Sayani will never be replicated by a radio jockey anymore. The two brothers were stars. As a child, Usha had participated in their radio show. At that time, no one took Usha's childish tantrums to sing seriously. But she was a dark horse. Mahalia Jackson and Leela Nadhan, among others, must get the credit for encouraging the fascinating and joyous accident that is Usha.

After singing at the Nine Gems on Yashwant Vikamsi's request, Usha got another opportunity to sing for two weeks at Hotel Savera during that trip to Madras. The Savera people arranged for Usha's up and down flight tickets from Bombay. Back in the day the one-way airfare was Rs 126. This was Usha's first journey by air. Hotel Savera's owner, Shyamsundar Reddy, also owned a nightclub, Golden Bowls. Usha sang Tamil and English songs over there as well. But just before she was leaving for Madras, she received an unexpected offer from HMV to record 'Jambalaya', a song sung by American singer Hank Williams. The words went:

Goodbye, Joe, he gotta go, me oh my oh
He gotta go, pole the pirogue down the Bayou
His Yvonne the sweetest one, me oh my oh
Son of a gun, we'll have big fun on the Bayou

This song celebrates the festivity, feast and love of life on earth. Usually, the Creole community sings this song during their festivals. It is a mixed community of Europeans and Africans, a carefree and joyous bunch. Their language, Creole, has a touch of French, Spanish, African and native American languages. Hank Williams during the 1950s sang Creole songs. Usha was heard singing 'Jambalaya' by HMV's Vijay Kishore Dubey. He was so fascinated that he decided to sign her to record this song. But there was a small episode before the recording at the HMV studios. Famous Cine Laboratory's well-known sound engineer Minoo Katrak recorded Usha's songs one day. Minoo, an old friend of Usha's father, was from the Parsi community. After listening to Usha, a mesmerized Minoo said to Usha's Appa, 'Sami Saheb! This girl is like a tree full of songs.' Those days, the Bombay film industry was going through a slump. Due to some reason, the industry's workers were on strike. So, most studios were empty. Minoo Katrak told Usha's father that since there was no work happening in the studios, Usha could record some of her songs.

After Minoo's proposal, Usha along with the music group Conquerors went to the Famous Cine Laboratory. That day Minoo made Usha record ten songs. She sent the spool to HMV's Dubey. Among the ten songs, he loved four including 'Jambalaya' and 'Green Back Dollar'. A few days after that, he heard Usha singing 'Jambalaya' at an American event and everything came together. The year 1968 brought a lot of golden opportunities for Usha. There was a band called the Hecke Kingdom in Bombay. Hecke Kingdom himself played the saxophone in the band. Xavier Fernandes was on the piano and Arvi Double on bass. Florian played the drums. There was a big function in Bombay for the Americans and Hecke Kingdom had requested Usha to sing at the event. It was unimaginable for Usha to even think that HMV would make her such a prestigious offer in the evening. However, Usha still remembers how she finished recording 'Jambalaya' in one take. Joyously drenched in the happiness of the recording, Usha went to Madras where she was supposed to sing at Hotel Savera for two weeks.

Nine Gems doesn't exist anymore, but Hotel Savera is still there. Savera's owner Shyamsundar Reddy loved Usha like a daughter. Hotel Savera's memory continues to linger in Usha's mind. Her performances at the nightclubs in Madras were advertised as, 'Tonight . . . and every night Usha! No cover charge!' For special occasions, the restaurants were known to levy a cover charge. It's like an advance booking. Earlier, the restaurants had cover charges that ranged from Rs 100–150. Nowadays, the cover charge at a basic restaurant can go up to Rs 1000. This also takes care of dining and entertainment, but back in the day the nightclubs used to announce that there would be no cover charge for Usha's shows.

Usha gets emotional even today when she visits Madras. She says, 'The magic of Madras is evergreen. What's not to love about this Madras?' Enjoying the beautiful memories and adoration that she got from the city, she asks the audience, 'Have you ever tried the sundal?' 'Sundal? What is it?', the non-Tamil listeners ask with a sense of wonderment. Then Usha smiles, 'Ask this Madrasan. Sundal is a famous snack in Madras. It is made from roasted gram or lentil seeds along with spices. You can also prepare sundal with roasted peanuts or green pulses and sprinkle spices on it. There are many kinds of sundals made in Madras—konda kadalai sundal, sweet corn sundal and kadalai paruppu sundal. It's quite easy to prepare. But to learn the recipe, you will have to visit Madras.'

The audiences laugh with joy.

'And have you ever tasted kili mooku manga?', Usha smiles like Alice in Wonderland. 'The parrot-beak mango. The Madrasi mango which is shaped like a parrot's beak! Go and see how the tourists enjoy it served with salt and chilli on the beaches of Madras. Come over to my place someday, I will treat you to its pickle that you won't be able to resist once you have tried it. Instant pickle of kili mooku manga. This is our delicious mango that is available throughout the year. A city, coloured with traditions and rare forms of joy.'

Usha is right. By all means, Madras, or Chennai, is a traditional city. You can't imagine a woman without a nine-yard sari and the *mukkuti* nose pin that is worn on both sides. Usha dressed traditionally when she used to sing at Savera. She would receive Rs 750 as honorarium. It was good money. However, one evening when she was leaving Savera after a performance, she received an offer to sing at Little Hut, the nightclub at the Ritz in Bombay for three weeks.

In the third week of singing at Little Hut, she received a blue inland letter from Trincas, the famous nightclub in Calcutta. Trincas's owner had requested the Little Hut's owner that if Usha finds some time, they would love her to sing at their nightclub. Actually, one of the regular patrons of Trincas had heard Usha one evening at the Little Hut. He told Trincas's owner that if Usha sang there, it would add a feather to the nightclub's cap. That was how in 1969 Usha came to Calcutta on the invitation of Trincas and stayed on forever in the city of joy. Usha's intoxicating voice added to Trincas's stature and she never looked back. She made Calcutta her axis and her charm began to spread across the world. In 1969, she sang the title song for *Was it for this the clay grew tall?*, a Shyam Benegal production. Benegal's film was based on Gandhi and how we are overlooking his teachings in a free India. The poem 'Futility' by Wilfred Owen was beautifully used in the film. Usha's voice added depth to it . . .

Think how it wakes the seeds—
Woke once the clays of a cold star.
Are limbs, so dear-achieved, are sides
Full-nerved, still warm, too hard to stir?
Was it for this the clay grew tall?

And in Shyam Benegal's next film, *The Making of Mahatma* in 1996, she sang 'Vande Mataram' and lent it the beauty of a blooming starry night.

Usha's songs are replete with thrill, rhythm and joy. From 'Scotch and Soda', 'Fever', 'Hari Om Hari', 'Pouring Rain', 'Doston Se Pyaar Kiya . . . Dushmanon Se Badla Liya', 'One Two Cha Cha Cha', 'Rambha Ho', 'Tu Mujhe Jaan Se Bhi Pyara Hai', 'Gulabi Chehra', 'Uri Uri Baba', 'Darling', 'Hai Ye Maya', 'Bolo Ta Ra Ra Ra', 'Ye Raat Monalisa', 'Aami Shotti Bolchi', 'Koi Yahan Nache', to 'Hai Yahi Prarthana', 'Vande Mataram', Christmas carols and Karadi rhymes for children. These and other countless songs are drizzled with Usha's one-of-a-kind style of singing. She is evergreen. Her voice is eternal like the spring. Unlike Lata Mangeshkar and Asha Bhosle, Usha might not have sung unlimited number of Bollywood songs but she has unlimited fans, and her voice has touched people across the world.

She never got the safety net of film songs, but despite that her songs have mass appeal because of the festivity in her voice. It is said her vocal style ushers in joy and is trouble for sadness. That's why during her shows when she asks her audience, 'Okay? Ready to rock?', the reply is always in the affirmative. On the map of popular music, Usha has been the queen for decades. Yet she is modest and often smiles and says, 'In films, I have mostly sung for the bad girls. But it's God's grace that despite that, people have always loved my songs.' Then after a pause she smiles in the same enticing manner and says, 'You know what the cat sitting on the tree says to Alice in *Alice in Wonderland*? It says, "Well behaved women rarely make history." I love to sing wild songs.'

In the beginning, Usha used to wonder as to what kind of singer should she be to be accepted by the people. Neither could she be called a playback singer entirely nor a nightclub singer. But in time, she was recognized as a pop singer. It was the common belief that a pop song means a fast-paced and loud English song. Slowly and steadily she successfully broke this misconception and proved that pop songs do not have to be necessarily in English. Also, that pop songs aren't always loud, but can also be melodious and meaningful. Many famous songs sung by her like 'Fever', 'California Dreaming', 'Godfather', 'Love Story', and the most recent of songs, 'Skyfall', aren't fast-moving at all.

She also sang many popular songs in a variety of Indian languages and believed that they conveyed a message. She started asking audiences during her performances, 'The lines of "Rambha Ho" . . . *Jitna tum pyaar se jee loge utni hii zindagi* . . . The time lived with love is life . . . Is that meaningless? *Doston se pyaar kiya* . . . We loved our friends. Is that just an entertaining noise? In the film *Kudrat*, the song I sang, "Hume Tumse Pyaar Kitna . . ." Is that meaningless? In the same film another song sung by me . . . *"Dukh sukh ki har mala kudrat hi piroti hai, Haathon ki lakeeron mein ye jaagti aur soti hai* . . ." Nature binds the thread that holds both joy and sadness. It wakes up and sleeps on the lines of fate on our hands. Is that meaningless?' In direct conversations with the audience, she addressed and dismissed the objectionable connotations associated with pop songs and evoked respect for them in people's hearts.

However, in the last few years during interviews when she was asked, 'Are you an ethnic singer? Are you a jazz singer? Or are you a pop singer?' Her response was, 'I am a people's singer. I am totally a gypsy. I am a nomad of music.'

November 8, 1947, marked an interesting coincidence. Two magical voices were born on that day. One was Usha Uthup in

Bombay and the other Minnie Riperton in Chicago. Minnie who died at thirty-two on 12 July 1979, had many timeless songs to her credit. But her song 'Loving You' enjoyed much popularity. Its lines are very touching:

> *Lovin' you is easy 'cause you're beautiful*
> *Makin' love with you is all I wanna do*
> *Stay with me while we grow old*
> *And we will live each day in springtime*
> *No one else can make me feel*
> *The colours that you bring*
> *Stay with me while we grow old . . .*

A perfect mix of love and compassion, Usha loves this song released in 1975. Five years before that she evoked similar feelings of love in the film *Bombay to Goa* when she performed a cover of the song *Rain* made popular by Jose Felicino:

> *Listen to the pouring rain*
> *Listen to it fall!*
> *And with every drop of rain*
> *You know I love you more!*
> *Let it rain all night long*
> *Let my love for you grow strong!*
> *As long as we are together*
> *Who cares about the weather?*
> *Listen to the rain Listen to it fall . . .*

Minnie Riperton and Usha Uthup, one could say, were like twins born on different sides of the globe and blessed with passionate voices. Minnie unfortunately departed four decades ago, but Usha's voice continues to inspire and glow, like glimmering raindrops under the tropical sky.

4

The Eternal Five Women

There were many personalities who visited or were associated with the Shanti household who left a deep impression on Usha Uthup. Among them was petite and fair Swarnam aka Swarnambal or Chinni. She smoked Marlboro cigarettes like a European empress. There was a regal air about her when she released smoke out of her nose or blew smoke rings in the air. She also regaled everyone with her trunk full of stories. One was about the brand she smoked: 'There was a cigarette maker named Philip Morris in London. He was behind creating the Marlboro brand. Actually, he had a small cigarette factory in a lane in London called Marlboro. That's how he chose Marlboro as the brand name. Phillip Morris made these cigarettes first for women. The company put a fine red line on the rim of the cigarettes so as to conceal lipstick marks left on the cigarettes. The red band was projected as, "Beauty tips to keep the paper from your lips."' When she narrated such nuggets, Chinni looked like the amla and pomegranate trees loaded with flowers. She continued, 'My God! For generations, Marlboro had such heart-warming taglines—"Mild as May", "Come to where the flavour is. Come to Marlboro Country".'

She had stories lined up to share longer than the trails of ants in all the dharamshalas in Madras. Like a religious preacher, she would reel out countless stories and interesting anecdotes. Even on the Marlboro tagline she could hold forth for weeks with her listeners asking for more. Like her smoke rings, she had many rings of jokes. That's why during the holidays Usha and her brothers and sisters would desperately wait for Chinni's arrival at Shanti. Chinni's elder sibling Sister R.S. Subbalakshmi's house with a big establishment running in it was just a gallop away. Chinni used to live there with her famous sister.

Sister Subbalakshmi had five houses in her compound. She lived in one of them. Chinni in another, and the rest were occupied by their kinfolk. Covered with bougainvillea flowers, Sister Subbalakshmi's house was always endearing. Her veranda was quiet and serene, with a swing fixed in it. This was in keeping with the tradition followed by households in Madras. Sister Subbalakshmi could often be seen on the swing in all her magnificence like a goddess.

She was a living legend during her lifetime due to her pivotal campaign for young widows in Tamil Nadu. The Sharda Act of 1930 abolishing child marriages had Sister Subbalakshmi's hard struggle behind it. Girls getting married at a tender age, getting pregnant and passing away during labour used to agonize her since childhood.

The Chinni who regaled children at Shanti with her captivating stories had several layers to her personality. The first of these was being Sister Subbalakshmi younger sibling. Since she had so much influence over Usha, one has to understand Chinni. And to know Chinni, it is essential to know Sister Subbalakshmi's story.

Sister Subbalakshmi's father, R.V. Subramania Iyer, was a civil engineer who worked in the Public Development Department of the Madras Presidency. Her mother, Vishalakshi, was a simple traditional woman. While staying at home, she gained profound knowledge of Sanskrit and Tamil literature. Subbalakshmi's aunt, Chitti Walambal, who was untimely widowed, stayed with

Subbalakshmi's parents and had a good knowledge of Sanskrit and Tamil literature as well. Growing up in the laps of her mother and aunt, Subbalakshmi and her four sisters—Balammal, Savitri, Swarnam and Nityananda—acquired the essence of Tamil and Sanskrit languages.

Subbalakshmi's mother Vishalakshi was so pious and traditional that when Subbalakshmi was to be born, her parents called for a doctor. It wasn't acceptable for Vishalakshi that another man touched her body. She was sixteen years old. Coincidently, there was a European lady doctor, Miss Scarleb, in Madras at that time who came home and handled the delivery. In the hope of a son, Vishalakshi gave birth to five daughters. Subbalakshmi was the eldest.

Due to poor health and constant transfers, Subbalakshmi's father resigned from his job and took on an assignment at the Government Agriculture College in Saidapet that was ten kilometres away from their home. The couple never had a son, but they were committed to giving the best of education to their five daughters. Those were the days when educating girls was unimaginable. To uphold the Tamil Brahmanical traditions, Subbalakshmi was married off as a child, but she was widowed at the age of twelve. That deeply pained her parents who wanted her to receive good English-medium education and become independent.

That Subbalakshmi and her sisters were pursuing higher education left her grandmother, family members and well-wishers in a state of shock. But Subbalakshmi's parents never really bothered. While working at the Saidapet Agriculture College, her father had rented a house in Madras to facilitate Subbalakshmi's higher education and her aunt Chitti accompanied her to take care of her. Chitti was a fun-loving and sweet person.

Since childhood, Subbalakshmi had noticed that while her mother wore colourful silk sarees and decorated her braided hair with flowers, Chitti's hair was cut till the roots. She wore white sarees. Subbalakshmi had seen her grandmother in the same attire. It really saddened her to see Chitti living a widow's lonely life at such a young age. Subbalakshmi witnessed her own widowhood, Chitti's sad life and that of many young girls who were widowed. Among them were Amukutti and Parvati along with countless young widows. During those days, many boys died due to influenza and that caused the number of widows to grow. Subbalakshmi remembered that when she was widowed after a few years of marriage as a child, her wedding saree was cut and turned into frocks for her sisters so that she didn't relive her colourless past.

At the Presidency College in Madras, Subbalakshmi not only studied European history, physics, chemistry, mathematics, geography and English but also read Vedantic philosophy with great interest. Later on, when she came in touch with Miss Lynch and got into teaching, her vision widened. Madras's PT School, where she taught, was also where her sisters studied. At school, her sisters also addressed her as 'Sister'. One day, Subbalakshmi got emotional and said to the school's head, Miss Lynch, 'I also want to become a "Sister" to all the child widows.' Since that day, she was known as Sister Subbalakshmi. Slowly, her image transformed into that of a social reformer. Her name became synonymous with social change.

Her sister Swarnam, who was much younger to her, was personally quite dedicated to her. That's why despite her transferrable job as an inspector with the Education Department, she always took special care of her eldest sister. When her mother Vishalakshi asked Swarnam to get married, she refused saying that she would rather take care of her sister. But who would have thought that Swarnam's life would be more turbulent than she had ever imagined. After retiring from the Education Department, Swarnam was devoted to her sister full-time until her last breath. Sister Subbalakshmi died at the age of eighty-three in 1969. In her last few years, she had lost her eyesight and became hearing impaired. Swarnam was her sister's eyes and ears through those dark days. Swarnam visited Shanti once a week. She used to come in the morning and leave late afternoon. Usha and her siblings always reckoned that Swarnam was a close relative of their maternal family and that's why she blended so well among them.

Whenever the stylish and extroverted Chinni visited Shanti, she first enquired after everyone's well-being and then would head straight to the room of Usha's maternal grandfather, Nadhan. It appeared as if the six-foot-tall, fair and handsome Tatha (grandfather), Hallasya K. Nadhan, waited for her. Usha hasn't forgotten her Tatha's Greek god-like persona. With utmost adoration, Tatha would bake rice wafers on the electric burner for Usha and the other children. He also used to keep a glass jar on one of his racks filled with little red sweets. Usha and her siblings were alert like cats in getting sweets from Tatha.

Usha's grandfather, who was absolutely dashing in his days, with passing age had embraced simplicity in its purest form. He had lost some hair on his forehead. With his white hair and beard, he mostly dressed in a dhoti and *jubba* (kurta). There was a beautiful swing in his room on which he loved to sit. This was quite a different Tatha from the one dressed in a dapper suit and tie in the family album. His suited–booted pictures were from the Pune days where he worked as the chief director at the Public Development Department. Usha maternal grandmother Madras Patti said that their eldest child Meenambal aka Minnie was born in Pune on 5 November 1919. Meenambal got educated at the Saint Helena School in Pune. She always came first in her class and took her matriculation exam after marriage and topped that as well. The two principals at the school—Ms Evlyn C. Gaze and Ms C. Wilson—used to say that Meenambal took great care learning the lessons and remembered them well.

After retiring, Tatha came to live at Shanti permanently. There was a bedroom as well as a meditation room for Tatha where he read and thought while smoking cigars on the swing. Chinni while smoking her Marlboros used to enter that room which fused the cigarette smoke with the fragrance of the cigar. Tatha's and Chinni's harmony of cigar and cigarette was so marvellously mystical that the present-day Usha would have wondered about the strange fusion of the two streams of smoke.

Chinni was herself a living story. Whenever Chinni left Tatha's room, the children at Shanti would endearingly compel her to tell them a story. When Chinni was comfortably on the swing downstairs, she would scatter her stories like a rainbow. Chinni had an unending store. From the tales of gods, goddesses, kings and queens to delightful stories of birds and animals who behaved like humans. And stories of humans who behaved like animals. In Chinni's stories, rat, crow, lion, bear, Ram and Ravan, were all there. Even now Usha remembers Chinni, Tatha, Madras Patti Ma and the golden days at Shanti. She realizes how everything silently fades into infinity. But she also finds that memories of that time are deeply etched in time.

Usha remembers how when she and her siblings grew up and went to college, in some context Usha's maternal aunt Leela Nadhan aka Jippi Ma revealed that Chinni was Tatha's second wife and Peri Ambi was not Madras Patti Ma's son, but Chinni's. Jippi Ma dropped this bombshell in a matter-of-fact manner, but the information shocked and devastated the children. Suddenly at Shanti there were two Ambi Mamas with different mothers. The first one, the elder Ambi, V.H. Ram, was Chinni's son and the second, the younger Ambi, Balkrishna, was Madras Patti Ma's son. Both the Ambis lived at Shanti and were equally loved by Madras Patti Ma. Whenever Chinni visited Shanti, she would get similar respect from Peri Ambi and Chinn Ambi. From Jippi Ma's information, Usha figured that Chinni after giving birth to Peri

Ambi gave him to Madras Patti Ma to raise him. Apart from the elders in the family, everyone around thought that all of Hallasya K. Nadhan's children were from Madras Patti Ma.

At Shanti, the sense of discipline was such that there was nothing apart from love and respect for each other. Everyone respected Madras Patti Ma and Chinni received utmost regard as well. That's why whatever lay underneath, the Shanti household never faced any disquiet on the surface. Many decades later, Usha found out that the Shanti premises belonged to Chinni. Usha still remembers the photo on Shanti's wall in which Tatha, Madras Patti Ma and Chinni are seen with all the children. The memory of the black and white photo still makes Usha shiver. She wonders about Tatha's second marriage to Chinni and in what state of mind Madras Patti Ma would have given birth to Chinn Ambi? After getting to know of Tatha's relationship with Chinni, Usha felt anger towards Tatha in the beginning. Why was he so unfair towards such a dedicated wife as Madras Patti Ma? When she asked her mother Meenambal, she got this reply, 'Chinni married Appa in Pune.'

The delicate ties of relationships resolved for Usha when she grew up. Her Tatha Hallasya K. Nadhan's elder brother V.S. Sunderesh Iyer was married to Sister Subbalakshmi's sister, Ballambal aka Balam. Chinni often used to visit her elder sister Ballambal. Amid this, she met her brother-in-law's brother Hallasya many times. Due to close proximity with the family, Chinni was aware that Hallasya K. Nadhan was married with children. But the tall, broad and handsome Hallasya at the first look made a special place in Swarnam's heart. Swarnam was short in height and, like her name, was beautiful beyond belief. So Hallasya K. Nadhan was also enamoured by her. This attraction eventually concluded in marriage. There was another reason to Chinni and Hallasya K. Nadhan's closeness. Actually, Hallasya K. Nadhan was posted as an engineer in Pune and Chinni's father

Subramania Iyer also worked in the same Public Development Department in Pune. Chinni married Nadhan in Pune.

How the unrestrained desires and hopes of human beings come to terms with the reality of life! The case in point is Usha's Madras Patti Ma. She was definitely a skilled homemaker, a loving mother and a devout wife but she was nowhere close to her husband when it came to intellect. Swarnam aka Chinni was not only beautiful but intellectually inclined as well. The ownership of Shanti, the double-storey house, possibly added to her stature. But it was Madras Patti Ma who came into Tatha's life and held the household together. It was an *agraharam*-style Brahmanical household, and Madras Patti Ma fulfilled her duties with the utmost dignity.

Many such close and loved ones who came into Usha's life aroused many questions in her. Did Chinni fire Tatha's amorous desire or was she also an intellectual companion for him? And was Madras Patti Ma who stood up courageously reflect the song of sadness in Shanti? Usha believed that despite the storms that raged within it, there was always respect and love of the sense of collectiveness at Shanti. And the axis of Shanti was Usha's maternal grandmother, Madras Patti Ma. An epitome of patience and tolerance!

Dharmambal aka Madras Patti Ma, Swarnam aka Chinni, Amma aka Meenambal Sami, Tulsi Ma and the next-door neighbour in Bombay, Mrs Zakia Khan aka Pathan Aunty! In the mortal light of life, these five women dazzled Usha with their strength and endurance. These five women like pearls in a seashell residing deep in the sea, would seemingly ask Usha from the depth of their souls, 'Usha do you know the age of fire, water, darkness, wind and light? Is it the same as that of the universe?'

The age of fire! The tale of countless characters that come to our lives that not only startle and disturb but also provide a deep warmth the encompasses the earth's heat. Usha thinks that these five remarkable women's words run in her veins and arteries.

Remembering all five of them feels like a permeant sprinkle of chapatti, sweetness, stories, caresses and adoration. Usha deeply misses her grandmother who from morning to night at Shanti tended to everyone's needs, spinning like a top. Dusky, tall and lean Madras Patti Ma who despite being a traditional and conservative woman would go to any extent to fulfil the desires of her children and husband. She was a pure vegetarian and never entered the kitchen without a bath. But on the demand of her elder son Balram Nadhan, she wouldn't hesitate in preparing a flipped egg. Eggs flipped in a typical Italian style omelette that her son needed in the morning at any cost. Usha remembers the blue glass in which Madras Patti Ma would beat the eggs. Barlam was the apple of her eyes. She was ready to do anything and everything for him. But despite that, Balram was never happy with all her endeavours. For the blind love for her family, she gulped the unbearable sorrow and lived her life.

It was due to her limitless affection for the children that Madras Patti Ma, who had never stepped foot in a nightclub in her life, went to Hotel Savera to hear Usha sing. Tatha was a god-like figure for her. She was always attentive to his clothes, meals and medicines. Usha remembers how Madras Patti Ma would carefully serve Tatha's food and take it to his room upstairs herself. Whenever Chinni visited Tatha and while they were busy talking about philosophy, literature and worldly matters, Madras Patti Ma would bring endless cups of tea and coffee to Tatha's room. And during lunch, after serving Tatha's food, she would take Chinni's lunch to his room. In what state of mind would Madras Patti Ma be carrying a plate of food for Chinni? With a forced smile or in complete silence? Even decades later it is strange for Usha to determine what her grandmother's feelings were. It would be like assessing the dust, sand and cracks of an old landslide that happened years ago.

Time takes its toll. First Tatha passed away, then Chinni. Usha remembers how Chinni, who lost her eyesight in her last days, was in a miserable condition. After Chinni's demise, Madras Patti Ma was in a state of shock for days. And after a year or so, she also left the world. Usha reflects on how these two women who left the world with their pain were like a well full of moonlight. And it seemed the fragrance that emanated from these two women was like maulshree (Spanish cherry) flowers swinging in the breeze. Then there was Meenambal, Usha's sweet Amma and the Sami family's harbour. Meenambal was called Minnie in her maternal home. After marriage, the name on her passport was Minnie Sami. But Usha's Appa would call her Min out of love. Appa and Amma's was a love marriage.

Minnie had introduced her father Hallasya K. Nadhan to Chinni in Pune. In those days, Minnie's father was an electrical grid superintendent in Yerawada, outside Pune. At that time the tall, broad and dynamic Vaidyanath Someshwar Sami, after training at the Nasik Police Training School on 16 June 1931, had joined the Bombay City Police as a sub-inspector. During his police service, he came in contact with Sister Subbalakshmi and through her, he met Chinni. By then, Chinni was married to Hallasya K. Nadhan. Once when Vaidyanath Someshwar Sami visited Pune, Chinni introduced him to Minnie. And it was love at first sight. He was twenty-six then and Minnie was all of fifteen. Their love developed quickly and on 6 May 1934, on a Sunday, Minnie Nadhan and Vaidyanath Someshwar Sami got married at the Chidambaram temple.

On the fascinating mention of their marriage, Appa would smilingly tell the children about how he relished the moment he saw Minnie for the first time during a casual walk in Pune. How he suddenly saw the ever-so-charming Minnie in a beautiful garden and couldn't stop looking at her. Then Minnie also shyly looked at him. Appa used to say, 'Then I began to sing, "Should I reveal? What I feel? Should I confess I love you." And then everything fell into place. Minnie immediately said yes to me.' On hearing this juicy story, Amma would shyly say, 'Enough, enough! Stop this drama now.' However, the bottom line of this marriage was that both their families were truly happy. This is how a barely fifteen-year-old Minnie Nadhan became a housewife.

Dusky and well-built, Amma was a housewife who was always happy no matter what. Usha never saw her stepping down from the merry-go-round of joy. Among the six brothers and sisters, Usha inherited a sense of joy from her Amma. Usha doesn't remember if Amma ever spoke in a loud manner. Amma was very proud of her husband who was a police officer. However, Appa's salary was limited. But Amma without any complaint would run the household with six children happily.

Usha couldn't see her paternal grandfather, Someshwar Iyer. Usha's elder sisters, Indira and Uma, did see him. Because Someshwar Iyer would call his eldest granddaughter Indira 'Kiddy Kiddy' out of love, all the children in the house would call him Kiddy Kiddy Tatha. He died at an early age. However, Usha vividly remembers her paternal grandmother, Parvati Iyer. The children called her Bombay Patti Ma. She stayed with them. The dishes prepared by her were delicious. How Amma held Bombay Patti Ma in the highest regard is still clear in Usha's mind. Usha's Appa was also responsible for his siblings—brothers Sheshu, Chadrashekhar aka Chandru and Debu and their only sister, Sushila. He ensured their education and like a father got them married and settled. Generally, a wife doesn't like it when her husband goes out of his way to take care of his parents and siblings. But Minnie Sami was the exact opposite. She not only appreciated this effort and affection of Usha's Appa towards his family but also supported him by cutting down her household budget.

Usha believes that her Amma demonstrated such a rare practice of giving that it is difficult to replicate. If Appa was the Banyan tree of modesty and ethos, Amma was his verdant green earth. Amma had a melodious voice and whenever she used to sing at leisure, Usha listened mesmerized. Amma especially loved listening to Juthika Roy's songs like 'Ghoonghat Ke Pat Khol Re', 'Tujhe Piya Milenge' and '*Main toh prem diwani, main hansti ti ti ti, Main roti ti ti ti, Gaati hun main ti ti ti*' were her favourites. Usha remembers how Amma would sing one of Rabindranath Tagore's Bengali song '*Oyi Malotilata dole / more bhabona kothai hara megher mothon ja chale / Oyi maloti lata dole*', with such depth and resonance. And Amma had another favourite Bengali song as well, '*Aelo varsha je sahsa / mone tai / rim-jhim / jhim-rim / jhim-jhim gaan geye / aelo varsha . . .*'

Amma liked cooking as much as she liked singing her favourite songs. She relished preparing one-of-a-kind dishes, especially the new recipes that caught her attention. Even the simple meals prepared by her had great taste. Her deep adoration for her children and husband was much evident in each and every moment, but breaking discipline was unacceptable for her. Even her way of washing and drying clothes had such perfection to it. She would hang the washed clothes in such a manner that there was no chance of a crease appearing on any of them. Post-drying, the garments looked as if they were ironed. There were no electric irons those days, so she would use a traditional heavy ferrous iron to press clothes for nine people, including herself, six children, her husband and Bombay Patti Ma. She would tell her children to smoothen life as well without any creases.

Appa was smitten by Amma's sweet and well-assembled attitude towards everything. He believed that Min was his soulmate forever. He used to say, 'Min is dedicated to an extent of being a slave to her family.' As much as Appa loved her, Amma felt a lot more respect for him in comparison to his love for her. Appa was very respectful when it came to women. Whenever he went to any programme as the deputy commissioner of Bombay and if he saw a constable's wife standing, he would vacate his chair for her. Usha's elder brother Shyam Sundar Sami aka Shamu had seen Appa do it many times at the Police Ground.

For Appa, his sweet Min was above everything. Shamu remembers one particular event when intense communal riots were taking place in Maharashtra and Gujarat. An important political figure from the undivided province of Bombay was demanding special security for himself from the Bombay police. The latter had deployed all its resources to contain the riots and hence the politician came to Someshwar Sami's home in Byculla fuming with anger. Coincidently, her husband was not at home, and it was Minnie Sami who had to deal with him. The politician seated in the drawing room began yelling at Minnie Sami, saying how the Bombay Police has left him on his own to die. He continued screaming, 'Do you know who I am? I am a minister. I will get your husband punished if he doesn't grant me complete protection immediately. I will leave your house only when your husband gives me special security.' The minister's anger was such that tears came out of Minnie's eyes. Suddenly, her husband came back. It angered him seeing the minister creating a scene at his house but moderating himself he calmly said, 'Yes Sir! What can I do for you?' The minister repeated his demand for special security in a furious and arrogant manner. Mr Sami responded, 'You came to my house and insulted my wife and even now you are not coming to your senses. You get up and leave immediately. Right now, the entire Bombay police is busy in controlling the riots. You come to my chamber tomorrow and I will see how I can help you.'

'I can't wait until tomorrow,' the politician growled. Mr Sami immediately called Parab, the police official deployed at his premises, and ordered, 'Parab! Take this man outside this campus and make him sit in his car so that he can go home.' Usha remembers many such episodes and thinks how Amma represented a sense of eternal familial feeling for Appa.

Usha recalls her father's joyous and evergreen maulshree, the Spanish cherry tree, laden with flowers and her mother's love for gardening. In the Love Lane bungalow, there are still many trees that were planted by Amma. Appa used to say to Amma, 'Min! You have green fingers.' Amma was an accomplished gardener and had her eyes on each and every plant inside the campus. The wilted plants she touched would sprout fresh leaves. Amma was a lot of things and Usha feels that even if she is able to uphold one-fourth of the qualities that she inherited from her, that would be more than enough. When remembering Amma, Usha feels as if tender buds are slowly and happily germinating in her veins.

The five women in Usha's life were like the shielding seasons that protected her from bad omens. There are comforting warm feathers that envelopes Usha when she thinks of Zakia Pathan Aunty as she walks down memory lane. The bungalow situated in Bombay's Love Lane where Usha spent her childhood, was next to the bungalow where S.M.A. Pathan, the deputy commissioner of Bombay's traffic police, lived.

At that time, Usha's Appa was CID's deputy commissioner of Bombay Police (Crime Branch). Pathan Uncle and Appa were colleagues, neighbours and good friends. Both the families shared a wonderful friendship. Pathan Aunty was very close to Amma. The Pathan couple had seven children—Yusuf, Abbas, Asad, Suraiya, Tahira, Jameela and Shameem. Yusuf and Suraiya were the eldest of the children. The seven children of the Pathan family and the six children of the Sami family were thick friends. Among all the siblings, Usha was the closest to the Pathan family from whom she learnt a lot. This included the love for prayer, cultural rituals, preparing mouth-watering delicacies as well as the art of stitching a salwaar-kameez. After returning from school, there were two sources of enjoyment for Usha. One was the giant guava tree on whose triangular branches she would lie down and read comics, resting her head on a pillow. The other destination was

Pathan Uncle's house where Pathan Aunty waited with unlimited love. Usha would lovingly call her Ammijaan. Pathan Aunty's youngest daughter Shameem studied with Usha at the same school and they were close friends. But over time, Usha became closer to Shameem's elder sister Jameela who was much older to Usha but took Indian classical music lessons at home. So, despite the age difference, Usha really enjoyed her company.

Jameela had turned a corner room of the house into a music room. From harmonium to tabla, there were many musical instruments there. Famous singer Himesh Reshammiya's father, Vipin Reshammiya, would come at 9 p.m. to teach her music. Although Vipin was Jameela's classmate in college, he was skilled at the harmonium, and she would take regular lessons from him. Little Usha, without fail, would come at the same time, and would quietly sit in the music room and watch Jameela practise. Usha would joyously say to Jameela, 'One day, you will become a big singer. And I will tell everyone that she is my elder sister, I have seen her practise since the very beginning.'

Jameela Pathan was incomparably beautiful. Her voice was equally sweet. Music maestros like Shakeel Badayuni, Khayyam, Naushad, Shankar-Jaikishan were frequent visitors at the Pathan house as they were close to Jameela's Abba. Khayyam and Shankar-Jaikishan had also made several offers to Jameela to sing in films. But Jameela father never agreed to the same.

Jameela studied at the St Xavier's College in Bombay. Her admirers would follow her till there as well. One of the many was Suresh Malhotra who was enamoured by her. Even Jameela surrendered to Suresh's love. Suresh was interested in an acting career in films. One day Jameela told him, 'I don't trust those who act in films. Such people even though married have many affairs.' Hearing this Suresh said that he would drop the thought of acting in films for her. And Suresh did as promised and went into film production. Film star Rajesh Khanna partnered with him in this venture.

Pathan Uncle got wind of Jameela and Suresh's love affair. He was dead against their marriage. One day, Pathan Uncle said to his daughter, 'You have a good voice. I can allow you to sing in films. Only on one condition: if you forget the idea of marriage to Suresh.' But Jameela was one of a kind. She told Pathan Uncle in a brief but firm manner that she would not marry anyone else other than Suresh. That's how she became Jameela Malhotra. Jameela now lives in Bengaluru. Suresh passed away a few years ago. But she still remembers how thrilled Usha was when she found out about their wedding.

Jameela has always been a role model for Usha. Since childhood, Usha would copy Jameela's classical singing style and she pestered Amma and got a salwar–kameez–dupatta set stitched, just like Jameela's. Usha loved the sight of Pathan Aunty and Jameela praying. So, Usha also began praying with both of them. Jameela would sometimes affectionately call Usha 'Maddy'. Although Usha was absolutely fascinated with Jameela Apa's love for music, for playing games, loitering and fun-filled silliness, her constant companion was Jameela's younger sister Shameem. The games Usha and Shameem played were unique. Sometimes, they got into a lot of trouble as well.

Pathan Uncle and Aunty were fond of chewing paan made of betel leaves. Whenever Pathan Aunty was busy making paan for herself, Usha, like a smitten kitten, would look at her. Putting all the ingredients for preparing a paan—the leaf, catechu (kattha), pieces of betel nut (supari), sliced, roasted and moist betel nut, liquid tobacco (kimam), tobacco masala (zarda) and peppermint— was amusing to observe for Usha. Sometimes, Ammijaan would ask her, 'Will you have a paan?' Usha would say no to such an offer. But Ammijaan would make her a special paan with just roasted betel nuts and mouth freshener. Usha would put in in her mouth in a royal style. At times, when Ammijaan would be busy with household chores, Usha, along with Shameem, would play the game of paan–paan. In the game, Usha would put the dupatta on her head just like Ammijaan, and sit with the paan box (paandaan) just like her. She would talk to Shameem complaining about household matters while cutting betel nuts with a scissor-like tool, *sarauta*.

One day, during this game, Usha made a paan for Shameem. Because Usha didn't know how much catechu and other ingredients went into it, she applied a thick coat of slaked lime (chuna) on the leaf and sprinkled a lot of catechu along with betel nuts, liquid tobacco and too much of peppermint, and offered it to Shameem. After having that paan, Shameem's head began to spin. Looking at Shameem suffering, Usha's hands and feet froze. In a desperate moment, she screamed at Shameem, 'Spit it. Spit it out!' But Shameem said if she spat it out, everyone at home would find out. So, amid all the chaos, Usha took Shameem to the bathroom where she rinsed her mouth many times and washed her face. Ammijaan sensed that something was wrong and she came to the bathroom door. Usha and Shameem were severely scolded. Shameem's inside cheek was swollen due to excess slaked lime, but she never told anyone that Usha had made her such a life-threatening paan. Even now when Usha sees anyone having paan, she thinks of Ammijaan. When Ammijaan passed away, Usha asked for her old paandaan and beautifully etched sarauta. Filled with countless memories, that paandaan is still with Usha. The beautiful sarauta as well.

The Pathan family always remained a circle of joy for Usha. She occasionally stays in touch with Jameela and her siblings, reliving the sweet memories of childhood. She gained a lot from the Pathan family, including her command over Hindi and Urdu. At Usha's house, Tamil and English were spoken but she got the hang of Hindi songs from the Pathan family. They watched Hindi films on a small projector at their home and so Usha got to see movies like *Udankhatola*, *Aan*, *Baiju Bawra* and *Aag*. Hindi films and their songs were very close to Usha's heart during her teenage years. The big stars of the Hindi film industry like Dilip Kumar, Nargis and Meena Kumari were close to the Pathan family and would often visit them. Looking at these eminent film personalities, Usha would imagine herself as being one of them someday. During Milad Shareef, it was a sure thing for Dilip Kumar, Nargis and Meena Kumari to visit the Pathan family. Usha with a smile, remembers when these stars would visit them in royal style, she would stare at them like a lesser mortal. Usha and Shameem would play cinema–cinema, where at times Usha would be Dilip Kumar and Shameem, Meena Kumari. Similarly, Usha would become Dev Anand and Shameem would be Nargis. Many years later, when Usha gained name and fame, she met the 'Tragedy King' of Hindi cinema, Dilip Kumar, at an event. Usha reminded him that she met him as a child at Pathan Uncle's house. The thespian immediately held her cheeks and said, 'Oh! You are Maddy, that crazy girl who would jubilantly sing on the dhol along with Mrs Pathan's daughter, Jameela. Do you still get to meet Ammijaan?'

Ammijaan, who considered Usha as her own daughter, would introduce her to the film celebrities saying, 'She is our daughter.' She was immensely fond of Usha. As Usha's family was Tamil Brahmin and they were strictly vegetarian, Ammijaan would specially prepare khichda without meat for Usha. Well-settled in the Pathan family, Usha's day-to-day fun would annoy her brothers and sisters. They would say to Amma, 'She eats khichda at Pathan Uncle's and comes home asking you for rasam.' Minnie Sami would faintly smile at the complaints against her daughter. The Sami couple was very liberal in nature. They were quite open towards the idea of accepting and respecting the religious beliefs of others. Although at that time there was lot of insistence upon religious rituals and practices in Tamil Iyer Brahmin families, the Samis were far more relaxed in these matters.

Once while visiting the Mahalakshmi temple in Bombay, Usha asked Amma out of curiosity, 'Amma, why is it written in the temple that only Hindus are allowed inside the cirque?' On Usha's innocent inquiry, Amma said, 'Hinduism is a way of life. The way one understands the true meaning and values of life is Hindusim. It's not related only with worshipping and rituals.' Such thoughts of Amma and Appa had a deep impact upon Usha, and her subconscious easily registered the fact that generosity is the key mantra of humanity. Religion is not only about worshipping and rituals but it's a way of life. That's why Usha believes that the atmosphere in which she grew up in, nurtured by her parents and the Pathan family, never allowed even a scratch on her mind and soul. That's why she was able to do everything in life the way she wanted to.

The love between the Sami and Pathan family was a living example of a generous and joyful way of coexistence. Each and every member of the Pathan family was part of all the festivals the Sami family celebrated, and in the same way, the Sami family would be present at all the festivities and events at the Pathan house.

The Sami and Pathan families stayed away from communal complexities. Pathan Uncle's eldest son, Asad married a Hindu girl and Usha's constant companion Jameela wedded a Hindu, Suresh Malhotra. Something similar happened with Usha and her brothers and sisters. They studied at a Christian convent school. That's how they learnt English and French at school and Hindi, Urdu and Tamil at home and the neighbourhood. Usha often wondered while growing up what is it that separates religions across the world from each other. In time, Usha understood the differentiating factor among people practising different religions. It was manifest in their food habits, their prayers, their dress and the practices they followed. Usha feels that the environment at her home, the Pathan household as well as her proximity to schoolmates belonging to diverse religious communities left a deep impact on her. And this happened because Appa and Amma gave her the freedom to expand her personality. Appa and Amma in a way had strongly inculcated the idea in their children that to be a true Hindu is exactly like being a true Muslim, Sikh, Christian or a Jew. Usha believes that Amma and Appa taught them that being a good Hindu is all about being a good human being who listens to all and accepts their good thoughts.

Even today, when Usha remembers the Pathan family, she is reminded of the songs of Lalan Faqir. His songs are popular across Bengal. She has sung a lot of his songs:

> *Shob loke koy Lalon ki jaat sansaare Lalan bole jater ki roop?*
> *Dekhlam na ei nazore Sunnot dile hoye Musholman*
> *Narir jate ki hoye vidhan Bamun chini poiter promaan Bamani*
> *chini ke prokare?*
> *Shob loke koy Lalon ki jaat sansaare?*

Lalan notes that a Brahmin man can be recognized by his sacred thread but what about a Brahmin woman? Lalan's story goes that he was born in a Brahmin family but was afflicted by small pox as a child. He was in a miserable close-to-death situation and his parents abandoned him. A Muslim fakir picked him up and raised him. That's how a Brahmin Lalan became a Muslim. Usha still remembers how the Pathan family's fragrance became a part of her life because of the love and affection she shared with them.

The childhood spent at the Byculla bungalow was truly magical. At home, where Appa worshipped Lord Ganesha, Amma prayed to Goddesses Lakshmi and Saraswati. When Usha would pray, mimicking Amma at home, everyone would laugh uncontrollably. But it was the same Usha who would copy Jameela offering namaz and the Sisters kneeling down and praying at the chapel. The Love Lane still has the Mankeshwar temple and the Gloria Church where Usha would leisurely pray before her exams. Usha was a little weak in mathematics so she would go to the

Shiva mandir and offer two to three coconuts bought from the money saved from her allowance whenever she would pass her exam. She would also light ten candles kneeling down near the Rosary Grotto at her school chapel.

The European style bungalow is still vivid in Usha's memories. Most recently, the additional director general of the Anti-Corruption Bureau, Vivek Fansalkar, was living there. IPS Krishnaprakash lives in the bungalow right next to it where Pathan uncle used to live. Statues of Lord Ganesha and Lord Krishna now stand at the entry of the bungalow. Even today, it more or less stands there in its full glory but many things around it have changed. Usha's childhood home had the police warehouse right next to it. But for the last fifteen years, Sulochana Pawar has been running a women's police canteen there, which offers lunch, breakfast, tea and coffee among other things. According to Sulochana, she got the space under a police welfare scheme There is a water dispensing structure right next to the police canteen in the memory of the late Ummedmalji Hazaarimalji Rathorwali Rajasthan. But four water taps have dried at the structure. This footpath, touching the European bungalow, is covered with almond trees.

Just opposite the bungalow, across the road lies the big old premises of Regina Pacis Religious of Mary Immaculate. There runs the Regina Pacis Convent High School for girls and the Gloria Church right behind the property. There is a mosque in front of the church and a Hanuman temple next to it. Next to Regina Immaculate is the Masina Hospital run by a Parsi community trust which has an ancient brick-like textured entrance. After Gloria Chowk, there is Miyan Ahmed Darvesh Chowk which is also called Savta Marg. There is a school for young and special children that has been run for decades by the Gloria Church.

Usha came to the same church to pray before her exams. Next to the Love Lane is the Hansraj Lane, where stands the 150-year-old Shri Mankeshwar Shiva Mandir where the vibrant Usha's joy continues to dwell. This was the same temple where she would offer coconuts after getting good grades in school exams. A train line runs next to the temple. Usha still hasn't forgotten the duet of the sound of the echoes of the temple bells with the clickety-clack of the trains.

Shri Mankeshwar Shiva Mandir is managed by people from the Gujarati community. The makers of the temple, Seth Hansraj Karamshi Ranmal Charitable Trust's main trustee Praveen Bhai, and the temple's head priest, Shri Shri Mahesh Maharaj, are aware of the fact that Usha used to visit this temple as a child. Inside the temple premises, Nand Singh who hails from Nepal's Achham district sells flowers says with a charming smile, 'I also heard that Usha Didi used to come here as a child.'

Indeed, time flew by touching so many passages of life, but Byculla's Love Lane is still in Usha's veins. All community festivals were celebrated with utmost excitement. People from every community would participate with a deep sense of belonging. Even now Love Lane continues to be a 'Little India' where people of Hindu, Muslim, Sikh, Christian, Parsi and Yehudi faiths coexist. Usha, whenever she remembers the Pathan family's Eid, loses herself in the happiness of those beautiful old times. Usha still hasn't forgotten that silly and hilarious incident when she decided to give Pathan uncle an Eid Mubarak card.

After saving some money from her pocket money with great difficulty, she went to the Zafar Book Store that was located near the Gloria church from where she would often borrow comic books for a small fee. However, before Eid that year Usha bought an Urdu-scribbled Eid card for two annas for Pathan uncle. His children addressed him as Abbajaan as did Usha. Anyway, Usha decorated the card and gave it to Abbajaan. After reading the lines in Urdu on the card, Abbajaan burst into laughter and said, 'You mad girl, what card are you giving me?' Then, Ammijaan, Suraiya, Tahira and Jameela saw the card and began laughing at Usha's innocence. The Urdu lines on the card said, 'Eid Mubarak, my beloved!' and the lines in Urdu inside the card went something like this, 'It's Eid today, give me a hug today you heartless! It's a worldly ritual, we also have the opportunity and it's expected.' Looking at everyone laughing crazily, Usha, completely aghast, kept staring at their faces wondering what she had possibly done for all of them to laugh at her. Jameela says, 'Even today, Usha's childhood innocence remains alive within her.'

The fragrance of those memories! Usha cannot forget sweet Tulsima. She was always there during Usha's childhood with her boundless love, despite a rugged and lifeless personal desert throbbing in her veins. She never let anyone get a sense of this while she worked for the Sami family. The fifth woman in Usha's life, Tulsima, influenced her inner world. It was Tulsima who made Usha realize and register naturally in her subconscious that there was glory in being a giver. In Usha's eyes her Tulsima was the most generous person in the world. From washing Usha's and her siblings' clothes to being particular about their meals and even offering one or two annas for something that Usha would throw a tantrum for, Tulsima took care of everything.

When Usha's brother Shamu was about to be born, Sister Subbalakshmi had sent the twenty-five-year-old Tulsima to Minnie Sami in Bombay from Madras. Tulsima was a child widow. After Tulsima came to the Sami family, she never went back to her husband's home. Whenever Tulsima would go down memory lane, she would talk about visiting her maternal home in Kumbakonam in Tamil Nadu. Before leaving for Kumbakonam, she would say that everytime she intended to spend the rest of her life there, her eternal bond with the Sami family always brought her back sooner than expected. The children would dance with joy when she returned. Then Tulsima in a hush-hush tone would say to Minnie Sami, 'What do I say? I am not able to stay in Kumbakonam without these kids.' It was Tulsima who packed the lunch boxes diligently for all the children with sambhar rice, curd rice, rasam and vegetables. Usha was the closest to her, so she would secretly give her one or two annas, which she tied to a corner of her saree. This loving gesture was from her monthly salary.

When Someshwar Sami moved to the police quarters in Worli, Tulsima moved there as well. After her marriage, Usha shifted to Calcutta. But whenever she visited Bombay, there would be no end to Tulsima's excitement. As she grew old, she had difficulty in walking but hearing Usha's voice she would approach slowly and rest her head on Usha's chest while hugging her. Then she would place Usha's suitcase carefully under the bed. Appa would laugh and say to Usha, 'Yes, yes. Keep your house clean and spread junk in our house.' Tulsima would smile at Appa's banter and then would string one or two lines in English to welcome Usha. 'You need coffee, Usha?' she would inquire and prepare coffee and sit with Usha on the dining table. But should Appa cross the room, she would immediately get up. From such mannerisms that Usha noticed in Tulsima, she was able to understand that a person should always be aware of his or her status. Usha, at some point, had put up a message in her old studio: 'If you feel you are unwanted . . . you are!' Usha believes that a person is his own measure. And she also believes that she learnt this from Tulsima.

Usha grew up in a big family. It was not possible to provide independent rooms to everyone. Tulsima would always alert Usha and her sisters that a woman should never sleep flat on her back. She used to say that women should always sleep on their side. During train journeys, Tulsima would somehow cover Usha and her sisters with bedsheets. That's the reason that despite singing at nightclubs, Usha was always seen wearing a full-sleeve blouse paired with the saree and went to the extent of covering the mic with the corner of her saree while singing. Usha also learnt to prepare dosa, idli, rasam etc. from Tulsima who used to say that women should be skilled in the art of cooking.

Tulsima was always loving but at times Usha saw the sadness in her eyes. Perhaps that was because she was left with no blood relatives in the end. Appa would safely get her salary deposited at the post office, but one of Tulsima's distant relatives had conned a lot of money from her with a fake sob story. But she never regretted that she lost money. 'She needed the money more than I,' she said with grace.

Tulsima passed away after Appa and Amma left the world. In their last days, Appa and Amma lived at Worli's Deenath Court. Tulsima fulfilled her duties to them till their last breath. When Tulsima passed away, Usha visited Bombay. Usha's brother Shamu performed the last rites. When the priest enquired about the dead's gotra, her lineage, Shamu told him his own—Kaushik. Even after Appa and Amma's demise, she never forgot her love and gratitude towards the Sami family. Usha remembers how Tulsima would cut the newspaper clippings of any event or news that featured her and treasure them. Usha took Tulsima a few times to her shows at the Bombay's Oberoi hotel where Tulsima had cried with happiness.

Such small and precious memories of the past in which so many loving people figured. People, who Usha knows, won't come back to life. The triagonal branches of the lovely guava tree won't be found again where the little and carefree Usha would read her comics resting on a pillow on its boughs. And those five women won't be there who shaped her with their love during her childhood. Usha's eyes well up. She instinctively remembers the lines of the heart-wrenching pop song 'First of May' from the album *Odessa* released by the Bee Gees in 1969. It is a song that soaks the soul in deep introspection:

> *When I was small and Christmas trees were tall*
> *We used to love while others used to play*
> *Don't ask me why, but time has passed us by*

Someone else moved in from far away
Now we are tall and Christmas trees are small
And you don't ask the time of day
But you and I our love will never die
But guess we'll cry come first of May.

How, even many decades later, does a pop song suddenly reappear on the apex of the soul's surface? All those who loved left one by one. Eyes get wet remembering each one of them. Who will cry during Christmas, drenched with the tears and capped by memories? Usha Vaidyanath Someshwar Sami? Usha Iyer? Usha Uthup? Bombay's Love Lane? Swarnam? Madras Patti Ma? Amma? Pathan Aunty? Or Tulsima? Usha feels that they will all cry together—crying out of love.

5

Bombay Police's Sherlock Holmes

The Gamdevi Police Station at Grant Road in Bombay was swarming with people in the morning hours. The previous night, Car Mart's owner, sixty-year-old Mohammad Siddiqui Chunawala, his forty-five-year-old wife Fatimabai, eight-year-old grandson Sajid and the house help, Annie, were murdered in their ground-floor flat in a multi-storeyed building located on Owen Dunn Road in South Bombay.

Chunawala's son lived in Germany and his daughter was based in Aden. The strangest thing was that the murderers didn't touch a thing at the apartment. The Chunawala family was murdered without leaving much of a trace. After the murder, the blood-stained floor was wiped clean. The criminals were wearing gloves. But during the murder, the clothes worn by the killers might have been stained in the process of controlling the chaos and the family's terrorized state. That's why the murderers took their clothes, spattered with blood to the kitchen and burnt them. It was the year 1967 and Bombay Police's CID deputy commissioner Vaidyanath Someshwar Sami was going to retire soon.

Mohammad Siddiqui Chunawala was a big businessman and his murder had put the Gamdevi Police Station in a deep shock. Curfew was enforced in the area under the police station's jurisdiction. Ultimately, seeing no developments in this puzzling murder case, the inspector of the Gamdevi Police Station called Vaidyanath Someshwar Sami and communicated the gravity of the situation. He requested the latter to help in the investigation.

After receiving the details, Sami—Bombay Police's Sherlock Holmes—without wasting any time reached the Gamdevi Police Station and along with the inspector went to the murder spot and examined each and every corner of the house. As the murderers had cleaned the house after killing the entire Chunawala family, it was extremely difficult to identify any clue or evidence. Suddenly, Vaidyanath Sami's sharp eyes met with the burnt pieces of clothes in the kitchen. He asked the policemen to collect the ashes and place them carefully in front of him. Even if they found a thread that didn't burn, they had to take it out safely. So, two policemen got their heads together and began a fine inspection. In a trice, one of them found a half-burnt cloth piece in the ashes and showed it to Vaidyanath Sami. It was the tailor's tag stitched on the collar of a shirt.

Vaidyanath Sami, taking a confident deep breath, said to the Gamdevi police inspector, 'Now this case will be solved.' The inspector's disappointed face was lit with hope. He said, ' Sir! The adapted poem that you often quote is true: "Lives of master criminals all remind us . . . That we might do a bit of time . . . And departing leave behind us . . . Thumbprints on the charts of crime." Really salute you, sir!' Renowned poet H.W. Longfellow's famous poem was the basis of cracking the toughest cases and it was quite popular among Bombay's policemen. Gamdevi's police inspector said, 'Sir, today you practically showed me what this poem stands for!'

'Good! Now you must have understood the way forward,' Vaidyanath Someshwar Sami said, his razor-sharp eyes on the inspector.

'Yes! Got it, sir. This collar that had this tag will be caught even if he is hiding in hell. With this key evidence, we will get to the Chunawala murderers,' the inspector said optimistically.

'That's great!' Sami responded.

Bombay's famous deputy commissioner was a firm believer in the theory that no matter how much time it takes to research a case, there will be a result if one is constantly at it. The Chunawala murder mystery was one of the most bizarre and serious cases in Sami's long police career that came to him right before his retirement. With that half-burnt collar tag and rigorous investigation for months, the culprits were caught. In his police service, Vaidyanath Someshwar Sami had solved many unresolved mysteries in ruthless criminal cases. And the strange part of it was that Sami had never imagined that he would join the police force.

His father Someshwar Iyer, who hailed from an affluent Diwan Sheshadri family, had to face a severe financial crisis at one point. He was the descendant of Sir Kumarpuram Sheshadri Iyer who was Mysore's Diwan for a long time and hadn't ever imagined adverse times. The family enjoyed a prestigious position among Iyer Brahmins. A lawyer by profession and later on the Diwan of Mysore, it was Sheshadri Iyer who laid the foundation of the now modern Bengaluru. Be it the governance of southern India or in the education, art and cultural domains, the Iyer Brahmins have always contributed to being at the forefront. It is noteworthy that Iyer Brahmins of Tamil origin are followers of the Advaita philosophy established by Adi Shankaracharya. They are one of the five Brahmin communities, Pancha Dravida as classified in *Rajatarangini,* a historical chronicle written by Kashmiri historian, Kalhana in the twelfth century CE. The Iyer population is still mainly in Tamil Nadu, although many in the community are settled in Karnataka and Kerala as well. After Independence, the Iyer Brahmins also moved to Bombay and Delhi.

Strictly vegetarian and lovers of coffee and curd, the Iyer Brahmins have always been staunch traditionalists. The patrons of Bharat Natya Shastra and Bharatanatyam, south India's Iyer Brahmins have been dominant benefactors of dance and music in their society. Due to their strong command over Tamil and English, they were essential to the British Raj as well. While remembering his family's golden past and struggling for identity in Bombay, Someshwar had no one to share his agony with.

During the 1900s, he was working for a tram company. In those days, trams were pulled by horses. Vaidyanath Sami was born in Bombay on 21 November 1908. From the very beginning, he had witnessed how his mother Parvati and father Someshwar were pulling the household tram with great difficulty. However, after years of working for the Bombay Tram Company, Vaidyanath's father, Someshwar Iyer, returned to Mysore with his family. Thus most of Vaidyanath's schooling happened in Bangalore. He studied at the Government High School, Malleshwaram, Bangalore, and later did his college education from St Joseph's College. During those days Someshwar Iyer once again fell on bad days and one by one, his wife Parvati had to sell all her jewellery.

As Vaidyanath was the eldest, he was witness to this crisis. Since he had completed his college education, he moved to Bombay intending to find a job to hep his family through its bad times. Initially, he found employment as a screen puller at the Opera House theatre. But he wasn't able to continue there for long. He also worked as an insurance agent for some time. Coincidently, during those days in the 1930s, the Nasik Police Training School had advertised for those domiciled in Bombay to apply for the police force. As Vaidyanath Sami was born in Bombay, he had a birth certificate from the same city. So, he applied and was enrolled as a cadet officer. After training, Vaidyanath Someshwar Sami joined the Bombay Police in 1931 as a sub-inspector. He was unmarried and lived at the Byculla's sub-inspectors' quarters. From 1931 to 1967, Vaidyanath Someshwar Sami served the police in various capacities.

As a sub-inspector he served at many police stations in Bombay during the 1930s. At that time he was also transferred to Pune for a brief stint. It was there that he met Swarnambal aka Chinni at an event. Chinni introduced him to Meenambal aka Minnie. It was love at first sight. Minnie and Vaidyanath lost no time in deciding to be life partners. Minnie was Hallasya K. Nadhan's eldest daughter among seven children. She was born in Pune and was educated at the St Helena's School. Her teacher as well as the principal Ms Evelyn C. Gaze and Ms C. Wilson were great admirers of Minnie's sharp mind. When Minnie told her father about her romance and marriage plans, he was taken aback as he wanted his daughter to pursue higher education. The Nadhan family's life in Pune had many ups and downs. It was in Pune where Hallasya K. Nadhan made Chinni his second wife, which Minnie's mother Dharmambal quietly accepted with deep pain. Perhaps, Minnie opted for a love marriage with Vaidyanath Sami at a young age to avenge her father's second marriage.

Such impulsive love marriages often fail, but luckily Minnie had found a dedicated life partner. Vaidyanath Sami proved to be an ideal husband. In 1936, after two years of marriage, Vaidyanath and Minnie had a daughter, Indira. Then in 1938, a second daughter Uma and in 1940, son Shyam Sundar aka Shamu was born. By then, Vaidyanath Sami was transferred back to Bombay. Actually, many senior officials in the police department were impressed by Sami's attentive and dedicated work ethic and that's why in 1939 he was made a part of the Bombay's CID. It was a momentous turning point of his career. He was associated with the Bombay Police's crime branch for twenty-eight years and retired as deputy commissioner towards the end of his career. His image in the Bombay Police was that of an impossible and yet, intelligent officer. However, he had to step away twice from the CID department when in 1943 he was promoted as a deputy inspector and was posted at the Mahim and Lamington Road police stations. Then two years later, in 1945, he was recalled to the CID.

Seven years later, in 1952, when he was appointed as the police superintendent, he was transferred to the prohibition department for a few years. But Mr Sami's relationship with the CID was like that of fish with water. The newspapers also noticed how serious crime was tackled when Bombay's Sherlock Holmes, Vaidyanath Sami, was in the CID. On 26 August 1955, a daily in its editorial wondered why a police officer with so much expertise has been given an extended stint in the prohibition department. It speculated that perhaps the bigwigs in government did not give due importance to solving murders, robbery and other grave criminal acts and were only interested in prohibition. To his credit, Vaidyanath Someshwar Sami with his ability and hard work had swiftly resolved many pending cases in the prohibition department and given it a new shine. He even nailed Mumbai's notorious alcohol mafia.

Before being appointed at the prohibition department, Sami was with the Bombay CID from 1945 to 1951 and had solved several nerve-wracking cases and caught wanted criminals in the Turf Soda Factory murder case, Bombay Central Bank robbery, Lloyds Bank robbery case, Kuldeep murder case and the Bombay House robbery case, among others. That was the reason officials at the Bombay CID wanted him back after he was posted elsewhere after his promotion. It was the time when the Bombay Police's morale was at its peak because of valiant police officers like Billimoria, Kadampande and Rajadhakshya. The Bombay Police was considered as the ideal force in the country. These esteemed police officers always boosted their colleagues' morale and kept them focused on their goals so that the Bombay Police persistently maintained its diligent and dutiful status. Similarly, with valorous officers like Bombay CID's deputy commissioner Kwilter to Paranjpe, Pendekar, Fremroz, Bodhanwala, Razdan, Lobo, Potdaar, Samant, Nayar, Korde and Khan, Bombay CID was famous as one of the best investigative agencies. Such officers, including Sami, were the spine of the department. Such bravery and dedication is a rarity in today's police officers. The way the Bombay CID decoded and closed many serious criminal cases led to it being compared to the world's best, the Scotland Yard.

Bombay's Central Bank robbery was a case in point. It had left the city's residents in a shock. But the way Vaidyanath Sami caught the gang responsible for the robbery, with his sharp mind and diligence, made headlines in the newspapers and remained a topic of discussion for a long time. In the beginning there were no clues. But Vaidyanath Sami had spotted an unclaimed car parked on Mohammad Ali Road in the same week of the bank robbery. The car covered in dust was parked outside a Muslim man's house. Vaidyanath Sami saw that children were playing on top of that unidentified car.

While researching a case Sami would often visit the local tea shops and salons on street corners. He believed that an investigation was like hunting with deep patience. One has to keep one's sixth sense in a complete state of alertness. During the quest, he would also fully utilize Bombay Police's Fingerprint Bureau and the Police Dog Squad. He placed informers in almost all the colonies in Bombay. He would only rest once he had enough evidence against the accused so that they wouldn't get away in the court for the lack of it. However, he was against the practice of third-degree torture of criminals as he found it quite inhuman. By solving the Bombay Central Bank robbery case with his sharp and attentive mind, Vaidyanath Sami had astounded officers in his department.

The robbers hadn't even left a strand of a clue after the crime. The police chief was losing his sanity over this case. Whenever angry, he would begin speaking in English. But Vaidyanath Sami in a relaxed tone reassured the chief, 'Sir, don't you worry. I will catch the criminals even if they are hiding in hell.' He immediately alerted all his informers across Bombay. Soon his informer from Mohammad Ali Road called and told him that there has been an unclaimed car parked outside a Muslim man's house on the road for a week now.

'You stay right there! I am leaving office right now,' Vaidyanath Sami said to the informer in a soft tone, 'My hope is alive now.'

Vaidyanath Sami reached Mohammad Ali Road in an hour. He saw the car covered with dust and the kids from the lane playing on top of it. Sami wondered how it would be possible to identify the fingerprints of the robbers amid countless fingerprints of the children playing on the car. Still, he felt he must give it a try. Along with the informer, Vaidyanath Sami went to the nearest phone booth and called the Fingerprint Bureau and asked them to come and take fingerprints. The Bureau took Mr Sami's call as seriously as an emergency, but the car was covered with too many fingerprints. Even the experts were sweating at the impossibility of the task. When the process was over, Sami opened the car door. Right below the car seat, he found a torn piece of an Urdu newspaper. When Sami was asking the Bureau to take fingerprints from it, suddenly out of nowhere he thought of a criminal called Ibu who was accused of stealing a revolver a few months ago. Without further delay, he called for Ibu's dossier. His suspicion became stronger when he discovered that Ibu's address was about 200 metres away from Mohammad Ali Road. After that, the detective inside Sami was ready for action. He sent Ibu's bail bond to the Fingerprint Bureau to check if his fingerprints were on the car and the piece of newspaper recovered from inside it. After checking the countless fingerprints on the car and the torn piece of the newspaper, the Bureau called Sami with utmost excitement, 'Sir, It's Ibu's! We are sending you the report.' Ibu was arrested in a hurry and all the other criminals involved in the Bombay Central Bank robbery were caught. Vaidyanath Sami used to say, 'Most of the time, our intuition is stronger than evidence.'

In 1945, Vaidyanath Sami similarly solved The Turf Soda Factory murder case. Khan Bahadur Pardiwal, a respectable

Parsi of Bombay, was the owner of The Turf Soda Factory. Due to his noble heartedness, he was not only admired in the Parsi community but in other communities as well. It was a rain-drenched morning in 1947 when Khan Bahadur's sick wife went to his room and screamed at the sight of his blood-stained dead body on the bed. Khan Bahadur usually woke up at dawn, but that morning his wife had gone to his room because there was no sign of him moving about. After looking at her husband's dead body, she rushed outside in an unstable state. People crowded outside the house hearing Begum Khan Bahadur's cries. The news of the murder spread like wildfire. The police also reached the spot without delay, and when they inspected the dead body they found that Khan Bahadur had been fatally stabbed in the neck.

Inquiries revealed that Khan Bahadur had hired two young Sikh men at his factory who were now missing. What was quite strange was that nothing was stolen from the factory or the house. The Parsi community was in deep shock after the murder. Ultimately, the case was handed over to the CID. The two men were arrested in Ahmedabad and were brought to Bombay for trial. Both confessed that they had their eyes on the jewellery kept in Khan Bahadur's bedroom locker. They had entered Khan Bhahadur's room via the window on the night of the murder. Both got into a major scuffle with him. And when they failed to snatch the locker keys from Khan Bahadur, they killed him out of frustrated rage. When they saw a massive flow of blood spurt out of the victim's neck, they both admitted being jittery with fear and hence quietly fled through the window. It was Vaidyanath Sami who cracked the case and arrested the two men in Ahmedabad.

In 1947 Vaidyanath Sami left the people of Bombay startled by solving the mysterious case of a headless body. On 11 September, the Railway Police at Shamgadh station near Bombay found a big unidentified black trunk from the bogie of a train. At first the policemen thought that it contained drugs. But when they broke the lock, they found a robust man's dead body inside it. The Railway Police forwarded the case to the CID for further investigation. When one of the officers in the CID failed to solve the case, it was given to inspector Vaidyanath Sami to investigate. In the past one and half months, despite all efforts the dead body in the trunk had not been identified. Inspector Sami began by conducting a thorough inquiry at the Bombay Central Station, following which he sent a photo of the dead person to all the stations near Shamgadh where the dead body was found in a black trunk inside a train compartment.

After an extensive investigation, Inspector Sami found out that the dead person was a man named Kuldeep who came to Bombay to start a business a few years ago. In the beginning he was introduced to VC India Ltd's owner, Amreek Singh Malik. Amreek allowed Kuldeep to work from a portion of his office. In a short time, Kuldeep's hard work paid off and his business struck roots. When Inspector Sami found out about Kuldeep's family during the investigation he called for Kuldeep's elder brother Dhanwant from Lahore. Dhanwant was shocked looking at the image of his brother's dead body. He said Kuldeep had stopped writing letters for a while, and so his parents and folks thought that maybe he was busy in his business. But they couldn't imagine in their wildest dreams that Kuldeep was murdered in such a mysterious way. Dhanwant told the inspector that Kuldeep would always mention his friend Amreek Singh Malik in all the letters he wrote to his family in the past.

Inspector Sami called Amreek Singh Malik to the headquarters for further questioning. Whatever Malik said during the interrogation related to Kuldeep sounded contradictory. So, Inspector Sami without any delay decided that there should be an immediate raid at Amreek Singh Malik's house and office. He didn't allow Malik any time. Taking Malik with him, he went to his PM Road office. He also raided his Colaba home. An unlicensed revolver was found at Amreek's office. Each and every corner of Malik's house was checked. Inspector Sami noticed that Malik's house was freshly painted. So, he got a team of labourers and got the newly painted walls scratched. He was astounded to see splattered blood spots on the walls. The police also found a letter written in Urdu at Amreek's house, which was written by his employee Ram Singh. There was nothing significant as such in the letter, but one particular line was repeated thrice in it: 'There is nothing to worry.' Inspector Sami was intrigued by this line. It was found that Ram Singh had been changing his name as per his convenience.

Inspector Sami was certain that without arresting Ram Singh the murder mystery could not be solved. So, he sent one of his trusted associates, Inspector Salvi to Jammu to find out about Ram Singh. Inspector Salvi donned an army uniform for this mission and the army was alerted in Jammu. Ram Singh was caught and after much grilling he admitted to murdering Kuldeep on his employer Amreek Singh Malik's orders. Ram Singh was brought back to Bombay. Malik was questioned. He initially denied everything, but broke down later. He told the police about the coolie who carried the trunk from his Colaba apartment to the railway station. Inspector Sami also found the shop where the trunk was purchased. That's how Inspector Sami collected all the evidence and presented it at the court. Amreek and his employee Ram Singh were sentenced to death by hanging.

Sami's colleagues couldn't often figure out his ways of investigation. He solved the Bombay Llyods Bank robbery case with the help of a clue given by a schoolgirl! During the early days, his department's head was G.J.W. Kwilter, and Vaidyanath Sami was called Kwilter's 'brain trust' by the department. When Inspector Sami solved the sensational Bruce Bank robbery in 1949, the report on the front page of the newspapers said—'Kwilter's brain trust worked with quick and quiet efficiency'. Kwilter was synonymous with terror for the criminals in Bombay. He and his close associate Vaidyanath Sami's name was enough to shake up the big dons of that time. After retirement, Kwilter went to Australia with his family. But his love for the Sami family was so deep that even after twenty-five years when his son and daughter-in-law were visiting Bombay for some work, he told his son, 'Do meet Vaidyanath Sami and give him my blessings.' So, Kwilter's son and daughter-in-law came to see Uncle Sami at his Worli home and told him how their father talked fondly of him.

Sami also fondly remembered police chief, A.G. Rajadhyaksh. When Sami retired in the second week of November 1967, presiding over his farewell ceremony, A.G. Rajadhyaksh said, 'Vaidyanath Someshwar Sami is the pride of the Indian police. His sense of discipline, courage and dedication is exemplary for every police officer.' Indeed, from 1931 until 1967, for thirty-six long years, Vaidyanath Sami had given 100 per cent to his work. Most of his career was spent at the Bombay CID. He was so well-respected that he even got a two-year extension. During his service period, he received four gold medals.

There were other proud feathers in his cap. One was the Bombay House robbery case which Vaidyanath Sami solved. The year 1949 had just begun and employees were supposed to be paid as usual on 10 January at the Tata Sons & Company Limited-owned Swadesi Mills at Kurla. So, Rs 3,49,265 were withdrawn from the bank and kept safely in a big trunk at the Tata's headquarter in Bombay House. But the criminals overwhelmed the guards at the stroke of midnight and left with the box. A robbery, that too at Bombay House, was unimaginable. Bombay CID's deputy commissioner was assigned the case. The boss, Kwilter asked his most trusted right hand, Inspector Sami, to get on with the investigation. Inspector Sami took each case as a challenge and this was a big one in which Tata Sons was targeted. Inspector Sami alerted all his informers.

The very next day an interesting coincidence took place. Inspector Sami was at the tramway stop around 8 p.m. when he saw three young men glaring at each other and having a heated argument. The onlookers surely saw them but chose not to get involved. Inspector Sami had his eyes on them from a distance. The angry men boarded a bus. Inspector Sami took a taxi and asked the driver to follow the bus. The three men got off at the Gowalia Tank bus stop. Inspector Sami asked the cabbie to park his car at some distance from the bus. Then he started following the three of them maintaining a distance. Three of them entered a big building. Inspector Sami drove in the taxi and immediately reached the area's police station and along with the police force he went back to the building. One of the men had left the building by then but the other two, Fali and Bali, were apprehended and brought to the Gamdevi Police Station for further questioning. Inspector Sami never preferred third-degree during interrogation, but his way of questioning was such that the accused often confessed. During the questioning, Fali and Bali revealed that the third man was Lorry Pinto who was a champion boxer.

Fali and Bali admitted that it was they along with Lorry who stole the trunk full of money from Bombay House. Fali during the interrogation revealed that they were fighting over the stolen money. On further investigation, the police found out that Lorry Pinto was working with Fali and Bali for the past four months on the robbery. As Fali and Bali were Parsi, it was easy for them to get inside Bombay House. However, it was the Parsi duo who gave Lorry the blueprint of the robbery plan. Lorry assured Fali and Bali that with his boxing techniques, he would knock down the security guards, and during that time Fali and Bali would be able to get away with the money. The most noteworthy thing in all this was how Fali and Bali took the Bombay House's invoice clerk Jamshed P. Surti and two more workers into confidence, promising them a share in the loot. The Bombay CID finally captured Lorry Pinto and Bombay House's invoice clerk Surti, and the other two staffers who were involved were arrested as well. After the final investigation, the police concluded that an infamous criminal Sher Khan who was serving his seven-year jail term at the Bombay Central Jail was their ringmaster and half the money was delivered at the location ordered by Sher Khan. The police raided that location too but unfortunately, nothing came of it. After a lot of trouble, the police somehow recovered Rs 1,28,000. The newspapers in Inspector Sami's praise wrote, 'Had it not been for Mr Sami, the stolen money from Bombay House would have never been recovered.'

Similarly, some thieves had stolen the goddess's jewellery from Bombay's famous Mahalakshmi Temple. Yet again, Inspector Sami caught and arrested them and recovered the jewellery and got it reassembled on the goddess's figurine.

It was said that Vaidyanath Sami could smell a criminal even if he was hiding in the corners of hell. It was the month of April in 1949 when a gardener watering pots in an apartment in Malabar Hill spotted a young woman's dead body hidden in the bushes. For a moment, the gardener turned pale with fear. He informed the residents of the building, and the police was alerted immediately. It became clear that the woman didn't live in the same building. She was murdered elsewhere and the killer had hidden her dead body in the bushes at night. The woman's dead body had nothing else apart from a petticoat. She had no bruises either and the police believed that she was murdered by suffocating her. She remained unidentified for two days. The police officials were fed up trying to identify her by showing her photograph in almost 300 houses in the area. Ultimately, the Bombay CID was roped into the case. Through his sources, Inspector Sami located the dead woman's sister. After investigation, he found out that the dead woman was a policeman's lover. He killed her by pressing her mouth and hid the body in the bushes downstairs in the Malabar Hill-situated building with the help of a local barber. Inspector Sami arrested the policeman in question. But he wasn't ready to confess his crime. Inspector Sami then began looking for the barber who was missing from Bombay. After much trouble, he was traced and arrested. The barber was hiding in the caves of the Ratnagiri jungles. The policeman and the barber were sentenced to death.

The exploits of Vaidyanath Sami, are endless. He was truly dynamic and full of valour. His daughter Usha is a replica of her father. When Usha holds the mic and sings her famous song 'Doston se pyaar kiya, dushmanon se badla liya, jo bhi kiya, humne kiya shaan se . . .' it seems like Vaidyanath Sami's gracious heroic stature is echoing in India's pop music queen's voice. When Usha begins her joyful blast of 'Nakabandi . . . Areh Nakabandi', it feels like Vaidyanath Sami is proudly smiling from backstage. Accomplished as her father was as a police official, he was an equally dedicated and loving family man. Usha has inherited all his qualities. She too is upright, meticulous, courageous, hardworking and ready to live and die for her loved ones. That's why her fellow-workers, friends, acquaintances and well-wishers are soaked in her love. Like her Appa, being there for people in their good and bad times is in Usha's nature.

Usha remembers her close maternal cousin Chikku's wedding. The Sami family reached Madras from Bombay a week before the wedding. Chikku's mother, Usha's loving maternal aunt Mrs Leela Nadhan, had made arrangements for the Sami family at a good guest house. Actually, Leela Mami didn't want the family's son-in-law, Vaidyanath Sami to stay at home whirring with wedding preparations and face any sort of discomfort. But Sami Pa wasn't ready to stay at the guest house. Fun-loving Vaidyanath Sami was Sami Pa to some at Shanti, Sami Tatha to a few others. So, Sami Pa smiled and said to Leela, 'Min and I will stay at Shanti. How is it possible to feel uncomfortable at our own home?'

From the very beginning, Shanti, his wife's family home, was close to Vaidyanath Sami's heart. At Shanti, the eldest son-in-law of the family was given the best room on the top floor of the house. When Minnie Sami would come downstairs after getting ready, Madras Patti Ma would be preparing coffee for everyone at home. She would send a coffee-filled tumbler with Minnie for her eldest son-in-law. Following that, Vaidyanath Sami would leave for his morning walk. While leaving, he would pet Chikku's two adorable dogs, Simon and Viklin, and would bring them biscuits while returning from the walk. That was the reason that along with the family members, even the pets would rejoice his arrival.

During that visit, he took the wedding responsibilities in his hand. His eye for detail at festivals and functions was marvellous. For Chikku's wedding, he held a family meeting at the balcony of Shanti. He assigned jobs to everyone. For example, he gave the flower decoration duty along with the task of welcoming guests from the groom's family at the station and escorting them to the venue to Indira's son Ajay and Uma's son Adi. Sumati and Premu were given the responsibility of putting *jamkalam* in the wedding hall and taking care of the wedding guests at the entrance and serving them lime juice. The girls Munna, Anu, Tinu and Poppy were given the task of making jasmine garlands, manjal, kumkum and sandal paste along with preparing small *thambulam* (bags) or pouches. Sanju and Vikram were asked to collect coconut husk sacks and betel leaves. When Sami Pa divided wedding duties among all the family members, the youngest member of Shanti, Usha's brother Babu's son, Rahul, started crying as he wasn't given any job to do. Then Sami Pa took his little grandson on his lap and said, 'You have the most important duty. You will clean the betel leaves for the thambulam.'

Mrs Leela Nadhan then said in a loving tone, 'Sami Pa! Magic! Everyone is feeling proud and important!' Leela was the only Kannada-speaking person among the Tamil-speaking family at Shanti, and Vaidyanath Sami was the only family member who could begin talking in Kannada with great ease and sweetness the moment he would meet Leela. Usha inherited the command over languages from her Appa, and she used this ability to sing in different languages.

'Languages are the viridescent branches of our personality,' says Usha's eldest sister, Indira. Indira was very dear to Appa. Usha recalls, 'She was always in the driving seat as she was the eldest among the six of us.' Indira was familiar with each and every sign and hint that Appa's eyes would convey. Even now when Indru remembers Appa, with a delightful smile she says, 'To know Appa you have to love him. If you were not able to love him, you surely had a connection with the underworld.' This is how Indru describes why Appa's six children loved him so much, 'As Appa was in the police service, he was always short of time. But he would always manage to find time to go watch a film or a musical event with us to make the children happy. Yes, he also gave clear instructions before going to the cinema that there shouldn't be any unnecessary demands over there. Still, during the interval all of us brothers and sisters would forget our promise when ice-cream and chocolate vendors entered the hall. After enjoying the ice cream and chocolates, out of guilt of breaking the promise made to Appa, I would fake sleep just before the movie got over. Then Appa would pick me up and take me to the car, and once we reached home, he would pick me up again and take me to our bedroom and put me to bed.'

'Like other kids, we didn't get any regular pocket money. How Appa managed everything in such a limited salary is beyond our imagination. Every evening we would eagerly wait for Appa to come back from work so that we could grab the change from his pocket. Now we feel that Appa would bring back change so that the children would jump with joy and like bees get stuck to him with love.'

Indru continues, 'Appa and Amma had a huge circle of friends. So, picnics and meet-up plans were made despite various busy engagements. Many a time Appa would make everyone beyond happy when he would come home and ask Amma, "Min, I am going to Pune. If you all want, come along." Then in an hour or so we would all be on the road in our small Ford BMX-3901. All the brothers and sisters loved this car. Uma and I would call our car 'Gallant Base'. Usha was little then, so Amma would ask her to sleep on a giant pillow placed on the car's floor area. Usha would fall asleep peacefully on the go.' Apart from those sudden trips, Indru also remembers the family's festivities, 'Appa definitely had limited money, but he wouldn't fail to make us happy on occasions. He would bring us crackers the day before Diwali. He knew that if he brings the crackers a few days ahead of the festival, we would burn them beforehand and then make a sad face on Diwali day. Similarly, all of us would desperately wait for the Vishu festival. Amma would place grains, fruits, vegetables, jewellery and some money in front of a mirror on a tray a night before the festival. No one was allowed to look at it till the next morning when the whole family would get up and take a look. On Vishu day the highlight used to be the one rupee that each of us would get from Appa.'

Indru remembers how proud Appa was when she began her job with Trans World Airlines (TWA). Indru would get Rs 350 as her monthly salary. There was lot of pressure at work, which would often get over late in the evening. Appa had a deep sense of dedication towards his work. But seeing Indu's work pressure would wake up the caring and loving father within, and he would say, 'Indru, if it's troubling you, quit!' And Indru would smile and say, 'Are you saying this Appa! You, who works so hard.' Indru worked with the TWA for long. Indru remembers when her children would throw a tantrum and she would get angry at them, Appa would smilingly look at Amma and say, 'Min, is it possible to have grandchildren without having children?'

Along with his brothers and sisters, Appa had bottomless love for his children and grandchildren. Uma who is elder to Usha remembers how their grandmother, Bombay Patti Ma, would get emotional at the mention of her daughter Sushila's wedding. She would say, 'Uma! When your Sushila Ethe (*bua*) was going to get married, I wanted to sell my gold bangles and earrings so that there would be little more money for her wedding. But your Appa didn't listen to me and he organized such a grand wedding for his one and only sister.'

Vaidyanath Someshwar Sami was like an earthly surface for his family, community and friends where their love, happiness and sadness would get shelter. The eldest daughter Indira's eighteen-year-old son Viju died in 1980 due to an electric shock. She stayed with her parents for many days. Amma and Appa kept her safe and provided her solace. Indru remembers how Appa didn't cry even once in front of her. In between, he had to leave for Madras when Madras Patti Ma passed away. Indru hasn't forgotten how Appa quietly came near Viju's photo. He stood there drenched in his own tears.

The coming years brought bad tidings. In 1985, five years after Indu's son's death, Usha's brother Tyaagraj Sami, aka Babu, died of cancer after years of painful struggle. Appa couldn't bear the loss. Even today, when Usha revisits those memories, she is unable to control her tears. She still remembers the day (14 November 1985) when Babu was struggling to breathe and how he was provided with an oxygen mask. Appa had a feeling that Babu won't survive. That night Appa returned from the hospital deeply saddened. He bathed and offered prayers. After getting up from his prayers he got a brain stroke and went into a coma.

There was no way he could have known that his son was no more. Three days after Babu passed away, Appa took his last breath while comatose. On 18 November 1985, one of Bombay Police's finest officers left the world. When his eldest son Shyamsundar, aka Shamu, was performing his last rites accompanied by a twenty-one gun salute from the police, the entire department became emotional. Even after many years of retirement, the respect that Vaidyanath Someshwar Sami evoked was very much intact.

6

Sami Sisters

The unbridled and colourful birds of memories have kept the horizons of the past adorned with love. Usha relishes colours as much as she loves music and Usha's two elder sisters were like two singing birds glistening over lightning and colouring playful clouds. They were the famous Sami Sisters—Indira and Uma. During the 1950s, while Lata Mangeshkar and Asha Bhosle made their mark in the domain of Hindi songs, the Sami Sisters were in vogue at elite events where English tracks were enjoyed. Lata and Asha never used to sing together but the Sami Sisters dressed in traditional Indian sarees with their hair done in twin braids would bloom together on stage like a pair of Kadamba flowers.

In those heady days, they were perhaps the first two Indian girls singing English songs. People started referring to Indira and Uma as India's Andrews Sisters. Three American sisters—Patricia (Patty) Andrews, LaVerne Andrews and Maxene Andrews—used to sing as the Close Harmony Singing Group. It was the sprightly wave of Swing and Boogie Woogie music in America. The three sisters created such magic by singing together that they ended up selling 75 million records. The Andrews Sisters sang from 1925 until 1968. Similarly, Indira and Uma sang from 1950 until 1968. Those eighteen years were unforgettable.

Usha who was almost twelve years younger to Indira and Uma would be ready from the morning to go to each of their shows with Amma and Appa. There was not much of an age difference between Indru and Uma. At that time, Indru was twenty-three and Uma twenty-one. Both weren't married and were studying.

Indira, Usha's Indru Didi, was pursuing BA in English from Bombay's St. Xavier's and Uma had just enrolled in Seth Gordhandas Sunderdas Medical College affiliated to King Edward Memorial Hospital for medical studies. Everyone in the family had their personal craze for music. Indira and Uma decided to learn Carnatic music and hence took lessons from music teacher Patu Vadhyar for a while. But their heart also belonged to English music. Radio Ceylon's English music programme was very dear to Indira and Uma. Maybe that was the reason that they stopped practising Carnatic music and soon focused entirely on English songs. Usha still feels a sense of exuberance when recalling memories of those childhood days when she would sit in Amma-Appa's lap in her pigtails and watch her elder sisters singing in Bombay's auditoriums. Even today she remembers two or three songs from those days that Indira and Uma would rehearse at home. Watching her sisters practise and seeing them perform at shows was the most captivating sight for little Usha. One such song was Irving Berlin's 'Sisters, Sisters' that she truly loved:

Sisters, sisters
There were never such devoted sisters
Those who've seen us
Know that not a thing could come between us
Sister, Sister

When Indira and Uma would be getting ready for the show, an elated Usha would fix their saree pleats in her own style. She also loved Indira and Uma's high heels. Most of Indira and Uma's shows took place at the Police Club, Cricket Club of India, National Sports Club of India and the Catholic Gymkhana. The duo were the only ones who sang English songs. They would get a string of invitations to sing at many institutions in Bombay. But it wasn't okay with Vaidyanath Sami that his daughters sing at any other place apart from cultural and dignified platforms in Bombay.

Through these programmes the uniqueness of the Sami Sisters spread widely through word of mouth. Their performances were even demanded in Sri Lanka. The fee for the Sami Sisters' performances was a flower bouquet. After every performance, they would accept the bouquet with a big smile and say, 'We sing so that the branches of your lives are filled with flowers. Then, we will also get some flowers.' The audience knew that the Sami Sisters would sing their last song for the evening—'Side by Side', made popular by Pat and Shirley Boone:

Oh! We ain't got a barrel of money
Maybe we're ragged and funny
But we'll travel along
Singing a song side by side
Don't know what's coming tomorrow
Maybe it's trouble and sorrow
But we'll travel the road
Sharing our load side by side

Backing Indira and Uma were the band Bombay's Hallgreens and musicians like Chic Chocolate, Goody Silver, Ken Mac, Maurice Concessio and Micky Korea. The sisters had their own distinctive talent and when together they would make the evenings more lustrous. Indira's voice was deep and velvety and full of warmth, while Uma had a voice which was soft like silk. She was also associated with Parsi–Gujarati theatre. Her 1971 song 'Bombay Meri Hai' was a super hit and remains a memorable number for many. The song was released on 45 R.P.M. Two of Uma's songs, 'Hi Pori Nonnachi' in Goan and 'Bombay Duck' in English, are still fondly remembered by old-timers. After her husband Jimmy Ardehsar Pocha's death in 1996, Uma stopped singing. Only one record of hers was released which was 'Bombay Meri Hai'.

Whatever Uma did, she did it wholeheartedly. That is why most of her songs still hold the same appeal. Uma had a magical quality of transforming and flipping songs as per the mood of the audience. Indira and Uma sang a lot until the 1970s. Then with time both sisters got busy with their jobs and household duties. But the people of those times still recall some selected songs sung by the Sami Sisters like 'Autumn Leaves', 'My Heart Belongs to Daddy', 'Bisem Mucho', 'Hello Dolly' and 'I Left My Heart in San Francisco'. Indira revisiting those old times says, 'Back in 1954–55 when the Police Club's secretary Mr Saxby heard our songs on Radio Ceylon, he requested Appa that we sing at the club on Christmas Eve. Appa agreed. After Christmas, it was time for the New Year, and we sang at the club for that as well with the Hallgreens band. Back then, Usha was quite young. I would fondly call her Ush. She happens to be eleven years younger to me, and she would come to our programmes with Amma and Appa.

'Most of our performances were for charity. We would also sing at the Taj hotel on Christmas. I still remember that we first sang outside Bombay in 1957. For Christmas, Uma and I were invited to sing at Calcutta's Monsoon Square Gardens. Amma had accompanied us to Calcutta. Until 1962, Uma and I sang together. But after my marriage, I got busy with my family life and the Sami Sisters broke up. After that, we never had a duet performance, although I began singing solo in Calcutta. In fact, I got an offer to perform at the Flury's nightclub in the city. One evening, the Oberoi hotel's manager heard me sing. He offered me a contract to sing at his hotel. But my children were quite small, so I agreed to sing only on Fridays and Saturdays at the Oberoi.

That was in 1969 when Usha began singing at Trincas. I also sang at the Hindustan International Hotel in Calcutta for some time.'

Turning the pages of her memories, Indira has this story from her Delhi days: 'In 1972, my husband got transferred to Delhi. The Ashoka hotel in Delhi wanted to know if I was ready to sing since they were interested in opening a nightclub at the hotel. I offered the management two days a week, Fridays and Saturdays. And that's how for the first time, the nightclub 'Supper Club' opened in Delhi. For three long years I sang at Delhi's Ashoka and would travel at times for solo shows outside the city. Uma's, Usha's and my solo shows always took place in the four metropolitan cities of India—Delhi, Bombay, Calcutta and Madras. This continued until 1980. My record of four songs was also released.'

Eighty-two-year-old Indira Srinivasan lives in Bengaluru with her husband. Even now at people's demand, she does a few solo shows. After several requests from the Bengaluru Catholic Club, she performed a solo show on 16 July 2019. But she says that Uma and herself didn't give music enough time like Usha did.

Remembering Amma, Indira says, 'Amma was far more melodious as compared to us. Trincas's director Omi Puri used to say that all our voices were pale in front of Amma's. Appa and Amma were great music lovers. Appa would regularly buy records. He would also take us to all the musical programmes in Bombay even if at times we weren't up for it.' Whenever she thinks of the old times, she remembers her favourite song 'Autumn Leaves':

> *The falling leaves drift by my window*
> *The autumn leaves of red and gold*
> *I see your lips, the summer kisses*
> *The sun-burned hands I used to hold*

So many decades have gone by! The old lovers of music still believe that the Sami Sisters could have sung in full glory for ten more years.

Indira and Uma did many solo shows that were truly loved. But any form of art demands continuity. It's not enough that you are a good singer. It demands life-long dedication. The Sami Sisters paused along the way, though both were immensely talented and enjoyed stardom in such a short time. But perhaps they did not take their singing career seriously. That's why in their lifetime, they became a tale of the past in the world of music. The Sami family believes that the duo could have continued their singing career as even after marriage they were in Bombay for a long time.

Whereas Indu's husband, N. Srinivasan, was the managing director of Asbestos Cement in Bombay, Indira was in a job at TWA. N. Srinivasan aka Chinu always encouraged her music. Uma was a doctor by profession and her husband Jimmy Ardeshar Pocha was a talented actor who worked with Adi Marzban's Parsi theatre. On her husband Jimmy Pocha's request, Uma sang quite a few times for the Gujarati–Parsi theatre. But Dr Uma Ardeshar Pocha got busy in her medical profession. That's how the era of the Sami Sisters came to an end. Just when Indira and Uma were going easy with their music, Usha took over.

Usha was neither trained in music like her elder sisters, nor did her family and friends ever imagine that she would grab the mic and create musical history for decades to come. Indira and Uma despite creating their identity by giving such fantastic performances didn't embody music as a matter of life and death. But even without any professional training and guidance, Usha took music in all seriousness and performed live with complete dedication. Usha studied at the JJ School of Arts. Canvas and colours could well have been her world. However, everything naturally moved in an entirely different direction. Usha began splashing melodious colours on her canvas of sound. The splendour of the Sami Sisters became a part of Usha's aura.

Usha loved listening to Radio Ceylon, BBC and Voice of America. But fundamentally, Radio Ceylon was her guiding light. Similarly, she didn't only passionately listen to Jamaican–American singer Harry Belafonte but also internalized his songs completely. And not just Belafonte, Frank Sinatra, Elvis Presley, India-born British singer Cliff Richards, Ela Fitzgerald and many others were also close to Usha's heart. Usha constantly soaked in their voices.

Usha's Amma and Appa also loved listening to English songs, but their favourite singers included Indian classical exponents like Kumar Gandharva, Pandit Jasraj, the Dagar Brothers, Kishori Amonkar, K.C. Dey and K.L. Saigal.

Usha was a guitar player since her school days. Her brother Shyamsundar also played the guitar and the flute. The second brother Tyaagraj aka Babu played the guitar as well. When Usha began singing at the nightclubs, the guitar was her companion that helped her get rid of the initial nervousness. Being a Sami Sister, she possessed the Sami mannerisms. Usha developed the wonderful art of setting up a dialogue with the audience during a song. She took inspiration from her sister Uma Pocha in writing songs and tuning compositions. Uma was a natural at writing songs that delightfully struck the inner chords, filling the heart with joy. One of the perfect examples was her song 'Bombay Meri Hai'. Usha also wrote quite a few songs for herself during the early days of singing. When she would sing famous English songs, she would also try out her own compositions on her audiences.

Usha's parents couldn't imagine Indira and Uma singing at a nightclub. Vaidyanath Sami had only allowed them to sing at prestigious places. But Usha had it completely different. She began singing at nightclubs and even after coming to Calcutta, she continued singing at the Trincas. Multiple roadblocks had to be overcome in Madras, Bombay and Calcutta. But Usha never mentioned anywhere about her days of struggle and the internal conflicts that she had to go through. For every successful performance and happiness of her soul, she kept merging herself unendingly into a whole array of emotions. That coalesced state was something that not only birthed new and exciting curiosities but also nurtured the desire to experience new sides.

For Usha it was crystal clear from the very beginning that one's performance was everything. In Usha's words, 'Ultimate is the personality of performance! Even if you sing songs of your despair before audiences, you will ultimately be judged by your act.' That's why Usha did each show like it was her last one. This is why during her shows, the audience becomes one with the infinite and unique sounds scattered across the universe. Sometimes it enters Alibaba's mysterious cave with the magic of The Beatles, sometimes feeling the morning washed in the rain with the prayer song 'Raghupati Raghav Rajaram' or at times with 'Rambha Ho' and 'Shaan Se' it would taste the immortal nectar of the love within, startled by the wind and storm. Usha's shows like those of magician P.C. Sarkar's were filled with eagerness, joy, thrill, excitement, love and the sonorous sound of chirping birds waking up at dawn. But all this was knotted into the garland of her soulful discourses with the audience.

From the beginning, she knew how to chart her journey by shaping herself with the soil of her identity in the mould of her own unique voice. Usha was also well aware that it wouldn't be easy to get recognition for a deep female voice among Indian audiences who were used to the soft and thin voices of Geeta Dutt, Lata Mangeshkar and Asha Bhosle. There was only one way which was by staying focused on the goal till the last breath. Usha was not in a hurry. But in time, her resolution started giving her results. A girl from a well-to-do family singing regularly at a nightclub was almost unimaginable back in the day. But God had created such a road map for Usha that there were only surprises along the way. Usha made her parents agree. There won't be any disgrace in singing with dignity.

The nightclub crowd really loved Usha's singing. Usha wiped off the notion in her first-round itself that women who sing at nightclubs are obscene. Slowly, she became popular in the music industry. In this recognition, there was no reference associating her with the Sami Sisters. She was emerging as the new face of a new wave in music.

During the 1970s, Usha's youngest sister Maya had also begun singing before her marriage. In height, build and voice, Maya was just like Usha. That's the reason why many strangers would interrupt and tell her that she looks like Usha Uthup's real sister. Then Maya would laugh and say, 'Not like a real sister, I am her real sister.' Like Usha, Maya's eyes are deeply expressive and beautiful. Usha absolutely adores Maya and believes she was her granted wish. The story goes like that: when Maya was to be born Usha stuck to her mother and would say, 'Amma! I want a sister.' Usha's brother Tyaagraj as in Babu would say to Amma touching her pregnant belly, 'No Amma! I need a younger brother.' Amma would keep smiling at this childlike demand. And when Maya was born, where Usha was jumping out of limitless joy, Babu was upset with Amma for days because she didn't listen to him but fulfilled Usha's wish. Usha looks back with a contemplative smile, 'After Indru Di was born, Uma Di was born to give her company. After her, my brother Shyamsundar was born. To give Shyamsundar company, Tyaagraj was born. Among the six brothers and sisters, I came in the fifth position. Possibly, I was Amma and Appa's mistake. However, my Amma would say, "Usha is my most good baby." Maybe to compensate for this mistake and to give me company, Maya was born.'

Maya is six years younger to Usha. Both are friends, along with being sisters. The younger sister shared the same fondness for stitching and ironing clothes as did Usha. Till the time the clothes that came from the drycleaners weren't pressed again, Maya would not sit in peace. During childhood, Usha and Maya would play a game called Lalita and Gita. Usha was Gita and Maya would be Lalita. In the game, the two sisters would have a one-better-than-the-other series of amusing conversations in which there would be lot of fun talk from cinema and cricket to bubble gum. Not only Usha and Maya's siblings but all those living in the Love Lane Bungalow would eagerly wait to catch this most entertaining household show.

Usha and Maya not only shared the same school but also the fun after school. For instance, from sharing a bubble gum to buying moong dal and samosas they were together. A Muslim man ran a shop which served Pyali or white peas chaat (a savoury street snack mixed with tamarind juice, chopped coriander leaves and potato chunks). According to Amma, there was always the danger of falling sick during the monsoons if one binged on street food. But despite her warning, Usha and Maya's mouths would be drawn towards street snacks. At times it was watermelon juice and ice cream that lured the kids. Other times apple berries and candy floss. Maya says, 'Whenever Usha was surrounded by friends after school hours and I was with her, she would say, "You go home. I am coming." In which case I laid down a condition that she get me some goodies. Helpless, Usha had to buy me something. Those were such priceless days full of flavour.'

Maya revisits the time when Usha went to Cochin and then Calcutta and how they would regularly exchange letters. And these letters weren't two-page ones but ran into fifteen to twenty pages and took a week to write. Appa would jokingly tease them saying, 'Both of you please send postcards or at best an inland letter to me. I don't have the patience to read a letter that runs into twenty pages.' Usha and Maya still have those letters which they have saved as if they have some heritage value. Even today, Usha has the same love for Maya. 'A couple of times when all the Sami Sisters came to sing together on stage, Usha, with great enthusiasm introduced me, "And now my baby sister, Maya!" And after that, the audience would burst into laughter looking at the fifty-year-old baby sister,' recalls Maya. She mostly sings in English, French and Spanish and has a unique style, just like her sister Usha. Just like the other sisters, she also comes on stage wearing a saree, bindi and bangles. She also possesses the Sami Sisters' mannerisms. But as a singer, she couldn't bring a sense of continuity to her music like Usha and went into advertising. Says Maya, 'Yes, I sing to the gallery. I do shows with tickets worth five rupees and also shows that have tickets for Rs 10,000.'

On her musical journey Usha has this to say, 'I was not afraid of being destroyed as I had the land of love and sky of faith. Despite all the sadness and pain in life, there is melody, nectar, rhythm and beauty—I have always tried to convey this thought of mine through music.' Usha still remembers how Indira and Uma would fondly sing Dorris Day's song 'Sentimental Journey' with the very same thought in their hearts:

Gonna take a sentimental journey
Gonna set my heart at ease
Gonna make a sentimental journey
To renew old memories

Remembering things past is sweet as well as thrilling. Usha revisits that afternoon when Appa who never lost his cool, flung his plate of food in anger. It was some holiday on that day and Amma went into Appa's room carrying his plate. Finding the right moment, Amma said in a quiet tone, 'Uma has decided to get married.'

'With whom?'

'There is a Parsi boy—Jimmy Ardeshar Pocha. He does theatre. Uma likes him.'

A loud clanging was heard after that. Appa threw his plate while he was eating. Amma was sobbing. Hearing that, a twelve or thirteen-year-old Usha came running from her room. She had never seen so much anger on Appa's face before. Amma who was crying pulled Usha into her arms. Appa checked himself immediately, became normal and lovingly caressed Usha's head. Usha noticed that his eyes were wet. Appa and tears! This was also an unthinkable moment for Usha. Later in the evening, Usha found out from Indru Di and Amma's conversation that Uma Di was going to marry Jamshedji Ardeshar Pocha, a theatre actor.

Amma was really hurt on two counts. Firstly, Uma was younger than Indru who wasn't married and she was getting married before her elder sister. Secondly, Uma marrying outside the community was not acceptable to Appa. However, Appa didn't attend Uma's wedding, but Amma and the family did go for it. Uma's wedding was organized at a small hotel called Mirabel. Despite all the anger, Appa sent a bouquet for Uma on her big day. Uma Di's wedding in 1961 is still vivid in Usha's memory. As also Appa's anger and ache. After a few days when Appa got over his displeasure, he happily threw a grand reception for Uma and Jimmy—Usha cannot forget that evening as well.

After Uma's marriage, Appa was naturally anxious about Indira's wedding. With adoration and faith, Appa would say of Indira, 'Indru is the captain of the ship.' All the brothers and sisters would keep Indru Di on that pedestal. Appa loved Indru Di a little more than the other kids. In Usha's words, 'There was one grain of more salt for her.' After Uma's wedding, Appa began feeling that Indira has been insulted. He began looking for a suitable boy from a Tamil Brahmin family on a war footing. Indru was born on 6 December 1936. She had turned twenty-five, which was the age for a girl to marry. That's why Appa didn't want to delay it any further.

Tall and lean, Indru was definitely slightly dusky, but her eyes were beautiful, and her nose was finely carved. Appa would smile and say, 'Ushi Muku!', which meant a nose pointed like a needle. Overall, Indru could be easily accepted as a sweet and pretty girl. She did her schooling from Byculla's Convent of Jesus and Mary. She also had a bachelor's degree in English from Bombay's St

Xavier's College. Ultimately, Appa liked a boy from a prestigious Tamil Brahmin family. He was N. Srinivasan, fondly called Chinu by his family. He had five brothers—Rajamani, Srinivasan, Kumar, Kiccha and Ramaswami aka Ramu. Chinu had an elder sister— Lalita. Appa liked Chinu and his family and in 1962, Indru and Chinu got married in a grand ceremony.

The wedding brought a new wave of happiness at home. After Indu's marriage, both families would visit each other. Chinu's youngest brother, Ramaswami aka Ramu, became close to the Sami family. The tall, lean, fair and cheerful Ramu would visit the Samis every day and play badminton with Usha. At times, he would also teach her maths, a subject she had trouble with. Days went by and Amma had an intuition that Ramu and Usha would make a good pair.

Their eldest daughter had married into the same family. So there would be no other family as tried and tested as this one. On top of that, carefree and playful Usha got along well with Ramu. The two families discussed the wedding proposal and six days after Usha's eighteenth birthday, on 14 November 1965, she got married to Indu's youngest brother-in-law Ramaswami or Ramu Iyer. By that time, Vaidyanath Someshwar Sami had left Byculla's Love Lane Bungalow and moved to the Worli area with the family. Interestingly, when the marriage was finalized, the Love Lane Bungalow wasn't allocated to anyone. So, it was decided that Usha's wedding could take place there. It was a magnificent wedding.

Many years after Usha's marriage, Maya fell in love and married Biren Ghosh. The bridegroom's father held a senior position in Ceat Tyres, and the family was a highly respected one. But Maya and Biren's marriage couldn't sustain for long. A few years later she got married to Raghusudan of Punjabi–Jewish origin. Raghu was into business. But now, after saying goodbye to business, Raghusudan is busy with his interest in photography and homoeopathy. Maya continues to be in advertising. She was Everest Advertising's creative head for a long time. Maya had no children. Usha also had no children with Ramu Iyer.

Indu's husband N. Srinivasan, aka Chinu, became Asbestos Cement's managing director. Indru and Chinu had three children—Ajay, Vijay and Priya. Vijay died of an electric shock at the age of 18. Indu's son Ajay is with a Birla group company. Priya or Poppy runs her own business. Ajay and Priya are both married. Ajay's wife, Moyna comes from a Punjabi family. Uma is no longer in this world. Her son Ardeshar Pocha and daughter Tina are married as well. Ardeshar's wife Avantika is also a Punjabi. Tina is married to an American, Peter. Tina is an English professor and lives in California.

Adi, Tina, Ajay, Poppy all dearly love their Usha Masi who is always there for her sisters' children and their happiness. Adi says, 'I called her Bukka Masi when I was a kid and since then she has remained Bukka Masi for me. While we were growing up she had become a famous pop star. On many evenings in Bombay, we all would get together and begin our music session with her. All of us children would be eager to take loose change from her purse. Maybe, she knowingly brought change for us in her purse. Bukka Masi would say that she will give all the change to the kid who guesses the correct amount of change money in her purse.

'Those days feel like a dream now. Our entire family was blessed with art. My eldest Masi, Indira, along with my mother began singing on the stage. As all the sisters would call Indira Masi "Akka", I also started calling her the same. Even at that age, Akka's voice was firm with depth. My father Jimmy Pocha died in 1996 but he was associated with theatre till his last days. He was a powerful comedian. The entire hall echoed with laughter just listening to his voice.

'And Bukka Masi was also one of a kind. She gave direction to my career. After graduating in physics I had no sense of what

I should pursue. During that time, Bukka Masi invited me to Calcutta. Masi knew that I wrote music since my student days. Masi said to me, "Write jingles." I wrote jingles for Dunlop Red Star and recorded them at Studio Vibrations. I received Rs 1000 as remuneration for all the work. Then I returned to Bombay and began my career in advertising. All this was possible because of Bukka Masi,' says Adi. Reflecting upon the good old days, Adi continues, 'When I was working with Lintas, I was fortunately transferred to Calcutta. It was at that time that Bukka Masi got the *Pop Time* programme on Doordarshan. Masi made me a part of the programme as well. I made many videos for it. Naturally, this gave a boost to my self-confidence.' Adi now owns Squirkle, a film production company in Bombay. 'Ma is no more but Bukka Masi always fills in for her,' he says.

Like Adi, his maternal cousin Indira Srinivasan's son Ajay Srinivasan also worships Usha Masi. He is a senior official with the Aditya Birla Group. Ajay remembers how Usha Masi would dress him up in a bow tie and Bambino shorts when he was young. She would bring special clothes and toys for him. Ajay remembers a moment from 1998, when his friends wanted to hear Usha Masi. So, when Usha Masi came to Bombay, Ajay requested her and she went to Ajay's place. She sang for long and made that evening an unforgettable one. Similarly, Ajay was posted in Hong Kong after a few years when Usha Masi came there for a show. Some of Ajay's friends requested a private singing session and Usha Masi obliged.

The Sami Sisters' children belong to the new age. Indira and Uma, the original Sami Sisters, left singing by the 1970s. But interestingly, the music of the Sami Sisters seems eternal. Auckland, New Zealand, now has three Sami Sisters—Madelene, Anji and Priya—who have made their mark in music there. Their 2011 debut album *Happy Heartbreak* attracted much notice. Though they are not related to Usha's family, she smiles when she hears about the new Sami Sisters and says, 'The Sami Sisters are

forever. There were never such devoted sisters.' Then she hums
an impromptu tune, 'All kind of weather/ the Sami Sisters stick
together! The same in the rain and sun . . . two different phases!
But in tight places . . . we think, and we act as one—the Sami
Sisters . . .'

7

Matilda

One of the first organized suburbs of Bombay was Dadar. It became a busy residential area with the hustle and bustle of the market next to it. By mid-November in 1965, Usha had come to her in-laws' house situated in Dadar. Appa had left Byculla's Love Lane Bungalow. But Usha would miss its greenery and Appa and Amma at her new home. Young and happy-go-lucky, the eighteen-year-old Usha hadn't come to terms with the fact that she had taken on a new role as the Iyer family's daughter-in-law. She wasn't even aware of the fact that Uma and Indu's wedding episodes had tied her wings at adolescence. She would often remember Love Lane's old jackfruit, banyan, mahogany and wild almond trees when she looked at the banyan, mahogany and wild almond trees at her new home in Dadar.

During those days Usha was a student at the JJ School of Arts. In 1965, she joined the art school after completing her school education. She felt that she would have a future in painting and got deeply involved in her art studies. She admired the lines of Amrita Sher-Gil, Souza, Jagdish Swaminathan, K.G. Subramanyan, M.F. Husain and Tayeb Mehta.

Usha admired Maqbool Fida Husain who depicted the colours of Indian life on his canvas. Raza's sentimentality touched her.

She found Van Gogh, Michelangelo and Francis Bacon's colours magical. She would often look at the photograph of Amrita Sher-Gil, daughter of an Indian father and a Hungarian mother. She found Amrita's beauty to be pure and mysterious. Usha wished she could go back in time and be with Amrita. She could then have met Amrita, her father, Sardar Umrao Singh Sher-Gil, and her mother, Marie Antoinette Gottesmann. She could then have formed a friendship with the family. If Amrita was alive in 1965, Usha would have written a letter to her in the same way she wrote to singer Frank Sinatra many years ago. Like Van Gogh's masterpiece *Starry Night,* glowing stars kept glistening across her inner sky. Usha's dreams were scattered like stars in the sky even as time was passing by. Dadar was well connected by bus and train. She took a bus to JJ School and back home every day.

November was a very pleasant month in Bombay. At times the rain would surprise the city. Usha enjoyed capturing the many facets of Bombay getting drenched in the rain. She mostly liked painting with watercolours. Once she got an order to make New Year cards for Thacker & Company and then it became a yearly routine. She would get Rs 100 for each design. She hadn't forgotten Appa's childhood lesson to work and earn, which is why alongside her painting she also stitched clothes for her sisters Indru and Uma's children. She also tailored clothes for the legendary film actor Rajendra Kumar's daughter Dimple. She had a classmate at JJ School who was close to the star's family. Hearing of Usha's tailoring skills, Rajendra Kumar's wife, Shukla, immediately placed an order with Usha to stitch her daughter Dimple's (now Dimple Patel) frocks. Rajendra Kumar Tuli aka Rajendra Kumar was a softspoken person and his wife Shukla was also delightful. She was producer–director O.P. Ralhan's sister.

After class, Usha would take the bus from the stop near JJ School of Arts to deliver Dimple's frocks at Rajendra Kumar's bungalow in Bandra. If at times Rajendra Kumar was at home, he would ask Usha about her how she was getting on with her painting. Usha would tell him that even though she was studying art, music was her first love. There was a big piano at Rajendra Kumar's house. Looking at it Usha wished she had a similar piano. Shukla would pay her Rs 80 per frock, which was quite a handsome sum for that time. Usha was also good at stitching salwar–kameezes, shorts and shirts for young boys. Even now, Usha never misses an opportunity to stitch at home. People ask her if she hadn't been a singer, what would she have been. She promptly says a teacher or a tailor.

When Usha took admission at the JJ School of Arts, Appa wasn't really happy. He wanted his daughter to pursue a regular college education and secure a good job. But that wasn't acceptable to Usha who disliked walking on the beaten track. However, Appa had faith in a corner of his heart that Usha would finally do something worthwhile and be independent. That's why he would jokingly tell Usha's Amma, 'Min, there is a lot of struggle in the world of painting. Artists have to wait many years for success. But Usha will manage to survive with the money she will make from being a cobbler or a tailor during her days of struggle.'

Usha had no sense of struggle at that age. She was even oblivious to the idea of the relationship between a husband and wife. Even after marriage they continued to be friends who played badminton. Meanwhile, Usha diligently and intently listened to Radio Ceylon and Ameen and Hamid Sayani's programmes. Her art studies were going on and although she enjoyed painting, music was flowing through her veins. There was a constant haze, a dilemma vis-à-vis painting versus music within her which was cleared in time.

While 1965–66 was spent with the syllabus and art workshops at the JJ School, 1967 saw things taking a turn. On Leela Mami's invitation, Usha came to Madras with her husband Ramu Iyer. One evening when Usha sang at Yashwant Vikamsi's Nine Gems at Leela Mami's insistence, people loved her performance. This unforgettable evening boosted her self-confidence and morale. In the coming months fate began opening doors for her dreams and wishes to come true. The high point was one evening in 1969 when the Queen of Gospel, Mahalia Jackson, blessed her and made Usha sing along with her on stage in Bombay. That event cleared any doubts Usha had about her real calling.

Music became that colour of her life. Usha participated in the Wills cigarette's famous 'Made for Each Other' music show and the 'Simla Beat Contest' during which Usha's unique voice and singing style caught the attention of many leading advertising professionals present at the shows. In 1968, Usha began to sing ad jingles. Her first one was for A1 Dust Tea, composed by the famous Vanraj Bhatia. It was a difficult jingle, but Vanraj who wrote the music for most of Shyam Benegal's films was certain that Usha would be able to handle it. Incidentally, the jingle was not composed keeping Usha in mind. Vanraj Bhatia had signed up budding jazz singer Asha Putli for it, but she had to travel suddenly to the US for a show. Vanraj waited for her, and when she did record the jingle Vanraj was not impressed. Instantly, Usha came to his mind, and he thought he ought to try out the new girl. That is how Usha got her first chance at a jingle. Its words went like this:

Tingle!
Want to hear a lovely jingle?
It's time for tea
Not just any tea
It's time for A1 Dust Tea . . .

Vanraj Bhatia loved the jingle sung by Usha and it became popular. Subsequently, there began a series of offers to sing ad jingles. Actress Durga Khote had a production house, Durga

Khote Productions, which produced all the jingles for Cadbury and Usha was chosen for all of them. From 1967 to 1970, there were a string of jingles—Sway Detergent and the Tinopal jingle made her famous. Old-timers will still remember Usha's Tinopal jingle: *'Itne ujale kapde, kiska hai kamaal? Tinopal . . . Tinopal.'*

When Tinopal changed its name to Ranipal, Usha sang the jingle along with Jagjit Singh—*'Ye kiska hai kamaal, Ranipal'*. Usha sang jingles for several brands including Close Up toothpaste, Nescafe, Bata shoes, Brook Bond tea, Bru coffee, Boroplus, Eveready torch, Maggi noodles, Lakme, Dabur, Baidyanath, Nawab vests, Janpriya Insurance, Glaxo, Binny, Monkey Brand toothpowder, Gold Spot, Thumps Up, Ponds company's products, Vicks and Dunlop. So prolific was her output, that the advertising world began calling her the Jingle Queen.

Usha's speciality was that she could sing a master jingle in as many as seventeen languages. Usha fondly remembers the Gold Spot jingle as it featured film star Rekha. Usha's jingles were so perfectly articulated that people wondered how a Tamilian girl could sing in so many languages with such versatility. A good voice and correct pronounciation were the primary reasons why she clicked when she sang jingles. She was taught to speak properly in English and Hindi by her schoolteachers. Usha remembers her teacher Ms Davidson admonishing her, 'Usha, don't eat up the last consonant. If you are so hungry, go home and eat something. But please don't eat the last consonant.' The school's Hindi teacher, Mr Kalra, wasn't behind in pointing out errors. He would always ask Usha not to swallow one syllable or the other.

Electronic media was yet to arrive and TV was no more than a novelty. Back in the day, a jingle would be recorded and readied for the short ad film shown in cinemas. The soundtrack would then be shortened as a jingle for the radio. Many small production houses didn't have big budgets to record jingles in many languages with new singers. So those with limited budgets would think of Usha as she was never rigid when it came to money. She was happy that she had an opportunity to sing in different languages as if they were her own. Famous Cine Laboratory's popular recording engineer Minoo Katrak had recorded ten songs with her. Usha met Radio Ceylon's acclaimed announcer, Vijay Kishore Dubey, who was associated with HMV after her recordings with Katrak. Those days Vijay Kishore Dubey was known as Dube Saheb in Bombay's music industry, and he was quite the connoisseur. In 1968, Vijay Kishore Dubey made Usha record two cover songs—'Jambalaya' and The Kingston Trio's 'Green Back Dollar' for HMV. At the same time, Usha also lent her voice to her version of the theme song from *Godfather* for HMV.

Those days the number of studios in Bombay could be counted on one's fingers. The prominent ones were Mehboob Studio, Famous Cine Laboratory, HMV Studio, Western Outdoor Studio, James Studio and Madhur Dhwani Studio. The Western Outdoor Studio belonged to Daman Sood, who was a noted recording engineer. Madhur Dhwani Studio was owned by actress Madhubala's sister. As advertising jingles were recorded at film studios, Usha would often get to meet many music directors. Apart from Vanraj Bhatia, Usha also did a lot of jingles with music director Baidyanathan. She would occasionally write the copy for ad jingles. It so happened that meetings with film people opened new doors for her, and Shyam Benegal signed Usha to sing the title song for the 1969 film *Was It for This, The Clay Grew Tall*, directed by him.

The year 1969 was an eventful year for Usha. HMV released a 45 RPM record of hers with the group The Flintstones. Then with the backing of Vijay Kishore Dubey, Usha's album *Scotch and Soda* was released as a long-playing (LP) record in 33 1/3 RPM. It included all the songs that were close to Usha's heart like 'Scotch and Soda', 'Rain', 'California Dreaming', 'Sunny',

'Hurry Sundown', 'Blue Prelude', 'Big Spender', 'Taste of Honey', 'I Left My Heart in San Francisco', 'Bye Bye Brown Eyes' and 'In the Midnight Hour'. All these songs were covers of tracks by world-famous singers, but Usha would impart to them her own soul and feel.

Thus when she sang 'Rain', her listeners felt the fondling strokes of clusters of clouds soaking within them. And 'Sunny' was like a misty dewdrop as the words rolled out: '*Sunny, yesterday my life was filled with rain/ Sunny, you smiled at me and really eased the pain/ The dark days are gone/ And the bright days are here/ My sunny one shines so sincere/Sunny one so true, I love you . . .*'

Whenever Usha sang this song, she thought that if she ever has a son, he will be called Sunny. After many years, this dream came true. Vijay Kishore Dubey had heard Usha sing all these songs. So, he proposed that all the iconic songs sung by Usha be put on an album. That's how the compilation *Scotch and Soda* came out.

On an evening of 1969, when Usha was singing at Hotel Savera in Madras, an elderly listener gifted her Puerto Rican singer José Feliciano's album. This is how Usha got her hands on the record and heard Feliciano sing his own composition 'Rain'. Usha became a big fan of his songs. 'Sunny' was also by him, and he covered 'California Dreaming'. José Feliciano was born blind. Usha would get goosebumps thinking about him. She would also get saddened thinking about another blind singer, Stevie Wonder. She wondered why God had denied these great singers the gift of sight. Tears rolled down Usha's cheeks whenever she listened to Feliciano's 'No Dogs Allowed', a song about a man who needed a guide dog because he was blind but found his dog was denied entry to places he wished to go to. Usha ardently practised several José Feliciano songs. His fans in India began saying that Usha reminds them of José. People even started liking her rendition of 'Rain' so much that it became Usha's signature song.

The year 1969 was really an ecstatic one for Usha. It was in that year that the owner of the Bombay nightclub Little Hut received a letter from Calcutta's famous nightclub Trincas requesting Usha to sing at the club. There was no end to Usha's happiness on getting an offer from Calcutta. Since childhood, she had heard great things about Calcutta's culture. Little did she know that once Calcutta embraced her, she would belong to the city forever. However, some people were worried for her because they had heard that the nightclubs of Calcutta were infamous. But Usha felt reassured as her husband Ramu was accompanying her. Ramu was working with the Bright Brothers, a company that manufactured plastic products, but he always gave utmost importance to Usha's music career.

Trincas was run in partnership by two friends—Ellis Joshua and Omi Puri. They had sent Usha two Bombay–Calcutta flight tickets. The flight to Calcutta was in the evening and when Usha and Ramu landed at the Calcutta airport a car was there to pick them up. Even today, Usha looks longingly at Park Street where Trincas was located. Park Street is still the same to her.

When Usha went to Calcutta with Ramu Iyer for the first time, Ramu's elder brother N. Srinivasan (Chinu) and Usha's elder sister Indru were also living in Calcutta. Chinu was working with the Asbestos Company in the city. But the Trincas people had made arrangements for Usha's stay. So, when Usha arrived at 87-J, Park Street in Trincas' grand car, Ellis Joshua and Omi Puri warmly welcomed her. Joshua and Puri lived together. Joshua was a Jew and Puri a Punjabi. Joshua was unmarried and Puri was married. Usha admired their closeness. A rare friendship.

The first evening itself, Joshua and Puri told Usha that they would begin rehearsals the next morning with the band at Trincas. But the next day, they both informed Usha that she would have to go along with them to the police headquarters in Lal Bazaar because without a licence she wouldn't be allowed to sing at the nightclub. At the Calcutta police headquarters Usha read the licence form and found it quite strange. Especially, two conditions: that singers can't go to the tables where guests are seated and that those performing will not get into any kind of relationship with guests. After reading the licence form, Usha was caught in a dilemma as she found the entire tone to be offensive. Sensing that, the officials at the police headquarters said, 'This is just a procedure for the licence. We are not raising any fingers on your character.' But Usha had figured by then that because of the bad reputation of nightclubs, such conditions were included in the licence form. However, no one, even Usha, didn't know that in the coming years, the perception about Calcutta's nightclubs would change. But this historical transition did happen because of Usha alone. The West Bengal government also began looking at nightclubs in a different light.

The Trincas contract was for three weeks and the pay Rs 750. Usha wanted her performance at Trincas to be perfect as she didn't want to disappoint Joshua and Puri who had invited her with so much faith. So, in those three weeks at Trincas, she regaled the regulars with her songs. The newspapers in Calcutta wrote that 'a Madrasi girl, Usha Iyer has come to sing at a nightclub in Calcutta.' In that first trip to Trincas Usha sang many songs by The Beatles—'A Hard Day's Night', 'Can't Be Me' and 'Yesterday'. She also sang 'Rain' and 'Summertime'.

It was on a Thursday that something happened. The band at Trincas was in full flight with Usha at the mic. Every table was mystified and mesmerized by Usha's singing. Ramu was sitting at a corner table far from the stage. During the recess, a tall good-looking man came up to Usha. 'I am Jani Chako Uthup! You are super tonight! Will you sing Harry Belafonte's "Matilda" tonight?' he requested.

'Not today,' Usha said with a hint of a smile, 'I will rehearse "Matilda" a bit. "Matilda" on Monday evening.'

'Thank you,' the man said and returned to his table.

After the interval, Usha began singing again. She was singing 'Killing Me Softly', a song made popular by Roberta Flack. The words were rather emotive:

Strumming my pain with his fingers
Singing my life with his words
Killing me softly with his song
Killing me softly with his song
Telling my whole life with his words
Killing me softly with his song.

It seemed as if Trincas itself was taking deep breaths as the night began to end. Usha was the last to leave with Ramu. But that night, 'Matilda' accompanied Usha. On her way back with Ramu, while walking slowly towards the house next to Joshua and Puri's home, Usha had made up her mind that she will rehearse 'Matilda' that night itself. It was truly a fascinating song. Someone had reminded her of this song after ages. The song overflowed with emotions and was dedicated to love. She could think of many like Matilda. Among them, poet Pablo Neruda's wife, Matilde Urrutia. She was an inspiration for his love poems. After marrying Pablo, she lived with him till her last breath. Usha had always loved Neruda's poetry. Usha revisited the poem addressed to Matilde:

I only want five things,
five chosen roots.
One is endless love.
Two is to see the autumn.
I cannot exist without leaves
flying and falling to earth.
Third is the solemn winter, the rain I loved,
the caress of fire in the rough cold.

My fourth is the summer,
plump as a watermelon.
And fifthly, your eyes.
Matilde, my dear love . . .

Apart from Neruda, there is British filmmaker and writer Dennis
Kelly's musical *Matilda*, based on Roald Dahl's novel for children
by the same name. The lines from Dennis Kelly's song 'This Is
from Matilda' is also very dear to Usha:

> *This is from*
> *This is from*
> *This is from Matilda*
> *Just like Johnny Flynn said, 'the breath I've taken and the one I must'*
> *to go on*
> *Put the grenade pin in your hand, so you understand who's*
> *boss*
> *My defeat sleeps top to toe with her success*
> *Oh this is from*
> *This is from*
> *This is from Matilda*
> *And she needs you*
> *This is for Matilda*
> *And she needs you*
> *This is for Matilda*

Usha's lips dance with a chuckle when she remembers singer Harry
Belafonte's song *Matilda*. Harry's Matilda was different from
Neruda's and Dennis's Matildas. Whenever Harry sang his song
on stage he would make people live the peak of joy and romance.
Since her early days, Usha was crazy about Harry Belafonte's vocal
style. Famous as the King of Calypso, Belafonte was celebrated for
taking Caribbean music and making it popular across the globe.

He was perfect at creating a dialogue with the audience. Usha was absolutely enthralled by his conversational style. She started internalizing it. Usha was very familiar with Belafonte's 'Matilda'. Each time Usha sang that song she felt Matilda, fluttering with fondness, was within her:

Hey
Matilda, Matilda, Matilda, she take me money and run
Venezuela
Once again now
Matilda, Matilda, Matilda, she take me money and run
Venezuela
Five hundred dollars, friends, I lost
Woman even sell me cart and horse
Heya! Matilda, she take me money and run Venezuela

Usha began rehearsing 'Matilda' late at night for Monday's performance. Ramu had slept by then.

Trincas was in its magical elements on Monday evening. The band began and so did Usha. While singing, Usha's eyes were looking for Jani Chako Uthup. She thought if she spotted him, she would sing 'Matilda'. But Jani didn't arrive till the end and didn't show up for the next four-five days.

Ramu asked Usha one night, 'You didn't sing "Matilda"?' Usha replied quietly, 'The one who asked for it didn't show up.'

On the last day, before Usha left for Bombay, Jani Chako Uthup was seen at a table at Trincas. And instinctively, the song 'Matilda' began dancing on Usha's lips. That night, Usha's voice was touching the stars. It was boundless music that filled each and every corner of Trincas with love.

'Fabulous!' Jani Chako Uthup's elated eyes met Usha's.

'Where is your moustache? It was there the last time,' Usha smiled and asked.

'It will grow again,' Jani's voice had a happy blushing tone. After a momentary pause, Jani asked, 'Should I grow it?'

'Yes please!' Usha laughed and the dimples that appeared on her cheeks brought out her beauty. Looking at these very dimpled cheeks, Madras Patti Ma had taken Usha in her arms after her birth and said, 'She is Usha. Her laughter beams with sunrise.'

'Will I get the chance of listening to you again?' Jani Uthup had asked her that evening.

'Don't know,' Usha said in a quiet tone. 'I am returning to Bombay tomorrow.'

8

That Monsoon in Calcutta

The Ritz Hotel, Bombay, stands stately in all its majesty behind the Eros Cinema on 5 Jamshedji Tata Road near Churchgate station. It was at the Little Hut, a small nightclub at the Ritz known for its jazz, that Usha once sang. It was from here that Usha journeyed to Calcutta's Trincas. Those were the days of blue inland letters and yellow postal envelopes carrying within them good and bad news. So, it was with some trepidation that Usha opened a yellow envelope addressed to her. It contained good tidings—an offer to sing for three weeks at Trincas, the nightclub on Calcutta's happening Park Street. Usha was visibly delighted with the contract, but replied saying that she didn't wear gowns and dresses as was the norm at nightclubs. She only wore sarees. The reply to her letter was prompt and precise saying, 'Come as you are! We want you just the way you are.' The three weeks in Calcutta would be treasured by Usha forever. Trincas exposed her to many fascinating experiences. The Lal Bazar, loving folks like Joshua and Puri, the owners of Trincas, and the man who loved Matilda!

After returning to Bombay Usha got busy with her evening shows at the Little Hut. She was already singing in English but began realizing the importance of crooning in a range of languages.

There were occasions when she sang in seventeen Indian and eight foreign languages. But after returning from Calcutta, all of a sudden Usha began focusing more on Hindi songs. One fine evening at Little Hut, she sang a beautiful rendition of a Hindi song sung by Mahendra Kapoor, *Dil karta . . . ho yaara dildara,* which was much appreciated. While performing for the Bombay audience, Usha felt that it was imperative to sing in Hindi and Marathi alongside English. That's how Usha got more confident singing in Hindi. She had learnt the guitar, but she quit the instrument later although she missed the guitar chords particularly while singing intense and emotional songs. Dealing with many forms of emotions was like handling a fleet of boundless clouds or preserving the misty drops resting on the petals of the soul.

It was the month of July in 1969 that Usha received a fresh contract with Trincas to sing for three weeks. She loved Calcutta from her first visit. There was a different fragrance and joy to life when compared to Bombay and Madras. Usha was naturally delighted on getting a second contract with Trincas. Like the last time, she received the flight tickets and there was a car waiting for her at Calcutta airport. Joshua and Puri welcomed Usha and they made arrangements for her stay. Ramu accompanied Usha during this trip as well. He was a bit reluctant, but he was there. As the Trincas band had become familiar with Usha, they didn't need any rehearsals. This time, she didn't have to go to the police headquarters in Lal Bazar either. On this trip, Usha had many rare songs in her repertoire which, even though they were her favourites, she hadn't sung them in a long time.

The monsoon season with the touch of the comforting rain infused a peculiar magic to the atmosphere. Job Charnock's Calcutta during the rainy season is far more ecstatic as compared to other cities. It was raining that evening when Usha sang at Trincas. The musicians with the band were charged up and Usha's songs spread warmth and joy. The atmosphere was electric. Ramu was sitting at a faraway corner table, but Usha also saw Jani Chako Uthup seated, resting his elbow on the nearby table. Usha was singing 'A Taste of Honey' made popular by The Beatles.

A taste of honey
Tasting much sweeter than wine
I dream of your first kiss, and then
I feel upon my lips again
A taste of honey
Tasting much sweeter than wine
Oh, I will return, yes, I'll return
I'll come back for the honey and you . . .

The song was transparent and full of joy. Like the honeysuckle flower swaying in the rain. An untamed desire seemed to be resonating in Usha's inner self as she sang, and a beautiful, infinite, irrepressible and restless desire began to take shape. The evening that was merging into the night turned into something like a dream. The besotted listeners at the tables were lost in the shadows of their souls. Usha stopped and so did the band. From a distance, Usha saw that Jani Chako Uthup was talking to Ramu on his way out. For whatever reason, Usha felt good seeing Ramu meet Jani. Ramu had told her that Jani Uthup works with the famous tea company J. Thomas & Company. Ramu seemed to have liked meeting Jani. Usha felt a sense of relief—at least Ramu had company. Someone he could spend time with in Calcutta.

Next afternoon, a few hours before the show, Ramu told Usha that Jani Uthup has invited him to a Chinese restaurant on Park Street. He would therefore meet her directly at Trincas. Usha only found out how Ramu and Jani's meeting went that afternoon when she reached her room after her show. During her performance Usha's eyes were constantly looking for Ramu. But he wasn't there, although Jani was present. After the show, Jani

Uthup walked up to Usha and said, 'I can't find Ramuji. Come, I will drop you home.' During the ride of a few minutes, Usha and Jani didn't talk. By that time, the rain had stopped.

Usha knocked on the door and Ramu opened it. His face turned pale looking at Jani standing behind Usha. Even as Usha stepped inside, Ramu said to Jani Uthup who was standing at the door, 'That's enough Mr Uthup! You can go.' Usha couldn't figure Ramu's uneasiness. What had happened to her husband who was normally very calm? Ramu slammed the door shut. That night, Ramu was unusually restless. Usha could see he was evidently disturbed. After being asked many times, he screamed and broke down. 'Do you know what Jani Uthup told me this afternoon at the Chinese restaurant? He said, "I don't know about Usha and her feelings, but I am in love with your wife."' As he said this Ramu was shaking with anger.

'Okay, he said that to you. So, what happened?' Usha said in a soft voice. 'He didn't say anything to me.'

'But what Jani said . . . is it true? Do you have the same feelings for him?' Ramu's voice was distraught.

'Yes!' Usha replied, pushing aside all fear.

It was a tortured night. Ramu flung the plate kept on the table at the wall and it shattered loudly into pieces. Usha cried almost until the crack of dawn. She didn't realize when she fell asleep. The throbbing wound inside her soul that she had lived with for the last five years was out in the open. The fear of society and what her family would think or say lay shattered to pieces.

In the five years of marriage, Ramu surely encouraged Usha's passion for music. But during the night, a strange immovable quiet, a darkness would descend on them. But that unbelievable conversation the previous night brought Usha out of the state of aching lifelessness.

Usha felt lighter the next morning. The sky over Calcutta was weighed down by clouds. Usha, however, was excited. Jani hadn't said anything to her directly. But what a feeling it was when she opened up and said what she had in her heart to Ramu. The events of the previous night kept reappearing in her mind. She thought of various scenarios that would follow.

She wondered what Amma–Appa would say when they find out. They were no doubt progressive but they could not remain silent bystanders after what had happened. Usha's elder brother-in-law, N. Srinivasan (Chinu) and elder sister Indira were living in Calcutta those days. Will Ramu share all that happened with Chinu and Indira? Many questions flitted through Usha's mind. But what also stood clearly was that people would talk. Appa's furious face when he found out about Uma Di's decision to marry the person she loved played out in her mind. Anyway, she hoped that whatever happened would be for the good.

The next two weeks were difficult. Ramu remained distant. He stopped going regularly for the evening shows at Trincas. But Jani would be there. A couple of evenings, Usha spotted him at Ramu's table, both talking to each other and it gave her some relief. Usha thought maybe things were getting better between them. But whatever happened had created a turbulence within her.

She wondered if it was possible to go any further with her frigid marriage of five years. When she looked back, Usha realized that she had spent the five years in gloom. She had never said anything to Amma, Appa or both her elder sisters. Music had helped her, but it could not dispel the darkness. The desire to embrace life was knocking on her door. When the three weeks contract with Trincas was over, Usha returned to Bombay with Ramu. Her fans at Little Hut were eagerly waiting for her to come back. Ramu did not mention the Calcutta incident to anyone, neither did Usha.

Towards the end of 1969 another invitation came from the owners of Trincas. This time Ramu wasn't ready to go with Usha. So, she decided to go alone to Calcutta. Trincas's owners, Joshua and Puri, were decent and loving. They said they would make arrangements for Usha's stay at their own place and would treat her like a daughter. Usha told Amma and Appa that going alone to Calcutta wasn't something to worry about. However, Ramu not accompanying Usha bothered her Amma–Appa and her in-laws. On his part, Ramu didn't clarify the reason why he was not accompanying his wife and Usha also avoided the matter saying that Ramu might be busy with work. But she knew why her husband was avoiding going to Calcutta.

After reaching Calcutta, Usha was in the thick of things. This time, she had more new songs for the audience. Usha had by now found a place in the hearts of the patrons of Trincas. The owners, Joshua and Puri, also noticed that whenever they announced Usha's performance schedule, the crowd doubled at Trincas from day one. In Bombay, the owners of Little Hut weren't happy with Usha's Calcutta trips.

On her latest visit Usha sang her heart out, and the guests at Trincas would impatiently wait for the evening to arrive. Among them was Jani Uthup as well, who after work would drive directly to Trincas. The early days of December were truly charming in Calcutta and there was a delightful nip in the night air. One evening Usha began singing her favourite track 'Big Spender' and everyone at the nightclub, including the band, were in the groove:

> The minute you walked in the joint
> I could see you were a man of distinction
> A real Big Spender,
> Good lookin', so refined.
> Say, wouldn't you like to know what's going on in my mind?
> So let me get right to the point
> I don't pop my cork for every man I see.
> Hey Big Spender, Spend a little time with me.

After the show that night when Jani Uthup was driving Usha back home, Usha smiled and asked him, 'I took your name today during the song. Did you like it?' He had an unexpected response: 'Usha, I don't particularly relish my name being spoken in public.' Usha felt that Jani who fearlessly claimed his love for Usha in front of Ramu was actually a shy and introverted person. During this trip, Usha and Jani would meet often during the evening shows at Trincas. And with each meeting, Usha was getting closer to taking a big decision in her life.

The first two weeks in Calcutta were absolutely grand. But there was an inner turmoil within Usha which aroused a sense of fear and foreboding that something unfortunate might happen. One morning Usha tried to pick up a heavy ashtray left on top of an antique table in her room. The ashtray fell on her left foot, and she sat down on the chair near the table for a moment. But when she tried to get up it seemed as if her left arm and foot had become lifeless. She panicked and was rushed to the Belle Vue Hospital. The doctors at the hospital after looking at Usha's condition concluded that this was a kind of partial paralysis that may take a long time to heal.

Usha requested Joshua to inform Jani Uthup about what had happened. Jani immediately reached the hospital and regularly visited Usha during her stay there, which was for almost a week. In the silence of the hospital room, Usha felt Jani's shoreless love and deep affection for her. In the five years of marriage with Ramu, she had never felt that. When Usha was getting discharged from the hospital, her doctor said that she will have to wear callipers on her feet and special leather shoes for a few months. The owners of Trincas wondered if Usha will be able to sing for long hours. Two weeks later, Usha stood in her callipers and sang for long and with such finesse that no one could even guess what Usha had gone through. She never mentioned the accident to Amma–Appa in Bombay or her sister Uma who was a doctor.

When Usha returned to Bombay she went directly to her in-laws' house in Dadar. Ramu expressed customary concern about her leg. But Usha's elder sister Uma Pocha took her to the King Edward Memorial Hospital. After a detailed investigation, the team of doctors said that this was a delayed impact of the polio fever that Usha had when she was a child. In medical terms—hemiparesis. Usha wore an ankle drop and a wrist drop on her left side. A steel plate was put on her left leg from the knee downwards. She had to wear callipers on her feet, and shoes specially made for people with this condition. Due to numbness in the left wrist, she had to wear wrist callipers. She underwent regular physiotherapy. For months, due to her condition she had difficulty getting on to the stage. In between, she flew to Calcutta to sing at Trincas. During this difficult period, Jani was her source of emotional support. The three distinctive qualities that Usha noticed in Jani Chako Uthup were his purity, honesty and his commitment to principles. But Usha would often wonder if there was any point in thinking about him when she was already married . . .

9

Listen to Your Voice

After all that had happened in Calcutta, Usha's room at the house in Dadar seemed sadder than before. The many puzzles related to the emptiness of the last five years became more apparent. How could she feel this unhappy and lost living with so many people at her in-laws' house? Why did she begin feeling such swelling loneliness in the house where she had spent her last five years? Usha used to think: will the future be any different? At times, she thought of asking Amma, 'Did you get my horoscope made? What does it say about me?'

It was 1970. An imagined future was occupying Usha's dreams. She had already sung two English songs at Bombay Talkies but getting into Hindi films was appearing tough to her. Luckily, the stars aligned in her favour, and she got regular offers to sing in films like *Kabhi Dhoop Kabhi Chaon*, *Hare Rama, Hare Krishna*, *Bombay to Goa*. As Usha had already sung so many advertisment jingles, the music directors were in two minds thinking if it would be a successful move to have a girl sing for Hindi films who came from a jingle-singing background. But eventually this doubt faded, and many offers came up to sing in Hindi films. Shyam Benegal's film was one such opportunity. But *Kabhi Dhoop, Kabhi Chaon* was the first Hindi film in which

Usha did playback singing. The song became popular—'Main Bhi Jalun, Tu Bhi Jale'.

This song was written by the famous film lyricist Pradeep and the music was by Chitragupta. When the film's producer called Usha for a meeting, she innocently asked if the song was in English, or a mix of Hindi and English? The producer laughed and said, 'The song is in Hindi. It's a lovely song.' Sitting along with the producer–director of the film, Chandrakant also couldn't hold back from smiling. Usha was given the song script. Usha actually liked the song—*Main bhi jalun . . . tu bhi jale . . . aaja sanam lag ja gale . . . aag se hi aag bujhe . . . bahon mein aake dekh le.*

The song reflected Usha's state of mind. She went to the studio for rehearsals. After that, she didn't go back to the house in Dadar but to Amma and Appa's home to share the good news that she had got a chance to sing for a Hindi film. Usha's brother Shyamsundar asked who will be enacting the song. Usha told him that this song will be picturized with Helen and Dara Singh. Shamu said jokingly, 'Oh okay! So, you will be singing for Dara Singh?' Such remarks were common between the siblings. Such lightheartedness ran in the Sami family. And Usha was ahead of everyone in humorous tricks. When *Kabhi Dhoop, Kabhi Chaon* was recorded, lyricist Pradeep was happy with the song's presentation. He said to Usha, 'I didn't expect you to sing this song so wonderfully.' This came as a welcome appreciation for Usha in 1970.

But amid this there remained an uneasy darkness between Ramu and Usha. They were in the fifth year of their marriage but there was still a desolated void between them. Ramu was always supportive of Usha's music career, but he was a quiet man by nature. Usha was full of life. And life was going on, chugging along the isolated quietness. But in her professional life the golden doors of opportunity had opened. The chance to sing in Dev Anand's *Hare Rama, Hare Krishna* was a sign of good luck. However, it was in Usha's horoscope that she would never attain anything without enduring difficulties. For the film, Dev Anand had brought Sachin Dev Burman, Rahul Dev Burman and Shashi Kapoor to Delhi along with the entire unit of Navketan.

This was during the last days of 1969. At that time, Usha was on a contract with Delhi's Oberoi International for two weeks. Dev Anand and the others were present at Usha's show. Shashi Kapoor's father-in-law ran the Shakespeareana theatre along with his daughter Jennifer Kendal. Due to that, Usha knew Shashi from before. When Usha's show got over, Shashi came to Usha and introduced her to Dev Anand. Dev Anand asked her, 'Usha, will you sing for *Hare Rama, Hare Krishna*? It's a duet song.' R.D. Burman told Usha, 'Lataji will be giving her voice to Mumtaz in this song and the girl with a Western outlook, Zeenat Aman will have your voice.' After Usha agreed, she was given the lyrics of *Dum Maro Dum*. Even Appa had tagged along when Usha had gone to the studio for rehearsals. It went well. But Usha was wondering as to why there was no news from Navketan. One day, when R.D. Burman spoke to Usha, he told her, 'What do I tell you! That song is not happening for you. Now Asha (Bhosle) will be singing it. But we have kept a song for you in the film *I Love You*.' Usha felt bad hearing this.

She had only heard stories about the politics that goes around in the industry, but this time she was experiencing it. The song that she had been rehearsing was given to Asha Bhosle. Usha, however, comforted herself by believing that what was destined for her would happen. She would sing the songs that were meant for her. However, the song 'I Love You', that was given to Usha, later on became a duet with Asha Bhosle. The English parts of the song were given to Usha and Asha got the Hindi parts. The song was written by Anand Bakshi and the music was by R.D. Burman. The song went like this:

Usha: *I love you*
can`t you see my blue eyes I really do . . . ooo
Oh, please give me another little chance
Dim duba dubaa, dim doobaa doobaa
Dim daaba daaba daaba daa
Asha: *Kya khushi kyaa gham, jab tak hai dum mein dum*
Arre aao kash pe kash lagaate jaao . . . galiyon mein ghooma, sadakon
pe jhooma, duniya ki khoob karo saair
Hare Krishna, Hare Ram
Hare Krishna, Hare Ram

This is how Usha, at an early stage, became a victim of the Mangeshkar sisters' dominance in playback singing in Bollywood. Whatever happened to the song 'I Love You', people till date believe that the song 'Dum Maro Dum' is sung by Usha Uthup.

Even R.D. Burman felt bad taking away 'Dum Maro Dum' from Usha after she was asked to sing it. That's why he wanted to make it up to her. From Bombay's famous nightclub Talk of the Town to Oberoi Sheraton, R.D. Burman along with Asha Bhosle had heard Usha sing 'Rain' many times. R.D. Burman would say each time, 'Usha, we must do something with this song.' He found a chance in the film *Bombay to Goa*. In a particular scene in the film, Amitabh Bachchan and Aruna Irani go to a nightclub following a tiff. In that scene, R.D. Burman had Usha singing 'Rain'. Even Amitabh Bachchan liked this song in Usha's voice. She was presented with her real name in the film sequence: 'And now ladies and gentlemen! We proudly present to you the one and only Usha Iyer!'

It was a fascinating period in film music that witnessed extraordinary lyricists, composers and singers. During that time, many unique experiments happened. Among the gifted musicians, the father-and-son duo of Sachin Dev Burman and Rahul Dev Burman had a special place. Earlier, R.D. Burman mostly worked at the Famous Cine Lab. Later on, he recorded at the Film Centre as well as Mehboob Studio. He had Usha record 'Rain' at the Film Centre in Tardeo. Back in the day, the lyricist, composer, singer and musicians came together and completed the recording. If there were any issues, the recording was done again. Times have changed with new digital technology which ensures technical perfection, but the endearing warmth and spontaneity of the old times are missing from the songs. This bothers Usha. She feels refining a song over and over again takes away its magic.

Indian cinema has had a long tradition of playback singing, whereas in Hollywood, songs featured only in musicals and the actors had to sing their own songs. Playback singing is a rooted tradition in Indian cinema that continues till today, and possibly into the future. Usha believes that to reach music to the masses one has to route it through cinema and politics, both worlds full of fantasies. Usha prefers simplicity over illusory presumptiveness—be it in life, in music or nature. She says that we cannot create a leaf, a drop of blood or even a tiny soil particle on our own.

From the very beginning of her musical journey, Usha found it essential to create a dialogue with the audience. To do so, one needed a good command over languages. During her schooldays, her teachers made her work on getting her languages up to the mark. Tamil was spoken at her house. There was an obvious insistence upon English as she studied in an English-medium school, where similar attention was given to Hindi and Marathi. There used to be a French class as well at Usha's school. Usha paid special attention to correct her pronunciation in these languages.

All this helped her when the golden doors of opportunities began opening. The music rehearsals for films and the singing at the nightclub were ceaselessly going hand in hand. Usha was getting ahead with the mantra that it's not important how good you are at singing but how original you are as a singer. Apart from offers to sing in films, Usha also began getting offers to record for non-film projects. Delhi's lyricist Jawahar Wattal offered Usha a song. Later on, many songs that Jawahar Wattal wrote for Daler Mehndi became hits. But to create a space in the musical scene, one needed backing from the film industry. When Usha's career was blossoming, film songs were quite a craze among people.

However, there wasn't much of a film-song trend in Kerala and Bengal as there were limited songs in Bengali and Malayali films. Non-film songs were much popular in these states. Non-film Bhojpuri songs were very popular in the Hindi belt—Uttar Pradesh and Bihar. But Bollywood compelled all of them to come under its canopy. The Marathi songs outside cinema were beaten down as they were not in sync with movies. The small music industry in languages including Hindi, Tamil, Telugu and Kannada, among others, were devoured by the film industry. In later years, the music albums also began to flop. All in all, the writing on the wall was clear—'No cinema, no success'. Usha also strengthened her command over singles. Singles in music was a successful western concept. The Beatles also tasted success with singles.

At that time, the Mangeshkar sisters had created a barricade when it came to Hindi cinema. Any new female playback singer was sent to oblivion only after a couple of songs. Usha was figuring out these roadblocks. But she had full faith in the originality of her voice. Usha says, 'I respect Lataji and Ashaji as my elder sisters. I have always received immense love from Lata Di. I never forget her birthday on 28 September. Once I asked her, "Didi, how is your voice this sweet?" Lata Di laughed and said, "Usha, I eat sugar candies every day." I said, so give me sugar candies too. And Lata Di actually sent me a kilogram of sugar candies. Even now when we talk, she smiles and asks, "Are you eating the sugar candies, Usha?"

'Asha Di's love is also unforgettable. I remember when I used to sing at Bombay's nightclub Talk of the Town, O.P. Nayyar

Saheb would visit often and Asha Bhosle would come along with him. Ashaji wore a big locket back in those days with O.P. Nayyar's picture on it. Even O.P. Nayyar himself was very loving. Nayyar Saheb would smilingly say, "You have a wonderful contralto voice Usha."'

Opera singers generally sing in soprano which is on a high octave. Female singing is mostly heard in soprano with the higher vocal range. The term soprano is derived from the Italian word *sopra* that means above or on top of. For a singer with such a voice, the notes available are from middle C to high A. The average peak of a female singer is from a small octave to the second octave. But Usha's singing voice is contralto as opposed to soprano which is a rarity in a female singer. Contralto, as compared to a high pitch, is a heavy and a uniquely deep voice in the lower octave. It's an invigorating thick, silky strong voice which is very close to a male singer. Western female pop singers blessed with a contralto include Patti Page, Joyce Berry, Timi Yuro, Dorris Day, Debbie Sims and Rosemary Clooney. And in India, the only representative of the contralto is Usha Uthup.

In the world of music, the lower octave and the higher octave are worth noticing. A male singer mostly focuses on the lower octave and the female singer on the higher octave. But Usha's voice is between three lower and higher octaves. That's why it is difficult for anyone to sing a duet with Usha. The two duet songs that she sang with Bappi Lahiri for the film *Vaardaat* are the only songs with a male singer in Usha's discography. 'Tu Mujhe Jaan Se Pyara Hai' and 'Na Main Hun Teri' were songs picturized with Mithun Chakraborty and Kalpana Iyer. The film *Vaardaat* didn't work at the box office but the two duet songs were big hits. Usha sang these songs on a lower octave and Bappi Lahiri on a higher octave in a thin voice.

After singing the two duet songs with Bappi Lahiri, Usha arrived at the conclusion that she could only sing duets with

S.P. Balasubrahmanyam and no one else. The image of a female singer in Hindi cinema is one who is dressed in a simple white saree looking like an emblem of purity singing holy songs or a sad song laden with tears. And that too in a high octave that is suitable for female singers. Usha refused to believe in such a structural norm and in the long run she got songs that were picturized on vamp characters in films, as in cabaret songs.

And what was marvellous was that Usha received great respect and love for singing these cabaret numbers. Usha believes that whatever work you get, if you give your everything to it, then there is nothing that can stop you from receiving love and respect. One can't sing a cabaret number like a prayer song and vice versa. The audience knows this. The way Usha embodies the rhythm with exhilarating sensuality reminds one of timeless singers like Juthika Roy and Geeta Dutt.

'The song is much bigger than the singer,' Usha often says. It is like a maxim: 'Any creation is much bigger than its creator multiple times. Van Gogh's eternal painting *Starry Night* is much bigger than him and Tolstoy's *War and Peace* is bigger than him.' Usha concludes, 'Music has shrunk the world and has brought all of us closer. So, sing anyway.' She emphasizes again, 'The song is much bigger than the singer!' This is the reason that she covered the song 'Skyfall', sung by Adele in the James Bond film, and made it unforgettable. She says that she can't be satisfied by singing like the Rolling Stones. She won't be content singing Tom Jones's famous 'Delilah' in his style. When she herself won't be able to enjoy the pleasure of singing, how would she make the audience dance with joy? Usha's admirers believe that Usha will be able to sing like the Welsh singer Tom Jones but he won't be able to sing like her.

Usha has a special affinity for the character James Bond. In her shows in 1969, she sang many songs from the James Bond film series—*Thunderball, You Only Live Twice* and *Diamonds Are*

Forever. What intrigued her about Bond was that you could have his number, take his name, but you would never have his heart. Usha was mysteriously attached to this James Bond credo. After reading James Bond books and watching the films based on them, these thoughts would often puzzle her. Didn't Bond wish to be loved, was he so stone-hearted? The James Bond theme appeared powerful to her in every way. But the highlight was when Usha decided to sing the Bond song sung by Adele in 2012 in her own style. Born on 5 May 1988, Adele is an endearing English pop singer. She has been conferred with many awards at a young age. Usha adores Adele. Usha sang Adele's song with absolute originality. 'Skyfall' in Usha's voice is spectacular.

> *This is the end*
> *Hold your breath and count to ten.*
> *Feel the Earth move and then*
> *Hear my heart burst again.*
> *For this is the end,*
> *I've drowned and dreamt this moment.*
> *So overdue, I owe them.*
> *Swept away, I'm stolen.*
> *Let the sky fall,*
> *When it crumbles,*
> *We will stand tall,*
> *Face it all together,*
> *Let the sky fall,*
> *When it crumbles,*
> *We will stand tall,*
> *Face it all together,*
> *At Skyfall.*

What a heart-wrenching song of life and death! Pop singers across the world like the Everly Brothers, Sam Cook, Simon and

Garfunkel, Dusty Springfield, Donna Summer, Robbie Williams, David Bowie, Jay Z, Marvin Gaye are like Usha's kin. That's why, on special occasions, Usha dedicates music to the iconic bands and singers during her shows.

One time in Madras when Usha sang 'Can't Buy Me Love' by The Beatles, everyone was overwhelmed:

Can't buy me love,
Oh love, oh
Can't buy me love, oh
I'll buy you a diamond ring, my friend
If it makes you feel all right
I'll get you anything my friend If it makes you feel all right
'Cause I don't care too much for money
For money can't buy me love.

Apart from celebrated pop singers, Usha also has immense respect for Geeta Dutt. Usha believes that due to Geeta Dutt's entrancing voice, like the Brahminy duck, she was Hindi films' ancient pop singer. She revisits the 1958 film *Howrah Bridge*'s song that was pictured on Helen and sung by Geeta Dutt:

Mera naam Chin-Chin-Chu Chin-Chin-Chu, baba Chin-Chin-
Chu
Raat chandni main aur tu, hello mister how do you do?
Babuji main Cheen se aayi, Cheeni jaisa dil laayi
Singapore ka joban mera, Shanghai ki angdaayi
Dil par rakh le haath zara
Ho na jaaye paagal tu . . .

Similarly, a song sung by Geeta Dutt in the 1959 film *Love Marriage* in which the Shankar–Jaikishan duo had given music is a fine sample of a pop song:

Kareeb aao, na tadpao
Humein kehna hai kuch tumse
Tumhare kaanon mein

Even now, in a leisurely moment, Usha gets mesmerized listening to the song sung by Geeta Dutt in the film *Night Club*, which Majrooh Sultanpuri had written and Madan Mohan had set to music:

Kahan phir hum kahan phir tum,
Kahan phir ye raatein,
Dhadkte dil se hojaye zara do batein.
Afsane nigahon ke sunta ja diwane,
Phir aaye ki na aaye milne ke zamane.
Kahan phir hum kahan phir tum.

Usha, looking at her country and the global landscape, believes that Geeta Dutt is matchless among the heirs of the great heritage of the music world. She has immense respect for her predecessors and unfathomable love for the new generation of singers. From Geeta Dutt and Lata Mangeshkar to new generation singers like Adele, India's Remo Fernandes and Susan D'Mello. The same Susan who at one point used to sing under the name of Suzie Q.

When the new generation of singers ask Usha how to sing, she says, 'Listen to your voice while singing. Don't try too hard to get to the song's next note. While singing and listening to your voice, you will get to that note. Get soaked in the song and its rhythm. Be happy while singing. Drink lots of water so that your throat doesn't get dry and stays moist.'

When Usha finishes a song, her fans shower her with a string of admirable words. For example, spell-bounding, captivating, mesmerizing, alluring, soul-touching and what not! But there is no satisfaction in these words. So, where lies the contentment? Usha has always felt that the ultimate fulfilment lies in listening to one's own voice while singing. She believes that when you listen to your voice the petals of your soul slowly blossom.

10

And Then, Usha Vaidyanath Sami

Merchant Ivory Production's English film *Bombay Talkie* was made in 1970. This film belonged to the genre of alternative cinema and was directed by Oscar winner James Ivory. Usha sung two songs for the film—'Hari Om Tatsat' and 'Good Times, Bad Times'. Both songs were in English. The famous duo Shankar–Jaikishan had given the music for the film which had a stellar cast that included Shashi Kapoor, Aparna Sen, Jennifer Kendal, Nadira, Jalal Agha, Pinchoo Kapoor, Sulochna and Utpal Dutt. It was the first and an important opportunity for Usha to sing in an international film. She was shown as a nightclub singer singing 'Hari Om Tatsat' in the film. *Bombay Talkie*, through the protagonist Lucia Lane, was a story about an English author researching the Bollywood film industry and falling in love with an Indian actor played by Sashi Kapoor. In the film, Lucia Lane is played by Jennifer Kendal.

Bombay Talkie was flooded with persons with formidable talent. During work sessions, Usha learned a lot from the composer duo Shankar–Jaikishan. They were among the rare ones who encouraged a new singer. Despite the dominance of the Mangeshkar sisters, Shankar–Jaikishan gave many singing opportunities to others, like Tamil-speaking Sharda Rajan Iyengar

during the 1960s. Sharda Rajan Iyengar who was famous as Sharda
sang the song 'Titli Udi . . . Udd Ke Chali' in the film *Suraj* (1960)
that remains an unforgettable hit song. Usha also got immense
encouragement from Shankar–Jaikishan. However, when Usha
was emerging as a recording artist, Shankar–Jaikishan's glory was
fading. On 12 September 1971, when Jaikishan passed away from
liver cirrhosis at the age of forty-one, this partnership came to
an end.

Usha remembers that it was the Shankar–Jaikishan duo that
was responsible for introducing jazz music in Hindi films. The
duo also laid the foundation of Indo–jazz music and released the
album *Raga Jazz Style* in which eleven songs based on Indian
ragas were recorded with saxophone, trumpet, sitar, tabla and bass.
After *Bombay Talkie* that was made in 1970, the next year 1971
that witnessed the loss of Jaikishan was heart-breaking for Usha as
well. If this duo had survived, Usha would have had more singing
opportunities in films.

Made for Western audiences, *Bombay Talkie* had four songs.
Two each in Hindi and English. One of the Hindi songs, 'Tum
Mere Pyaar Ki Duniya Mein', was sung by Mohammad Rafi. The
second Hindi song, 'Typewriter Tip . . . Tip . . . Tip . . .', was sung
by Asha Bhosle and Kishore Kumar. The two songs in English
were written and sung by Usha Iyer. One of the songs was typically
jazz, and echoed the hippy culture that flourished in those times.
The words went like this: *I will tell you of the vision . . . I saw last
night / I saw Hari Om Tatsat*. The second song, 'Good Times,
Bad Times', had these lyrics: *We have had good times / Although
sometimes / The bad times were not so bad/ Let's love through this
night / Let's just kiss and fight / And forever / And ever more / We will
say good night.*

The entire Bombay Talkie team was experienced and carefree.
Usha remembers Annabelle Crawford, an Anglo-Indian actor in
the film. One day during the shooting, she innocently asked Utpal

Dutt during a break, 'What do you do?' He replied in his typical witty style: 'I spy for China.' Annabelle's mouth was wide open as she stared at him in complete bewilderment and the others present on the set laughed uncontrollably.

Working with the Merchant Ivory Productions was not only a pleasant experience for Usha but also for the others. James Ivory was a film director of international repute who had a deep attachment to India. And the reason for this was that Ismail Noor Muhammad Abdul Rahman, aka Ismail Merchant, who was born and brought up in Bombay. In 1959, James Ivory met Ismail during the screening of James's documentary film *The Sword and the Flute*. Later on, they became thick friends. For forty-four years, they shared a harmonious relationship. They together launched the James Ivory Productions. There were actually three key members in the film production house that was established in 1961. One was Bombay-born Ismail Merchant, the producer. The second was American film director James Ivory. And the third was Germany-born Britisher and Booker Prize-winning writer Ruth Prawer Jhabvala. When this international trio got together, their primary goal was to make English films based on Indian narratives that catered to a global audience.

In India, Merchant Ivory Productions made fifty films. Ismail Merchant was the producer of most of the films, He once made an interesting comment about the trio that worked together: 'This company is like a strange marriage union; as I am an Indian Muslim, Ruth is a German Jew, and James is an American Protestant Christian. Someone called us a god with three heads. Some might also think of us as a devil with three heads.' This team also made many memorable films on life in Britain and America alongside Indian subjects. Iconic artists like Maggie Smith, Leela Naidu, Madhur Jaffrey, Aparna Sen, Shashi Kapoor, Jennifer Kendal, Hugh Grant, Emma Thompson and Natasha Richardson were associated with the James Ivory Productions. It made some notable films: *The Remains of the Day*, *A Room with a View*, *Maurice*, *Mr and Mrs Bridge*, *Shakespeare Wallah*, *The Golden Bowl*, *The White Countess*, among others. The association of James Ivory and Ismail Merchant lasted for forty-four years. In 2005, after the passing of Ismail Merchant, the production company fell apart. But the memory of *Bombay Talkie* is immortal in Usha's mind.

On 20 November 1970, there was a premiere of *Bombay Talkie* in Hyderabad. Shashi Kapoor had specially requested Usha to be present. Coincidently, Usha had a show in Mangalore right before the premiere. She decided that after the Mangalore show she would head to Hyderabad to attend the screening. When she was leaving her in-laws' home in Dadar she decided to only carry some essential clothes because her heart told her that she will never come back to the house. She felt no need to carry anything from a place towards which she felt no attachment. While leaving her room at the Dadar home, she looked at it with deep sadness. The vases kept in the room were never decorated with flowers.

She had occasional conversations with Jani Uthup over the phone during this time. He had told her that his company had temporarily transferred him for three–four months from Calcutta to Cochin. So, before leaving for Mangalore, Usha had called Jani to say after attending the film premiere she would be proceeding directly to Cochin. It was now clear to Jani that Usha was coming to him forever after freeing herself from the past. Jani called the head of his firm's Cochin office and asked if his friend Usha Iyer can stay at the company guest house for a few days. He happily agreed to it. After coming to Cochin, Usha felt as if after walking through a dark tunnel for the past five years, she has finally arrived at the kindled island of life.

Usha has gone to Cochin from Hyderabad to be with Jani. She had decided to never return to the Dadar home and this information somehow reached Usha's Appa. It obviously disturbed him. His eldest daughter Indira was also married in the same family. After putting many sources to work, Appa found out Jani's Cochin office details. Finally, he succeeded in getting in touch with Usha. At first, her brother Shyamsundar spoke to her and then handed the phone to Appa. Appa said a lot to her in very few words. 'Usha, the root cause of your problem is in Bombay. So, don't run away from Bombay. Come here and find your way.' Since childhood, Appa's words were like golden mantras for Usha. She told Jani that she must go to Bombay and file for divorce. Their marriage won't be possible without getting a divorce.

That's how, on Appa's word, Usha returned to Bombay. She straightaway went to see her parents. For the first time, she saw Appa restless and worried. He said, 'Usha, I won't be able to help you legally, financially or psychologically in this matter. Yes, you are my daughter. The doors to this house are always open for you. But I will always expect you to maintain the dignity of being a Sami daughter.' Appa also instructed her that in the present situation she wouldn't sing alone at any nightclub.

He said, 'Either your brothers will accompany you or I will be present over there.' Appa was apprehensive that in the current circumstances, Usha could be publicly insulted during a programme. Such a thing wouldn't happen as long as she was shielded by her family. Even today when Usha goes down memory lane, each and every day from those days is vivid in front of her eyes. All those days filled with unbearable moments, which were not only difficult to deal with but also impossible.

Regarding the divorce, Appa had already said that he wouldn't be able to help. However, Rallis India's managing director, Mr Panchu, who was also a family friend, spoke to a good lawyer, Mr Raichoudhry. It was in the month of February in 1971 when Usha met Mr Raichoudhry along with Jani. And a divorce case was filed. Jani was in Cochin. Usha would go alone on court dates. She was staying at Appa's house where the divorce was not even mentioned by mistake and the court dates went by. There was no protest from Ramu's side on the divorce matter. He also seemed to have understood that the five years was a mistake.

July 21, 1971, was a painful day for Usha as the final verdict was due on that date. She couldn't sleep the previous night. Who could she share her anxiety with at home? It rained through the night and morning. She got ready and reached the court on time. Of course, she was alone. The court proceedings began. The lawyer asked, 'What religion do you believe in? If you are a Hindu, then we will give you the Gita to swear by. If you are a Christian, then the Bible. If you are a Muslim, then the Quran. Tears began to flow ceaselessly from Usha's eyes. Glimpses of the past began to flash in front of her. Appa's puja, Appa's prayers, Madrasi Patti Ma's hymns. Her voice was choked. The lawyer came close to her and softly whispered, 'If you cry like this, your case will become weak. The court doesn't want to encourage a divorce.' Usha wiped her tears. Across her, Ramu was quietly present in the court. For a moment, Usha's eyes met Ramu's. She felt bad for him. But she had to look ahead. Ultimately, the judge announced the verdict, 'Marriage annulled.' While leaving the court, Usha couldn't hold back her tears.

After leaving the court, Usha came out and stood on the pavement. It had stopped raining by that time. She took a taxi and instructed the driver to take her to the Talk of the Town. This was the nightclub in Bombay where Usha used to sing some evenings. It was afternoon and the club was quiet. Usha made a lightning call to Jani from there.

'Who? Usha?' he enquired.

'Say my full name!' 'Yes, Usha! But Usha Sami! Now I am Usha Sami again.' 'Many congratulations,' said Jani.

Evening came by. Usha returned home. Amma was in the kitchen. Usha went to Amma and holding her she quietly murmured, 'Divorce is finalized.' Speechless, Amma started crying. And Usha too . . .

11

That Evening in Autumn

Autumn was awaited. The lawyer had suggested that nothing should be done in the next three months. Jani's birthday arrived on 4 September. Usha smiled and said to Jani, 'Jana, one shouldn't get married in their birthday month.' It was almost decided that the wedding will take place in Calcutta around mid-October. Jani informed his parents who raised strict objections to the proposed marriage. Jani hailed from a Christian community and Usha was a Tamil Brahmin. It was unacceptable for Jani's father, Chirrakrot Chako Uthup, who was a brigadier in the army, and his mother Thangamma Uthup that their son marry a non-Christian woman. Thangamma, like all Malayalis, lovingly called her son Mone. This decision of Mone's was unbearable for Thangamma in particular. But Brig. Uthup knew that his son was a one-track king whose decision was written in stone, impossible to change.

However, Jani's grandfather, Chako Chirrakrot Uthup, tried to explain to his son and daughter-in-law that they should not get involved in their adult and independent son's personal life. Chako Chirrakrot Uthup, who would tie a turban like a farmer, surely belonged to the conventional old times but he was very progressive in his beliefs. However, despite his efforts, his son and daughter-in-law remained rigid.

One morning when Usha was rehearsing for her evening show at Hotel Savera, suddenly three people entered the hotel. Two men and one woman. Savera at 9 a.m. was quiet and the hotel manager was also surprised to see visitors coming in that early. The guests told the manager that they want to meet Usha Iyer. When the manager informed Usha, who was busy with her rehearsal, she immediately stopped and went to meet them. A tall and broad old man asked Usha to take a seat while he introduced her to the other two guests. After the guests were acquainted with Usha, she was happy to know that they were Jani's parents, Brig. Uthup and Thangamma Uthup, along with Brig. Uthup's close friend Wing Commander John who lived in Madras. Usha out of courtesy asked them for tea or coffee. But saying no to that, they told her why they had come to see her. Jani Uthup's mother began in an angry tone. Thangamma's blazing temper primarily focused on one thing: 'You leave my son alone. You are a Hindu and in our Malayali Christian community there are already many good proposals that have come for Jani. Please know that we will never accept you as our daughter-in-law.'

Thangamma in Malayalam means gold! But fuming with anger, Thangamma's face was red. She was back in the day a beautiful woman. The twenty-three-year-old Usha was terribly shocked at this; while Thangamma was speaking, tears were constantly rolling from Usha's eyes.

When Thangamma was done talking, Usha in a quiet tone said to her, 'You ask your son to break all ties with me. I will lead my own life, Aunty.' Crying, Usha left. At that time, there were no mobile or email. Getting through to another city on the landline was almost impossible. When despite many efforts, no communication materialized with Jani, she wrote a letter to him on his Calcutta office address telling him about the incident. She wrote that his parents were against the relationship, so they must stop thinking about this any further. A response to that letter arrived soon in four to five lines. Jani out of love and closeness had begun calling Usha, Sutu. Maybe this was a short version of the word sweet. However, Jani's letter still remains vivid in Usha's memory after many decades:

Dear Sutu,
I hope that everything is okay over there.
Over here everything is fine.
I will tell my parents to mind their own business.
I will do what I have to do.
Love. JCU.

JCU as in Jani Chako Uthup's letter swept away Usha's sadness. She felt proud of Jani. A woman wants to have complete faith in her man. And Jani gave that to Usha. She read Jani's letter many times and her eyes welled up with tears. Jani's father was also well aware of his bold son's temperament. A resident of Kerala's Kottayam district's Kannikadi, Brig. Chirrakrot Chako Uthup (who was known as Brig. C. C. Uthup among his friends) however was a progressive man and he had immense love for his elder son. But he chose to be silent on Jani's marriage because of his wife Thangamma's anger. If it were only left to him, he would have already blessed Jani and Usha. Even today Usha remembers that Brig. Uthup had a large heart.

After marriage with Jani, Usha came to know from her mother-in-law that when Jani was born, Brig. Uthup was at the war front in Singapore. He had a Muslim friend over there called Jani who was martyred during the war. When Brig. Uthup returned from the front, he told Thangamma after looking at their new-born son, 'He will be named after my friend, Jani.' Jani's ancestral village is Chirrakrot. According to a tradition in Kerala, the name of the ancestral village is added to one's name. This was why Jani's grandfather's and father's names had the village name in their titles. And because of this, Jani was also supposed to add Chirrakrot to his name. But he never did that. He preferred to be called Jani Chako Uthup, Usha's Jana as in JCU.

Jani was the eldest of four siblings. He had a younger brother Ani, sister Rani and the youngest sister Ramani. Being the youngest one, Ramani was called Choti out of love. Kottayam's Uthup family was always inclined towards academics. Brig. Uthup was particular about giving his children the best possible education. He got Jani and Ani admitted to Lovedale School, Ooty in Nilgiri district. During childhood, Jani was an introvert, while Ani was playful and fun-loving, the exact opposite of him. Everything was going well for the Uthup family, but a sudden tragedy crushed Brig. Uthup and his wife Thangamma. At the young age of ten, they lost their daughter Rani to cancer. Despite every possible treatment in Delhi, she couldn't be saved. Brig. Uthup was so hurt by Rani's death that he requested a transfer out of the country for a few years. So, he was designated to the diplomatic corps and posted to England's Warminster town. Jani had passed his board exams at that time. After his father's transfer, he completed his plus two studies in England. Younger brother Ani and sister Ramani were also enrolled in a school in England. After some years when Jani completed his college education, he joined a famous tea company J. Thomas in England. But when his father's term got over in England, Jani also returned to India with him. Their daughter Ramani also returned to India with her parents.

In India, Jani luckily got a job in the same tea company at its Calcutta headquarters. But Jani's younger brother Ani stayed back in England. Ani wanted to build his career in England. However, this stubbornness on Ani's part wasn't well received by his parents. The Uthup family came back to India and over time, Ani became distant from his parents and siblings. He struggled a lot trying to create a life for himself in England. He took up many small jobs.

For a long time, Brig. Uthup or Jani weren't aware of what Ani was doing in England.

Once when Ani was standing in a queue at an employment exchange in London, an English girl, Anne, was standing in the same queue. Anne's life was also full of many difficulties. Ani and Anne met, and their relationship grew. At that time, Jani had met Usha and both were getting closer to each other. Through Jani, Usha found out how Ani was struggling in England. Coincidently, a few days later, Usha was among the few leading artists who were flown on Air India's inaugural jumbo jet flight to England. Usha took Ani's address from Jani and phoned him after reaching England. She told him that his family worried about him. Ani did speak to Usha over the phone 2–3 times but they couldn't meet. Maybe he didn't want to meet her. But at least Usha and Jani were able to establish communication with Ani over the phone. At times Ani would also send letters.

Once Jani received a letter from Ani that he had married his friend Anne. After three months of marriage, Jani received another letter from Ani saying that they had had a son. In response, Jani in a lighter vein wrote back congratulating his brother saying that in this jet age babies are born just three months after marriage. Ani and Anne had four sons—Jai, Saun Santosh, Marcus and Roy. After a long struggle in England, Ani got a job in British Railways. When Brig. Uthup got to know about it, he felt a little relieved. After that, on the mention of his younger son, he would say, 'My younger son is with British Railways. It's a very good job.' Anyway, these ups and downs carried on. But Ani's stars remained in darkness and it all culminated in Ani's passing away in an accident. He had gone to drop his kids in the car and as he stepped out, a milk van hit him. That was in 1983. At the age of forty Ani died. After Rani's death at the age of ten, Ani's death shook the Uthup family. As time passed, they lost touch with Anne as well. Unfortunately, Ani who fought with life till his last breath left a big void in the Uthup family. Jani's sister Ramani had a good life. She married Pranav Baruah from Assam who was employed in Kumar Mangalam Birla's company. Interestingly, Indira's eldest son, Ajay Srinivasan was also with the same company.

Brig. Uthup is no more. He passed away on 28 November 1995. Jani's mother Thangamma lives in Kottayam. She now loves Usha dearly, the same Thangamma who once was strictly against Usha and Jani's marriage. Today, when Thangamma revisits those days, she can't control her laughter. In the later years, Brig. Uthup would even say, 'Usha, you are like my son.' Usha believes that her father-in-law taught her a lot about the practicalities of life in his own unique way. After retiring from the army, he was the managing director of Modern Bakery for many years in Delhi.

After marriage, whenever Jani and Usha visited Delhi, Usha noticed that Jani had limited conversation with his parents. She found out that even before their marriage, Jani was a man of few words when it came to his parents. However, the same Jani was full of life and carefree with his friends. But quiet at home. His favourite corner at the Delhi house was the balcony where he enjoyed sitting in silence. By that time, their daughter Anjali was born. During a trip, little Anjali came along. Like always, Jani was sitting in the balcony with Anjali playing near him. Suddenly, Jani and Usha got into an argument. On seeing the situation getting out of control, Brig. Uthup said, 'Fights in love marriage too?' As he had been in the army for so many years, he preferred to speak in Hindi most of the time. So, he smiled and said, 'If husband and wife start having too many fights, they should begin to live like siblings. Look at me, Thangamma and I live like siblings.' Thangamma laughed at her husband's remark and pretended to sneer at him. After a few years of Jani and Usha's marriage, Brig. Uthup and Thangamma began giving Usha unbelievable love and the respect of being the eldest daughter-in-law.

Usha's daughter Anjali's baptism

Usha with Amma and Appa

Usha with her husband, Jani, and children, Anjali and Sunny

Usha's family

With A.P.J. Abdul Kalam

With American
actress Jane Fonda

With Asha Bhosle

With J. Jayalalithaa

With chief minister of Bengal,
Mamata Banerjee

With South African singer Miriam Makeba

With Mother Teresa

With Nelson Mandela

With R.D. Burman

With Raj Kapoor

Usha with school friends Umrana and Patsy

Usha with Shashi Kapoor

With Sonia Gandhi

With Shah Rukh Khan

Usha with her first band, Conquerors

With Atal Bihari Vajpayee

Usha in her younger days

With Rajiv Gandhi

Vaidyanath Someshwar Sami with Pandit Jawaharlal Nehru

With Prime Minister Narendra Modi

Usha and Jani

Usha with her younger sister Maya

With her mother-in-law

Usha's mother, Meenambal

With Chikku

Usha with daughter, Anjali

The Sami sisters

Usha with her brother Shamu

Usha with her son, Sunny

Usha's Tulsi Ma

Usha with her sisters,
Indira and Uma

Usha with husband
Jani and granddaughter
Ayesha

With her sister Uma

Usha's father, Vaidyanath
Someshwar Sami

Usha's daughter Anjali and son-in-law
John

Usha's family portrait with parents and siblings

Usha with her
granddaughter Ayesha

With mother-in-law and
sister-in-law Chotti

With sister-in-law Padma

Usha and Jani on
their wedding day

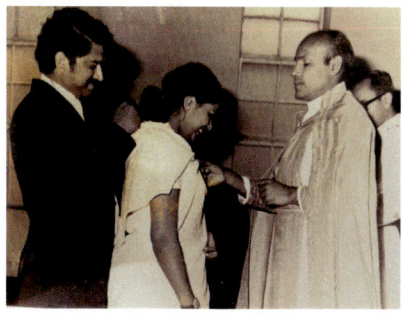

Usha with Jani, children and grandchildren

Usha with President Ram Nath Kovind

Dharmambal

Hallasya K. Nadhan

Shanti Home
in Madras

Usha with Pope John Paul II

Usha with her son, Sunny

Usha's grandson Riyad with Jani

With Farhan Akhtar

With Hrithik Roshan

Usha's childhood
home in Bombay's
Love Lane

With Amitabh Bachchan

With Kamal Haasan

With author
Vikas Kumar Jha

In the first week of October 1971, Usha got a new contract from Trincas. Like every year, the city of Calcutta was busy in preparation for the arrival of Navratras during the autumn season. Trincas's Joshua and Omi Puri were busy making arrangements for Usha and Jani's wedding. The date was fixed—16 October. It fell on a Saturday. Usha and Jani both wanted the wedding to be a simple affair. Mr Joshua and Mr Puri had organized everything at their 87 J, Park Street residence. On this occasion, Jani's parents didn't come but Usha's Appa–Amma and her brother Tyaagraj came and honoured the simple wedding. Mr Joshua and Mr Puri's friends with their presence brought exuberance to the brief wedding celebration. The marriage registrar carried on the procedure with utmost diligence. Then for dinner, everyone went to Hotel Hindustan International. Appa–Amma were elated at the joy on everyone's face who attended the wedding.

Appa remembered how a year ago, in 1970, he came to Calcutta with Amma. They wanted to see where Usha stayed during her visits to Calcutta. They felt satisfied seeing how Mr Joshua and Mr Puri took care of her as their own daughter. During that visit, they went to the Hotel Oberoi Grand for dinner. Usha had also asked Jani to come along. The dance and music was at its peak when they reached. People were dancing on the floor. When Jani asked Usha to dance, Usha looked at Appa with bent eyes and slight hesitance. So, Jani asked Appa, 'Sir, may I take your daughter for a dance?' Appa said with a smile, 'Sure.' On the wedding night during the dinner at Hotel Hindustan International, Appa laughed and reminded Jani of that night and said, 'Jani, I did not mean it seriously.' On this joyful joke of Appa's, Jani and Usha couldn't hold back their laughter.

The memory of that night on 16 October 1971 is still vivid in Usha's memories. After the dinner when all the guests left, Usha along with Jani went to Mr Joshua and Mr Puri's beautifully decorated room for the newly married couple. That autumn night was enchantingly drenched with love.

'Jana, happy now?' asked Usha, and Jani smiled.

'Jana, do you remember what you told me once?' Usha continued, 'You told me, "Usha, if you had walked back into your marriage, where would it leave me?" From today, all such questions are over.' Usha's voice was choked with emotion.

12

J.C.

After marriage, Usha and Jani began to live in a flat in Jassal House in Calcutta's Auckland Square. But at the beginning of 1972, Jani was yet again transferred to Cochin, Kerala. Naturally, there were limitations for Usha's music career in Cochin. There were no regular opportunities in this coastal city unlike Bombay, Madras and Calcutta. Usha decided that in the coming few years she would dedicate all her time to her family.

Kochi or Cochin has been a famous port city for centuries. Situated on the south-west coast and once colonized by the Portuguese because of its magnificent ports, it also witnessed engagement with the Dutch and English. That's why the city attracts international tourists. Life in Cochin was new for Usha. Jani had taken a house in the Fort Cochin area where those in the tea business mostly lived.

Life at the Cochin house was joyful, where Jani's friends would come and hang out in the evenings. Entertaining guests was difficult with limited resources, but Usha's warmth compensated for that. Mostly, the officials with the tea companies had a certain sense of lordliness to them, and Usha was well aware of that by now. That's why she learnt the art of setting the dining table in a formal fashion. While performing at the Hotel Oberoi and Trincas, she had noticed the art of positioning spoons and forks on the table. She got perfectly skilled at it while hosting at her house in Cochin. The years spent in Cochin were full of happiness. Jani and Usha's Cochin house was a favourite with their friends. A place where they could demand virtually anything.

Usha loved Cochin's hot and humid weather. However, there was no particular musical environment to be associated with. Still, some opportunities came up in the form of concerts. Slowly, she started getting proposals from Alleppey, Trivandrum, Calicut and Trichur. Then offers began rolling in from Trichy, Salem, Coimbatore and Madurai in Tamil Nadu. Pondicherry also joined the queue. This is how with the passage of time, Usha became busy in Cochin as well. Amid all this, her first child Anjali was born on 22 July 1972. Interestingly, Usha was doing shows until a week before Anjali was born.

Amma–Appa came to Cochin a week before Anjali was born and stayed for twelve days until the naming ceremony took place for the newly born baby. The doctor had predicted the third week of July for Anjali's birth. An apprehensive Usha had called Amma and said, 'Amma, I really hope Anjali doesn't come into this world on 21 July.' The year prior to that, in 1971, the court had given the final verdict on the same date. In life, some dates bring happiness and some remain as a wound on the subconscious. Usha's joy was doubled on 22 July when Anjali was born. Firstly, the joy of becoming a mother for the first time and secondly, Anjali being born on 22 July, a day after the tormenting 21 July. Anjali was named by Amma saying, 'She is a divine gift from God. That's why she is Anjali.'

Usha was lucky to find a nice, sweet girl to help her bring up Anjali. Her name was Alli. It was a quaint old British house near the Dutch church where the Uthup couple lived. The floor had a shiny wooden texture that added to the grandeur of the house. After morning tea, Usha would give Anjali a bath, wrap her in a towel and play Santana's music after putting the child on the floor. Usha would get busy sending Jani to work, while Alli would sit near Anjali. Little Anjali then got lost in the music playing near her.

The news of Anjali's birth was conveyed to Jani's parents, but they didn't come to Cochin. Usha felt that their anger hadn't subsided yet. They weren't present at the wedding. After the wedding, when the couple was headed to Srinagar for their honeymoon they went via Delhi. Brig. Uthup at that time was in Delhi working with Modern Bakery. After reaching Delhi, Jani had called his mother from a telephone booth and informed her, 'We are at the airport here.'

'Who is we?' Thangamma enquired. An annoyed Jani disconnected the phone. Usha and Jani had some time at Delhi. So, they took a taxi and went around the city and then took their flight to Srinagar. Jani's family's anger and sadness bothered Usha to the core. But this received some healing when Brig. Uthup visited them on a brief trip to Cochin 7–8 months after their wedding. Actually, Brig. Uthup was on his way to meet his father at his village in Kottayam. Also, he had to attend a family function over there. He got off at Cochin airport and thought of checking on his son's whereabouts. He had come alone on this trip. At that time, Usha was about to be a mother in a few months. Naturally, there was no end to Usha's happiness on Brig. Uthup's visit to Cochin. Usha came to know from her father-in-law how upset Jani's mother was at the news of their wedding. But his visit surely made things a little better.

Usha remembered how Appa told Jani after their wedding, 'Jani, never upset your father, because when I won't be there in this world, he will be there for you.'

Usha felt a little relief that the Uthup family had become soft towards their marriage when Brig. Uthup visited them in Cochin. But Thangamma Uthup was still very upset. After Anjali's birth,

Usha was hopeful that her child's grandparents would come to see her in Cochin. Anjali was the first child of their eldest son. But Brig. Uthup and his wife didn't visit them. Usha had learnt to be patient from her maternal grandmother, Madras Patti Ma. This teaching proved to be immensely helpful for her in normalizing the relationship with Jani's parents. When Anjali was three or four months old, Usha told Jani that she wishes to visit her in-laws in Delhi for a few days. But Jani said that if she wanted to go, she could, but he would not go along. However, Usha was firm and patient and nothing would stop her once she had made up her mind. She called her father-in-law and told him that she would be arriving on a particular flight to Delhi. This is how Usha along with Anjali and Alli came to Delhi. There was no end to Usha's happiness seeing her in-laws at Delhi airport. Their anger from the past days had vanished. This Delhi trip with Anjali proved to be a successful one for Usha. The lingering ache that festered from the insensitivity of her in-laws was gone forever.

Jani's younger sister Ramani was the happiest on Usha's arrival in Delhi with Anjali. Sixteen-year-old Ramani was studying at Lady Shri Ram College at that time. Ramani and her friends after returning from college loved playing with Anjali for hours. Even today, when Ramani revisits her first meeting with Usha in Delhi, she lights up with joy. She says, 'When I got to know about Usha's arrival, I was so excited as she had become a celebrity by then. She had fame. All my friends were going crazy to meet her. She had brought along many gifts. Even in the later years, she continued the tradition of bringing presents. That's why we started calling her the gift-bearing Usha, Mother Christmas.'

Diving in the sea of memories, Ramani says, 'Whenever I had a break in college, I would go and stay with Janiba and Usha in Cochin. Over there I met Usha's younger sister Maya and her cousin Chikku. Our holidays were full of fun and frolic with Usha and Janiba. Usha is the pride of our family. Two images are very grandly placed on the walls of our family home in Kottayam. One photo marks the moment when my father, C.C. Uthup received the AVSM from the then President of India, V.V. Giri, and the other photo is when Usha was honoured with the Padma Shri by the erstwhile President, Pratibha Patil.' Ramani says that it was Usha with her love and behaviour who came to Delhi and won over her upset parents.

A bridge had been forged with Jani's family and along with that, Usha wanted to resolve the puzzle that was troubling her. She had posed the question to Jani before their wedding about the religion their child will be raised under. This was a natural dilemma, as Jani's family was Christian and Usha was a Hindu. Jani never gave Usha an answer regarding this question. So, during the Delhi trip, Usha told her father-in-law that she wants her child to have a formal religion so that when she grows up, she shouldn't have any delusion or incompatibility in terms of religion. Brig. Uthup told Usha that he would like the child to be raised in line with her father's religious beliefs.

Being an army man, Brig. Uthup was progressive in his beliefs, but he found Usha's dilemma to be pertinent. He thought that whatever anger or pain was left in Thangamma regarding Jani and Usha's marriage will also fade away. He made Usha speak to Father Atayal at Delhi's Karol Bagh Mar Thoma Church. When the priest found out that Jani and Usha had a love marriage and Usha hadn't converted as yet, he told Brig. Uthup, 'To conduct your granddaughter's baptism ceremony, your daughter-in-law has to duly convert to Christianity. Firstly, Usha will be baptized. Then Usha and Jani will have to have a Christian marriage ceremony. Only after can Anjali be baptized.' After getting to know the whole religious process, Usha decided that she will come back to Delhi soon with Jani and Anjali and complete the formalities.

A few months later, after convincing Jani, Usha went back to Delhi with Anjali. Mar Thoma Church's Father Atayal gave the date of baptism and the wedding after a week. For the days in between he gave Usha some verses from the Bible to practice. There was a form that Usha had to sign. It said, 'From this moment on, I take Jesus Christ (J.C.) to be my only saviour.' Usha read the form again and again and she wondered if she was doing the right thing. Will it be correct for a girl from a religious Tamil Brahmin family who had lived twenty-six years of her life in that environment to change her faith? Her devoted Appa came to her mind. Her religious Madras Patti Ma and Amma also appeared. All the festivals and events of different faiths that were celebrated at home came back to her. But finally, she thought that religion is there to make life easier. Wasn't she doing all of this to keep life simple and easy?

Usha was experiencing faith like this for the first time. On the day of baptism at the Mar Thoma Church, she told Father Atayal, 'Father, I am more of a Christian than Jani's entire family. Like a true Christian who has love, care and a simple way of thinking.' While signing the form, an emotional Usha said, 'Father, on this form the short form of Jesus Christ in the bracket is mentioned as J.C. For me, my J.C. is my Jani Chako.' The entire Uthup family that was present over there was taken by surprise at Usha's passionate statement. It was a coincidence that Usha's brother-in-law, Indira's husband, was posted in Delhi at that time. That's why Indru Di was also in Delhi. She was present at the church for the wedding as a witness. Ramaswami Iyer, as in Ramu, was Indu's younger brother-in-law, with whom Usha had ended her relationship. This did bother Indru a bit. But she was there with Usha on such an important day of her life.

Whatever Usha had said to Father Atayal had left Indru taken aback. Even Father Atayal himself kept looking at Usha's face with wonderment. Ultimately, Usha put an end to that deep momentary silence and said, 'Father, shall we begin?' Father Atayal quietly began Usha's baptism. He said in a weighty tone that for the baptism, they will have to pick a name for Usha from the Bible. And so it happened that along with the baptism ritual Usha Vaidyanath Someshwar Sami got a new name —Usha Sarah Uthup. In Malayalam it was Usha Saramma Uthup. Usha now formally became a Syrian Christian. Along with her baptism, Jani and Usha's wedding rituals also commenced. Little Anjali at that time was in her aunt Ramani's lap, smiling and cooing completely unaware of what was going on. Usha said in an adoring tone, 'Anjali is so lucky. She is witnessing her parents' getting married.' After completing Usha and Jani's wedding ceremony, Father Atayal did Anjali's baptism. He gave her a new name, Anjali Elizabeth Uthup. In Kerala, the grandmother's name gets attached to the granddaughter's name and the grandfather's name is included in the son's name. Jani's mother's official name was Elizabeth. The priest naturally added her name to Anjali's new name. Then Appachan, as in Anjali's grandfather, took Anjali in his lap and smiled saying, 'Now see! This little Elizabeth!'

Both the trips to Delhi in a span of a few months proved to be truly satisfying for Usha. Both were like journeying through the Indian Ocean like it was for the crew of *Tarini*, a sailboat of the Indian Navy with an all-woman crew which circumnavigated the globe between 2017 and 2018. The initiative not only focused on encouraging sailing activities, but also showcased the Indian government's commitment to women empowerment. The crew of *Tarini* had not only to face the turbulent seas, but also exercise their perseverance. Usha thinks that every woman riding and grappling on a boat in the ocean of life is like a sailor on *Tarini*, searching for a safe harbour.

13

Cochin Days

Cochin is a big harbour city known by many endearing names. Kochi, Ernakulam and above all—the Queen of the Arabian Sea. A centre of the spice trade since the fourteenth century, this unique city in Kerala underwent changes through Portuguese, Dutch and British rule. It slowly took the shape of a metropolitan city. The wet, tropical climate gives the Queen of the Arabian Sea high levels of humidity. Amid ancient palaces, bungalows, forts and seashores, Cochin even today dwells in a mix of the past and the present.

It has within its fold the Dutch Palace, Bolgatty Palace, Hill Palace, Cherai Beach, Marine Drive, Pallipuram Fort and many others. Not only that, the smell of spices and fragrant trees pervades the atmosphere. For Usha, Cochin was like a gift of happiness, spilling with love like the translucent backwaters of Kerala. Usha's social life in Cochin mostly comprised people working with tea companies. Usha remembers her loving friends in Cochin in those days like Guddu Singh, Saroj Madhav, Rina Banerji and Ragini Menon along with whom time would fly like a bird. That era of festivals, celebrations, feasts and pleasant sittings would be soaked with joy.

Where Ragini was the better half of a literary friend Manju Menon, Guddu Singh's husband worked with the Brooke Bond tea company. Similarly, Saroj Madhav's husband was with Jani in J. Thomas tea company and Rina Banerji's husband worked at Tata Finley.

The atmosphere and environment in Cochin were magical. By coincidence, Jani before their marriage had introduced Usha to Elite Aces, a famous band in south India for a show with the Malayala Manorama group. On behalf of it, Mrs K.M. Matthew had invited Usha for the first time to Kottayam for a performance. This was Usha's first show in Kerala and it turned out to be very successful. When Usha came to live in Cochin, Elite Aces became her permanent backing band. There used to be an old nightclub within Cochin's Hotel Casino, and Elite Aces was associated with that club. Usha would occasionally sing over there. The tea company people who lived in Fort Cochin would mostly leave their cars on the jetty and take a ferry to go to work. But the officials at J. Thomas where Jani worked would mostly drive to work in their own cars and take the ferry to go home for lunch. Some of the J. Thomas executives would also go to Hotel Casino for lunch. During those afternoons, Usha was spotted there rehearsing for her evening shows. Whenever people found out that on a particular evening Usha was going to sing at Casino, that evening would light up with excitement. While singing along with the Elite Aces band, Usha would take everyone on an overwhelming journey. The listeners sitting at Casino would all of a sudden be transported to another world. Later on, Usha did several shows with Elite Aces in Shimla, Ludhiana, Bhopal and other centres.

Even after so many decades, the memories of the Cochin house are like the shelter of a tree under which she found much happiness. She experienced the wonder of motherhood there.

Those years in Cochin went by like a dream. The house near the Dutch Church where Usha and Jani lived has been turned into a hotel now. They went on to live in a big house owned by the Bishop's Parsonage. It was given to Jani by J. Thomas Company.

This house also had a royal demeanour to it. After Anjali's birth in 1972, Usha had a son, Sunny. This fulfilled Usha to the core. Now she had a complete family of four—Jani, their two children and she. Usha thinks of her own cherished childhood when she remembers Anjali and Sunny during their growing-up years. She also fondly recalls Alli, who was ever agile and always around as a household companion to help out Usha with the children.

Despite devoting time to Anjali and Sunny, Usha's creative side was active. Usha could do anything if she made up her mind and Jani was well aware of that. And during 1974–75, by starting a unique school called The Delta Study in Cochin, Usha took everyone by surprise. This one-of-a-kind school became a centre of attraction for children and their parents in no time.

When Anjali and Sunny grew up a little, Usha began sending them to a play school that was run by Mrs Painter in the Cochin Club campus. Usha began thinking about the teaching methodology that was followed at schools for children. Manju Menon and Ragini Menon were family friends to Jani and Usha. Both were sweet and loving. They had a son—Kabir. Manju Menon was deeply engaged in literature. He was an elderly and knowledgeable personality. Their familial timeline was also filled with scholars. Diminutive Manju Menon's thoughts were very profound, and Usha would listen to him with utmost attention. One day, on a random note, they began talking about the Scottish educator A.S. Neill and his book *Neill! Neill! Orange Peel!* and then turned their attention to the education system for children in the country.

Usha shared that there should be a good school in Cochin that focuses on newer ways of educating children that's different from the conventional ways of teaching. In those days, there were only two schools in the Fort Cochin area—St Mary's and Brito School. Both these schools were quite average. Manju Menon believed that the Britishers had most of their work on Willingdon Island where the tea companies were located in Cochin. So they didn't care much about Fort Cochin. The British employees in the area either sent their children to schools like Ooty's Lawrence School Lovedale or to England. The privileged Indians also copied the British in educating their children. Therefore, Manju Menon and Usha jointly decided that there should be a good school in the Fort Cochin area.

Lower income families were sending their children to substandard schools in Fort Cochin. Manju Menon asked Usha if she would like to send her children to a boarding school? Usha was crystal clear that she wouldn't. Usha told Manju Menon that surely there are many things from horse-riding, swimming to table manners and modern etiquette that children get to learn at fancy schools, but a sadness engulfs their hearts because of being away from their parents for long periods. She told Manju Menon that the school that they plan to open will not only focus on studies, sports and extracurriculars but also on the modalities of day-to-day life. Children must know the formal etiquettes like table manners along with their rooted cultural patterns. They should also feel happy eating on a banana leaf and enjoy eating rice, dal and sambhar with their hands. Usha added that elitism deprives us of many little pleasures in life. It limits one's scope of becoming a complete, well-adjusted person. The foundations laid during childhood are of great importance.

Manju Menon agreed with her that the new school would be established keeping the conventional course of study as well as modernity in mind. It was also decided that the children would be well-versed in Malayalam. Generally, in the schools of Kerala, the students were only taught Malayalam as a part of their course structure till the fifth standard. But in the school they would launch, stories would be narrated to children in Malayalam classes so that they would feel connected to their roots. It was also agreed upon that no exams will be held for Malayalam language as children would feel pressurized. Usha and Manju Menon went on many trips to Delhi's National Council of Educational Research and Training to discuss and plan the new school. After months of brainstorming, Usha and Manju Menon began a small school called The Delta Study near the post office in Fort Cochin. The school exists even today. But Usha regrets that the vision with which the school was started by both of them has digressed from its mission.

Usha remembers how she struggled to allocate finances for the school. She did many shows. And not only that, she also requested director Ramesh Sippy to hold a premiere of his film *Sholay* in Cochin.

The school began well. People noticed the new establishment. From studying nature to games like kite-flying and kabaddi were a pleasure for the children. The school's laboratory was also unique, where children learnt about the solar system in a playful fashion and also how buds sprout on trees and plants. But after some time, their guardians began to feel that the children would lag behind the central board standards. But some guardians liked this new pattern of educating children.

During Usha's stay in Cochin, she received parental love from Malayala Manorama's group head, K.M. Mathew and his wife. When Usha had come to Kerala for a show before her marriage to Jani, she had stayed with the Mathews. Mrs Mathew was a Gandhian figure for Usha who was dedicated towards women empowerment. She had brought together a group of women under a Gandhian organization called Kasturba. Over there, Mrs Mathew would get muruku, a delicious south Indian snack, made and then market it. This strengthened the economic condition of the women who came from poor families. During her days in Cochin, many tall and unique personalities came into Usha's life and inspired her.

Usha had whole-heartedly adapted to her life in Cochin, but in 1976 Jani Uthup was transferred back to Calcutta. At that time,

Anjali was five and Sunny was three and a half years old. After winding up her household in Cochin, Usha first went to Madras with Jani and the children. Then to Calcutta by the Coromandel Express. Their nanny Alli accompanied them as well. The train journey to Calcutta was a long and difficult one with two small kids. After reaching Calcutta, Usha went to Mr Joshua and Mr Puri's Park Street house with her family and luggage. She had informed them of her arrival over the phone. She stayed with them until a place was ready to live in Park Street's Queen Mansion. After living in Queen Mansion for a few years, Usha and Jani stayed in a rented flat on Lord Sinha Road. However, this time, Usha's arrival in Calcutta was like a new highway into the future. But such highways aren't easy to negotiate. It wasn't easy for Usha either.

14

The Dolan Champa Tree, Studio Vibrations

When Usha moved to Calcutta from Cochin, the flowers of dolan champa were in full bloom and the night flowering jasmine would be strewn on the ground in the morning. This was a new innings in Usha's career. Calcutta's lazy mornings, humid afternoons, chirpy soulful evenings and silent nights weren't new for Usha. From 1969 to 1971, she had sung at Trincas. But on her return to Calcutta this time, Usha felt that in the previous four to five years the nightclub scene in the city had slackened. During this time, the West Bengal government had unexpectedly increased entertainment tax. As a result, the number of musical bands playing in the clubs became limited. This is how music programmes at the nightclubs of Calcutta almost came to a halt.

Despite that, Mr Puri and Mr Joshua were really happy about Usha's return. Usha being in Calcutta meant the evenings at Trincas would perk up with Western music. Trincas was certainly a permanent stage for Usha, but this time she wanted to do something on a bigger canvas that would give longevity to her career. Slowly and steadily, she began working in that direction. It was a long-term dream for Usha to bring Western agility and a new wave of energy to the lax recording format in India. Usha's vision was clear in this regard that this change would not necessarily be concentrated on film recordings, but this experiment could be carried out in the domain of private recordings. What's astonishing is that Usha had foreseen the impact of marketing on music five decades ago. Usha appreciated the warmth, interest and excitement that Western music powerfully awakened. She had guessed that the new generation would spontaneously relate to this spirited warmth. Usha believed that whereas Indian music has splendour, Western music has speed. It has a tempo. Every generation has a thing for speed and tempo.

Usha found the vivifying element missing in Hindi film songs that excited the new generation. In the ever-changing times, the new generation looks for something in music that opens new doors and stairways. In Hindi films, the voice was given utmost importance and music was mostly sidelined. In Western songs, there was an equal division when it came to the singing voice and music. This was a balanced proportion. In India, there were many drawbacks to recording music. Western songs were much ahead of them in recording quality. Some years ago, when Usha had recorded 'Jambalaya' and 'Green Back Dollar' for HMV, she had noticed many shortcomings in the recording. Her Balram Mama was better than HMV engineers when it came to recording songs. Since childhood, she had witnessed his magical way of recording with finesse and an eye for detail despite limited equipment. His younger brother Ambi Mama was also an expert in recording music. It disheartened Usha that in India, an instrument like the bass guitar wasn't even used. Caught in the web of these thoughts, when Usha went to Calcutta from Cochin, she had decided that even though no one took her opinion in these matters, it was her fundamental right to work towards her dreams and implement her ideas.

Like Usha, Jani also loved the Park Street area. So, while living at Mr Joshua and Mr Puri's house, Jani began looking for a house in Park Street on a war footing. And finally, they spotted a lovely house at Queen's Mansion on the same street. When Usha entered the house for the first time, she got the feeling that this would be the place from where she would begin her journey towards her dreams. She kept getting memory flashes of Balram Mama in a peaceful corner at Shanti recording music. Balram Mama owned a Grundig tape recorder. Usha remembered that whenever she sang, be it at Madras's Hotel Savera or at the Music Academy, Balram Mama recorded all her songs. Usha noticed something extraordinary in those recordings. Music and voice never overpowered or encroached upon each other's territory.

This was a fascinating balance. Remembering those days, Usha began recording at home a few months before she came to live at Queen Mansion. The initial few months were definitely full of struggle. Every new beginning is like shooting an arrow in the dark. But Usha had a basic mantra—consistency. Whatever the result may be, raw or perfect, just keep at it with utmost dedication. It had disheartened Usha seeing the Sami Sisters, her elder sisters Indira and Uma, despite seeing so much success, damaging their music career due to lack of consistency. The evenings in Calcutta were again in full bloom at Trincas with Usha's music. She began getting new offers to sing in films. The door to opportunities also opened at Tollywood for Bengali films. Naturally, while singing for films, Usha again reconnected with film musicians, music engineers and music directors. Usha found that the people in the music industry weren't interested, excited or even prepared to bring something new to the young generation. They were satisfied with sticking to their old music. There were no signs of any change in the near future.

However, Usha was committed to her recordings despite being busy with household matters and professional opportunities. When she went to Dubai for a show, she bought a Teac tape recorder, one of the finest in the market and quite expensive. She already had three microphones. She was the first singer who owned such good microphones. She had earned all this with her hard work in music. Once during a trip to Sri Lanka, she had also bought a fine music mixer.

This is how after arranging microphones, the Teac tape recorder, music mixer and hi-fi Kenwood amplifier and speakers at home, Usha began recording on a regular basis. It was a wonderful coincidence that Usha got back together with the band Elite Aces in Calcutta. This was the same band that Jani had introduced her to for her first show in Kerala. With the passing years, Usha developed a close connection with the band. She got them regular contracts in Bombay's Hotel Oberoi and Calcutta's Trincas. Interestingly, when Usha had come to Calcutta from Cochin, this wasn't her favourite band.

Usha's little cottage music project began taking shape at home. She hadn't done a detailed study of sound like Balram Mama, but Usha was certain that if she worked wholeheartedly, her project would become a reality one day. Her experiments in the domain of sound would become successful. There were many roadblocks and questions before her. How far should the mic be placed while recording? What should be the intensity of the sound? How minutely should one pay attention to the mixing of sounds in the mixer? In time, the music industry began talking about Usha's 'home recording experiments' and also praised her for doing such exceptional work.

This worked like a magnet. She began getting big offers from popular brands for their advertising campaigns. One significant offer was from the Eveready brand. Then the Pond's Dreamflower talc's campaign. And to top all this, the Nescafe coffee campaign came to her.

During this cottage music industry phase, along with advertisement campaigns, Usha also got a significant offer from HMV. These were two Bengali songs—'Mon Krishna Bole' and 'Aha Tumi Sundari Kato Kolkata'. The first was written by the famous film lyricist Pulak Bandhopadhyay and the second by the well-known Miltu Ghosh. Ajit Ghosh gave music to these songs. Usha with great effort recorded both these songs at home. For some unknown reasons HMV didn't like the songs. However, the skilled recording engineers at HMV were astonished, wondering how such a good recording could be done at home. But it didn't appeal to the bosses at HMV. Usha was asked to record the songs at HMV's Calcutta studio. Usha did that and both the songs were big hits. But it bothered Usha as to why HMV didn't like the versions that were recorded at home.

In those days, HMV was the only noted company on the Indian music scene. This incident became like a challenge for Usha who was determined to prove that the recording at home was far better than the templated procedure at the HMV studio. And in time, Usha proved this as well.

Working from home was like walking the tightrope for Usha. The job of giving equal attention to the household, husband, kids and recording was demanding. The mornings began with rounds of tea. Getting Anjali and Sunny ready for school. Then preparing lunch for Jani and the children. Usha had the habit of waking up at 5 a.m. and getting ready for the day before her morning chores, which concluded 8.30 a.m. when Jani would leave for work. There were days when he would leave by 8 a.m. if there was a busy day at a tea auction. That half hour was like a bonus extra time for Usha.

Usha would come to the sitting room in her house by 9 a.m. and by then her efficient helpers, Meena and Durga, would come in to help her with housework. Jani had hired a good cook in Subhan for the kitchen. This is how Usha, with the help of the trio—Meena, Durga and Subhan—would transform her sitting room into a studio in no time. To soundproof the room, all the blankets in the house were hung across corners. The carpet was moved to the middle of the sitting room. Usha's studio would be ready as the clock struck 9.25 a.m. The band members would arrive by 9.30 a.m. From that minute till 1 p.m., a focused Usha would record for the next three and a half hours. By that time, she had to go pick Anjali and Sunny from school. She would leave for school and the band members would stop for their lunch break. By 1.30 p.m., Usha would be back from school with the kids. After feeding them, she would get back to the recording by 2.30 p.m. The next three hours would be intense, and the work would be wrapped up by 5.30 p.m. sharp before Jani came back from work. For months, Jani was unaware of the studio running at home. With this hide and seek game, Usha's cottage music industry had taken off.

One day, Jani came home before his regular time and was shocked to see the recording session in progress at home. Young and famous Bengali film actor Dhritiman Chatterjee's voice-over was being recorded. Jani looked at Dhritiman and said, 'Oh great! Wonderful voice-over buddy!'

Dhritiman's nickname was Sundar Chatterjee. He was one of Jani's regular friends at the club. A favourite with filmmakers like Satyajit Ray, Mrinal Sen and Aparna Sen, Dhritiman Chatterjee is remembered for his memorable performances in Satyajit Ray's *Pratidwandi* and Aparna Sen's much-talked-about film *36 Chowringhee Lane*. Even today, he remains one of Jani and Usha's closest friends.

However, during Jani's and Dhritiman's conversation the band members had left after getting Usha's signal for ending the session. At that time, Jani didn't say anything to Usha but later at night, he said, 'Usha, this is my home, not a recording studio. Please find another place.' Usha was hurt by Jani's words. As time passed by, Usha realized that what he said was for her own good. By the way, there was a dubbing scheduled the next day. But Usha had told her small team, including the band, that the dubbing would happen after a couple of days. But it troubled Usha as to how she would explain the delay to the client? Out of pride, Usha had postponed the dubbing and she was caught up in the web of worries. But God came to her rescue as the team that was supposed to be recording informed Usha one by one that they weren't prepared for it and so the session should be moved to later. This news brought relief for Usha. But it troubled her that her favourite band, Elite Aces, was going back to Kerala. Finding a new band got added to her list of concerns.

Usha began looking for an affordable place in Calcutta where she could record in peace. Two to three days later, a golden opportunity came by. One evening, Usha along with Jani went to attend an event at the Bengal Club. There she met two brothers, Sohanlal Saha and Mohanlal Saha who owned the recording company Inreco and their brand was known as Hindustan Records. The brothers were popular as S.L. Saha and M.L. Saha in Calcutta. Their father, the late C.C. Saha, had set up Inreco after years of struggle. This recording company's catalogue had illustrious singers like Kundan Lal Saigal and Pankaj Malik, among others. And not only that, Inreco also held sole rights to the recorded voice of poet Rabindranath Tagore.

While interacting with the Saha brothers, Usha was told by them that they liked both her Bengali songs that were recorded at HMV. Usha shared the entire recording episode with them as to how she had recorded both the songs at home for HMV and how they weren't satisfied with it and got it recorded again at their own studio. Usha told the Saha brothers that as they had already heard the songs, she would like them to hear the home-recorded version and share their feedback with her. The Saha brothers asked Usha whether she would like to continue pursuing this interest professionally? Usha responded with a definitive yes, but she also mentioned that she was looking for a proper place to set up a studio. She said she had tried running the studio from home for as many days as possible, but this was becoming difficult by the day. Undoubtedly, this was God's will that after listening to Usha, the Saha brothers said, 'Why don't you come over to Hindustan Studio?' It was as if Usha's wish had come true.

Hindustan Studio was located in Calcutta's Akrur Dutta Lane. The next day, after seeking an appointment, Usha went to the studio. Usha presented one condition during the meeting with the Saha brothers: she would work as a recording engineer in the studio and she would like to bring all her home-recording gear and set it up at the studio. The Saha brothers smiled while they heard Usha's condition and finally agreed to it saying that for every hour, she would be paid Rs 10 when her recording equipment would be used.

This was in 1977. Usha didn't haggle and agreed to the nominal payment. Thus she began her work at the Hindustan Studio. For a full day's work, Usha made Rs 50. But she was delightfully content as she was getting to do something close to her heart. Because of Usha's unique recording skills, the industry began talking about how the recording quality at Inreco had remarkably improved. With that, began the rain of offers. Legendary names in the music world—from Salil Chowdhury, Hemant Kumar, Manna De, Anup Ghosal, Yesudas, Sunil Ganguly and Aarti Mukherji to the famous tabla player Shankar Ghosh and sitar maestro Pandit Ravi Shankar—began coming to the Hindustan Studio for recording. In those days, Inreco had a renowned recording engineer—Nirodh Babu, who not only had recorded Saigal and Pankaj Malik, but also Rabindranath Tagore's voice. Nirodh Babu liked Usha's experimental and carefree recording style. With his encouragement and faith, Usha would sit on the mixer. One day, he said to the Saha brothers, 'She is the magic girl of recording.'

Usha became one with Inreco's environment. During that time, she got the good news that her favourite band, Elite Aces, was coming back to Calcutta from Cochin on a second contract with Trincas. She especially liked musician Emil Isaac's work. Issac was a band member. When the band arrived in Calcutta, they got in touch with Usha. Usha connected Emil Isaac with

Inreco's Hindustan Studio and put him on to recording. In the daytime, Emil would work at the studio and during the evenings, he would perform at Trincas. Usha was also regularly associated with Trincas. Usha made sure to furnish and equip the studio area at Inreco so that her team and the artists who came for recordings felt absolutely comfortable while working. When Usha had some money to spare, she air-conditioned the recording room. She also bought some new and modern equipment. That's how Usha in due course made her recording studio better than the best. Also, because of the new equipment, the quality of the recording was scaling up.

Usha soon had an Akai recording machine, two Revox tape recorders, a Tascam mixer, one Roland voice processor, two Tannoy speakers, two Auratone monitor speakers and many good microphones. Obviously, she couldn't have bought all this equipment from the Rs 10 an hour pay at Inreco. Usha had relentlessly acquired all this for the studio from the money that came from doing occasional shows. This was an unabated investment towards her passion.

From the beginning, Usha and Jani never discussed anything on two matters. One was religion and the other was money. They had established a great understanding between themselves. Both of them never asked about each other's income and expenses. That's why Usha got the entire studio floor air-conditioned with the money she earned from shows. It also pained Usha that most studios didn't provide a canteen or a clean bathroom for the artists. Usha provided both these facilities at the Hindustan Studio at her own expense. Usha had a long-standing dream of air-conditioning the entire main floor at the Hindustan Studio. This would require some changes to the floor's structure. The Saha brothers didn't agree with this plan. Usha realized that since she was already spending so much money, why not look for a place where she can do everything as per her wish.

So, after a long search, she found an ideal place at a service centre next to the Don Bosco Church. The top floor of this building was already given on rent to the Federal Bank. The ground floor had a warehouse. Usha took this place on a monthly rent of Rs 6000. She transformed the place as she had imagined and on 2 November 1982, she began her own outfit called Studio Vibrations. When Usha was leaving Inreco, she requested the manager Mr V. Balsara if she could take along his accountant and studio typist, Navin Ghosh. Navin, also known as Nobin, was a good tabla player. Usha needed an experienced person as her studio manager. Mr Balsara who belonged to the Parsi community was a skilled musician along with being the manager at Inreco and he also had a network in Bollywood. At Usha's request, Mr Balsara gave a green flag to Navin to join her studio.

As her new studio began, Usha was naturally flying on the wings of excitement. She was busy making her outfit efficient. Back in the day, when Usha recorded at home, she would often visit the famous electronics market Chandni in Calcutta. She would find spare parts for her equipment. And not only that, things like fuse, cables, connectors and screw drivers as well. One day while working, Usha had a sudden thought of adding four channels to the six-channel mixer. A mixer is a device that allows combining and processing recorded sounds to make it a perfect mix in its entirety. As if Balram Nadhan mama had taken over Usha's mind, she conducted impossible and strange experiments to upgrade the recording quality. One day, she randomly went to Chandni Market and got an aluminium tiffin box. She then took it to a technician and asked him to cut four grooves on top of the tiffin box and put four faders on them. She also got an electronic circuit on the inside walls of the tiffin box. The amused technician kept following her instructions. Finally, at the end of it, he touched Usha's feet acknowledging her technical dexterity.

In no time, Studio Vibrations caught on. Acclaimed artists, not only from Calcutta, but also from the North-eastern provinces Assam and Mizoram, and even Bangladesh, began coming to the studio for recording sessions. From the likes of Bangladesh's iconic singer Runa Laila to Sabina Yasmin, Alauddin Ali, Andrew Kishore and many others left satisfied after recording at Usha's studio. In those days, several music recording studios had come up in Calcutta. There was music director Salil Choudhury's outfit, Kishore Kumar's ex-wife Ruma Guha Thakurta's studio Ad Makers, Colonel Bose and Shravanti Majumdar's Living Sound, which had become famous after doing the Boroline ad. But all these studios, one after the other, began heading towards a slump. Col Bose's Living Sound studio and Ruma Guha Thakurta's Ad Makers, where most of the jingles were recorded, shut down. But due to Usha's perseverance, Studio Vibrations was making progress. This was Calcutta's first studio where multi-track recordings began.

For about two decades, Studio Vibrations kept running from the Service Centre near the Don Bosco Church. The rent went up every two years. Usha decided to get her own place for the studio. The quest for a space resumed. Usha's allies at the studio—Jackson, Dulal and Lakhinder—began exploring for a suitable place. During the hunt, they found that house number 4G was available for sale on Radhanath Chowdhury Road. This was a nursing home that belonged to a doctor, and he was planning to sell it and move away.

The doctor was contacted. And it all materialized in the end. In 2011, Studio Vibrations came to its very own home. A big studio was set up on the top floor, the second floor was for recording and the rest of the studio's work happened on the ground floor. Usha's room was also on the ground floor.

Usha felt a great sense of fulfilment when Studio Vibrations was settled and running at its new permanent location. The dolan champa sapling that she had planted in her musical dreams was growing into a bounteous tree, blooming with white ginger lily flowers. Studio Vibrations is like a close-knit family—from Sodepur's Samresh Karmkar and Shweraphuli's resident Navin Ghosh to Khokon Rai. Samresh is the man Friday. Nobin Ghosh (as he is known) is the manager at Studio Vibrations, and also a good tabla player. He is a disciple of Pandit Shankar Ghosh. Usha's secretary is Sandra Ashing who is from Calcutta and was previously with the Oberoi Grand. Gautam Basu who is the resident of Calcutta's Kankurgachi is the studio's recording engineer. Recordist Rajen Bose assists him. Dulal Mandal who hails from Howrah's Bagnan is the office assistant. Khokon Rai also works as an office assistant. Similarly, Madan Sana, Sukumar Haldar and Surjit Saha are committed assistants to the studio. Usha's 'Hanuman' as in her personal driver, Lakhinder Mahto, is from Bahilwara Bhual village in Muzaffarpur district, Bihar. On certain occasions, Lakhinder's younger brother Harendar also helps out with driving for any studio work. But in the list of the salary holders at Studio Vibrations, there is a talkative eighty-five-year-old woman Uma Das, one of her staff members. Usha also calls her Daku Singh out of love. Daku Singh, along with her daughter, comes to Studio Vibrations in the first week of every month to collect her salary envelope with great authority. If Usha is available at the studio at that time, Daku Singh will go to her and take some more money. And their endearing strife is a must.

'Tell me, who else will give money to me?' Daku Singh asks Usha with all the right she thinks she has. And a smiling Usha while giving the money to her says, 'You dacoit! You dacoit!'

15

Rambha Ho

'When shadows fall and stars appear,
A pain I feel I cannot bear,
If I could relive that faithful day,
I would not turn my love away,
I reveal how I do adore her.'

The song 'I Do Adore Her', sung and written by the King of Calypso, Harry Belafonte, is deeply close to Usha's heart. This is not the only song. Usha was a die-hard fan of all his songs including 'Matilda', 'Banana Boat Song', 'Will His Love Be Like His Rum' and 'Mama, Look at Boo Boo'. Usha always considered Harry Belafonte as her idol whose songs were simple, spilling with the little joys of life. Usha, who during her childhood days had written an innocent letter to Frank Sinatra and mailed it with her saved pocket money, has also sung many of American-Swiss singer Tina Turner's songs. Tina is now seventy-nine and lives in Switzerland.

As Usha became serious about her career, she had many doubts regarding her image. Finally, she found her ultimate answer in one name—Harry Belafonte. He was born in America on 1 March 1927 and lives in New York. He is ninety-two now and cognitively active. Harry Belafonte, who had a powerful creative journey through his music from 1949 to 2003, has been honoured by the Kennedy Center, and has been awarded the Emmy, Grammy and Tony awards. Famous as the King of Calypso, Belafonte always raised a voice against American consumerism. He was one of the significant names during the Civil Rights movement in America. His singing style, the art of holding a dialogue with the audience and his dedicated moral commitment towards society deeply influenced Usha. Despite not having a teacher in pop music, Usha intermittently worked on her craft, and in this journey of self-learning, Harry Belafonte was her lighthouse. If one finds symmetry with Caribbean music in India, then it is in folk music.

Dance and music born out of swinging joy! Like the folk song '*Sonajhuri bon he bandhu pata shoru . . . shoru*', glistening with fun and frolic. Even in the West, pop music came like a fresh, sparkling breeze of fast-paced music and took over the world. This pop music was people's music and symbolic of the new generation's rebellious attitude towards the establishment. The songs would excite the playful, carefree Usha. From the very beginning, she would intensely listen to the music of Elvis Presley, Cliff Richard, Stevie Wonder, Barbra Streisand, José Feliciano, The Beatles, Tom Jones, Frank Sinatra, Ella Fitzgerald, Shirley Bassey, Al Jarreau, Phil Collins, Neil Diamond, Elton John, Joan Baez, Randy Crawford, Dean Martin, Abba and The Carpenters. There were also icons like Harry Belafonte, Nancy Wilson, Eric Clapton, Santana, Mahalia Jackson and South African crusader Afro-pop singer, Zenzile Miriam Makeba, who consistently protested against apartheid and the white minority government in South Africa through her music. They inspired Usha every moment and remained a part of her inner world amid the melodious chirp of thousands of rhythmic notes. Usha would blissfully listen to these music giants, and she would dance and swing within, like a tree. Her elder sisters Indira and Uma's voices, blazing like the fire and fragrant like the flowers, would leave Usha astonished.

But the search for social interest flowing in the veins of the original ragas of music would graze her subconscious and simultaneously, she would drown in the enduring riddle about the nature of her tone. In such a fashion, wondering whether her great paternal grandmother and great maternal grandmother also had dimples like her? Like a boat of glee on the cheeks?

Did ten generations ago, any woman in the family have such enchanting cheekbones? Voice also has a body, like the human body.

It is also important to know the forefathers of melody. Usha has always admired the melodic voices of Lata Mangeshkar, Reshma, Kishori Amonkar and Begum Akhtar. At the same time, the songs of Mukesh, Kishore Kumar, Mohammad Rafi, Manna Dey and Mehdi Hasan have been very close to her heart. Interestingly, after playback legend Kishore Kumar, Usha was the other yodeler of her times among Indian singers. This is a style of singing where one suddenly changes from a normal singing voice to a falsetto and back. But Usha never tried to imitate any of them. She was aware of her limits and weaknesses from the beginning. Caught between her boundaries and determination, Usha had once said, 'Music is not my profession. I just make dialogues.'

After listening to the masters of Western pop, she realized that the music of Harry Belafonte is actually a conversation. And this art of dialogue is ultimate and fascinating. Usha studied painting at the Sir JJ School of Art. She was also inclined towards reading literature. Usha's vision was clear about these different dimensions of art—that art which does not communicate cannot be impactful. The Mona Lisa painting communicates with its viewer. Texts like the Mahabharata and Gita are powerful dialogues. All the immortal singers in the world always communicated with their listeners. When Usha started singing in 1968, Harry Belafonte's dialogue style was a model of presentation for her. When some of Usha's songs became popular, the *Illustrated Weekly* wrote about her. The magazine's editor and famous journalist Khushwant Singh described her as the Queen of Pop in an article entitled 'Pop Goes the Iyer'.

Usha was then Usha Iyer, Ramaswamy Iyer's wife. This was the 1970s when the country was in a state of disillusionment and youth resentment was rising. The hippie subculture of the 1960s, which took the West by storm, had reached the young generation in India. The word 'hippie' originated from the word 'hipster' and the idea was used by the beatniks who vociferously opposed stereotypes in society.

Before Usha emerged as a star, there was an event on 14 January 1967 in San Francisco's Golden Gate Park. Called the Human Be-In event, it welcomed the hippie culture. This was followed by the 'Summer of Love', a social phenomenon where many embraced the hippy culture's fashion and behaviour. In 1969, the Woodstock Festival was launched on the East Coast. In 1970, an elaborate hippie event was held in Chile called the Piedra Roja Festival. The 1970s was a decade of revolt globally. It was the same decade when the student movement took place in India. Indira Gandhi announced the Emergency and lost the next elections. This was the time when Amitabh Bachchan was emerging on the Indian silver screen as the angry young man. And this was the time when Usha, the 'pop queen' of India, had caught the imagination of the young mind, heartily breaking traditions. Usha was on time. She had promptly heard the heartbeat of the decade. Usha understood the blinkered era of the previous generation that blindly fancied slow, tearful songs. The new generation was in need of vigorous gaiety. Usha realized that her deep voice, once considered a weakness, suited the changing times. It became clear to her that it was time to transgress the boundaries. The evolving time needed euphoria, not tears. She was simply the singer of joy and the first pop singer in a land of Indian classical traditions. She surpassed the conventional barriers, awakening a hurricane of joy and leaving the young generation mesmerized.

It was also a new message to the women of that era that she won't remain silent anymore, helplessly shedding tears. The essence of a woman is happiness! Every possible happiness! Usha, a south Indian, belonged to a community which has been devotees and admirers of Carnatic music. English songs weren't treated with respect. Clearly, Usha's path was not easy. The world of English songs was very limited in those days. Whatever it was, it was limited to listening to singers from Western countries. In the 1960s there were only two programmes for those who liked English songs on Indian radio—Date with You and Sorts Request. All the songs were by European or American singers. When listeners heard the voice of an Indian pop singer on the radio, there was no end to their happiness. Usha covered songs by the same singers, but English songs by an Indian singer represented a big shift and took a little time for the public to understand.

Usha created a contemporary narrative of the new-age Indian woman. And not only that, she also introduced a new paradigm of the confident Indian woman—free and strong. India's pop queen dressing in a dignified traditional Indian attire sent the message that physical modernity is meaningless. What is important is mental modernity. Strangely, the old-fashioned Indian mind was not ready to accept the new idea of mental modernity. But was the stubborn Usha going to give up? As the new generation was exposed to Usha's magic, it became a never-ending dialogue. The philosophy and message of her famous song 'Rambha Ho' written by Indeevar became immensely popular. It was a lesson of magic for all the senses:

Rambha ho ho Sambha ho ho
Rambha ho ho Sambha ho ho

Sambha ho ho . . . Sambha ho ho ho
Main nachu tum nacho
Jitni tum pyar se jeeloge
Utni hi zindagi
Rambha ho ho . . . Sambha ho ho
Sun le o janeman janeman
Main teri mehbooba
Muskura muskura
Gham tum kyu
kyu dooba
Living we are living
Dancing ya ya dancing
Rambha ho ho Sambha ho ho
Main nachu tum nacho
Jitni tum pyar se jeeloge
Utni hi zindagi
Rambha ho ho . . . Sambha ho ho
Duniya me logon ke mele ye
Aayenge jayenge ho ho
Yaaro se milke hum jhumenge
Jhumege . . . gayenge
Chhayenge chhayenge ya ya
singing ya ya singing
All the people we love
Rambha ho ho . . . Sambha ho ho

Usha's songs, like 'Rambha Ho', 'Koi Yahan Naache Naache' and 'Shaan Se', continue to stir joy around the world. The attitude towards life, fearless grit and living with courage and grace is conveyed in all of her music. She is the proud voice of life. Usha once told Indian audiences that if The Beatles, Sir Cliff Richard or Elvis Presley were known to be international pop singers, then Kishore Kumar and Manna Dey from India are also pop singers and even better than Western pop artists. Geeta Dutt was no less.

The quality and demand for pop songs increased over time. More and more new tools became available to make songs effective. Of course, the path Usha took fifty years ago by performing at nightclubs and stage shows is now at its peak in the new millennium. For the past several decades, instead of soft, romantic and mournful songs, we are now seeing rhythms akin to 'Rambha Ho'. It must be satisfying for Usha that by singing pop in seventeen Indian languages, she has proved that pop music is not only owned by the West. There was a conservative perception among Indian listeners that pop songs are just 'hip hip hurray' songs, which make no sense. But Usha proved that Indian pop is far more meaningful and powerful. She believes that it's all about how we see it. Everything rests on our vision. Once, India's then prime minister Indira Gandhi had just released Usha's album *Beautiful Sunday*. During a programme, one attendee requested Usha to sing *Beautiful Sunday* like a devotional song. The lines of the songs were like this:

> *Sunday morning, up with the lark*
> *I think I'll take a walk in the park*
> *Hey hey hey, it's a beautiful day*
> *I've got someone waiting for me*
> *And when I see her I know that she'll say*
> *Hey hey hey, what a beautiful day.*

Before presenting this song as a devotional song, Usha said that Sunday is the holy day of Sabbath. 'If I go to the garden on this holy day and call Him, I am sure He will definitely come. That is, God will definitely come when invited on the day of Sabbath.' When Usha sang the song, all drowned in the spiritual sea, the audience was overwhelmed. In the course of her dialogue with the audience, Usha strongly shared that it is just an illusion that pop music has a bad effect on the younger generation. Actually, pop means change with joy. A happy change. In the early days, it was also the view that pop meant vagabond music steeped in sex and alcohol. Nightclub girls were also considered indecent. Usha entered the nightclub world when only men went there. Usha changed that image with her dignified performances.

Usha's voice was cast for the bad girls of the silver screen. It was a time when no Hindi film could be imagined without Helen, Kalpana Iyer, Padma Khanna, Jayashree T. and Prema Narayan. But by gradually filming songs like 'Choli Ke Peeche Kya Hai . . .' and 'Dhak Dhak Karne Laga', the lead actresses showed the door to cabaret dancers like Helen and Kalpana Iyer. No one would accuse the actresses of indecency and obscenity, like before. But at one time, Usha had to knock on the courtroom doors for one such grave charge.

16

Usha in Court

It was a summer afternoon in May 1983. Bangla film actress Geeta Dey, along with some of her friends, came to meet Usha at the studio. Truly beautiful and graceful, Geeta had always been active on social issues. Her dedication to society and culture always influenced Usha. Geeta told Usha that she was organizing a charity show on behalf of her organization Vinodini Satya Goshthi in support of Thakurpukur Cancer Research Institute. She wished to know if Usha would take some time out it.

'When?' Usha asked.

'If a date next month is convenient for you,' Geeta said with a smile.

'Where will the programme be?'

'At the Mahajati Sadan Auditorium,' Geeta replied.

'I will definitely come,' said Usha. 'You come to the studio tomorrow or the day after and I will tell you the date and time.'

Geeta Dey and her association colleagues left happily after having tea. Usha told Geeta that some of her relatives who were afflicted with cancer had left the world untimely. Hence she always felt committed to this cause.

'I came to you with the same belief,' an emotional Geeta said to Usha while leaving.

Two days later, the actress came to Usha's studio and Usha felt that she had come to firm up the date and time of the programme. Usha warmly welcomed her as usual. But there was a strange look of sadness on Geeta's face.

'Geeta Di, you look so sad, what happened?' Usha asked.

'What do I say, Usha? The minister is not permitting us use of the hall.'

'Which minister?' Usha was astounded.

'Jatin Chakraborty, minister of Public Works Department, Government of West Bengal. When he found out that you will be singing at our charity show, he rejected our request to hold the programme at the Mahajati Sadan and said that Usha Uthup is encouraging a form of decadent culture in West Bengal with her songs. The government will not give any hall for her programmes.'

'Okay!' Usha was speechless.

'Yes, Usha! Jatin Chakraborty told me that Usha Uthup, her songs, her fans, everything is against our culture. "I won't allow Usha to sing. And the government won't give any hall for the same."'

Geeta Dey took out a newspaper of the day and put it on the table before Usha. What a strange coincidence that Usha, who was accustomed to reading the morning newspaper, did not see it that morning as she was caught up in household work. The banner of the newspaper was, 'PWD minister Jatin Chakraborty bans pop singer Usha Uthup'. Usha called for all the newspapers and this news was one of the prime highlights in each of them. Usha couldn't hold back her tears.

'Leave it, Usha, leave it! We will hold the programme somewhere else. Let this storm settle down,' Geeta Dey said to comfort Usha.

'No Geeta Di, if I sing, it will be at the Mahajati Sadan. I will also see how they stop me from singing at a government hall. These ministers are there to serve us. They earn salaries from our tax money.' Suddenly Appa appeared before Usha's eyes. He always said that one should never tolerate any form of injustice.

When Geeta left the studio, Usha left immediately for the Writers' Building, the West Bengal government secretariat. She wanted to confront Jatin Chakraborty the same day. The door of his chamber was open. Usha stood at the door and waited. Jatin Chakraborty saw her but didn't ask her to come in. After waiting for several minutes, Usha asked the minister, 'Can I come in?' Jatin Chakraborty annoyingly said, 'Yes!' Usha entered the chamber and stood for a moment and finally asked,' May I sit?' Jatin Chakraborty continued to respond in a similar tone, 'Fine.'

'Dada, why do you do this to me?' Usha asked him even as he looked into his files.

'I will do what I want to do. Your songs are uncultured. It is against the culture of Bengal. As long as I am the minister of this department, you will not get any government auditorium to sing. This is final,' he said sternly, glaring at his desk.

'Dada, who nominated you as the saviour of the culture of Bengal?' Usha could not stop herself.

'I will see how you sing in a government auditorium.' Jatin Chakraborty's voice was trembling with rage. 'Go wherever you want to go. Take me to court. But the government auditorium will not be given to you to sing.'

'Okay, so now we will meet in court, Dada,' Usha said while leaving Jatin Chakraborty's chamber. Tears were rolling down her cheeks. Usha returned to the studio and decided to meet Calcutta's noted lawyer Subrata Roy Chowdhury. He was also associated with Indira Gandhi's Allahabad case.

Jani was friends with Subrata's son. So there was a familial friendship between them. When Usha went to meet Subrata in the evening, she took all the documents with her.

When she explained the matter to the lawyer, Subrata said, 'Usha, I will take up your case. Don't worry.'

'I hope you will get me justice.' Usha said, taking a deep breath. 'I am deeply hurt by this treatment.'

'What's it that has hurt you the most in this entire episode, Usha?' Subrata Roy Chowdhury asked in a comforting tone.

'Dirty accusations of promoting bad culture.' Usha's voice was choked. She then added, 'I have always been singing in traditional Indian attire. Even during the evenings at Trincas, I sing with dignity. My songs are never vulgar. No double meaning. Nevertheless, a minister of the government is hellbent on ending my freedom of expression.'

'And what else is bothering you?'

'The minister has banned me from singing in government auditoriums on charges of propagating bad culture, and this news is making headlines in the newspapers. I feel very humiliated by this. I don't sing to bring down the honour of my family, parents and relatives,' her eyes welled up.

'And what else seems unacceptable?' Subrata asked again, digging further.

'It pains me that the musicians in my team will lose their work,' Usha pointed out.

'All right, Usha. First we will file a case on the issue of freedom of expression. Then we will file a defamation suit against this news published in the newspapers. We will win this case Usha,' Subrata reiterated.

'Your fee, uncle?' Usha asked politely.

'Will I charge a fee from my daughter? This case is also a prestige issue for me. This is the first case in the country in which the government has banned a singer.' Subrata Roy Chowdhury responded, asking Usha to leave without any worry.

True to his word, he studied the case in great detail. He examined the history of the Aryans again. When did they arrive? What was their culture? His research turned into a thick file. He telephoned Usha after registering the case in the Calcutta High

Court and informed her that she should come to the court at every hearing, and he would take care of the rest.

Usha was present in the court when the first date of the case came up and the hearing took place. The following day, this news appeared in the newspapers of Calcutta. Jyoti Basu, the then chief minister of West Bengal, issued a statement that he had no knowledge of the matter. Jyoti Babu said that Usha Uthup is a good and respected singer. She did many charity shows to support the government of West Bengal. In fact, Jyoti Babu even named the shows that Usha had done for the Chief Minister's Assistance Fund and the Red Cross Society. After the CM's statement, the whole matter was reversed. The entire country was with Usha in the battle. Significant people from across the country gave statements in support of Usha.

During all these developments, Jatin Chakraborty remained tight-lipped. The case began in May 1983. Before every hearing, Usha made calls to Bombay to seek guidance from her appa. Finally, on 1 September 1983, the case was closed. Justice P.C. Borooah of the Calcutta High Court said in his lengthy judgment that the allegation made by the public works minister regarding Usha Uthup is totally invalid.

The Calcutta High Court's decision was an important and historical document for the Indian music industry. It was the first time in India that the government had banned a singer. The decision stated,

Mrs Usha Uthup vs. State of West Bengal and others. Dated September 1, 1983. The petitioner Usha Uthup does not require any introduction among music lovers of India and in many countries outside as well. Her charity shows have benefited the Red Cross, West Bengal Chief Minister's Assistance Fund, the Indian Navy and the institution of Mother Teresa from time to time. She has regularly sung for all the Doordarshan centres like Delhi, Bombay, Calcutta and Madras. She has often been presented by the Delhi Center in Doordarshan's national program. She has been seen and heard many times on US, Hong Kong and Singapore television. She has been frequently singing for various centres of the All India Radio. Usha Uthup has done many functions in several public halls in Calcutta, including the halls managed by the West Bengal government. West Bengal Governor, Chief Minister and Mother Teresa have also been present in these programs. Most of the major and minor records of her songs have been released in several Indian languages including English, Hindi and Bengali. She has also had the honour of presenting her music before the President of Kenya, Prime Minister of Mauritius and members of the British Parliament. No one has ever raised objections about her singing or her style of singing in India or globally. Yes, this is the first time that the Minister-in-charge of Public Works Department in the Government of West Bengal, Jatin Chakraborty (respondent No-5) objected, which was published by the Anand Bazar Patrika on 20 May 1983. The news said that defendant No-5 i.e. Jatin Chakraborty, as the chairman of the Board of Trustees of the Mahajati Sadan, managed by the West Bengal government, has prohibited Usha Uthup from doing the programme because they think Usha's songs and the disco that happens during that represent a degenerating culture. In this way, the songs that are sung by a distorted culture have a very low level and the listeners of such music are equally lowly. On June 18, 1983, in an interview to The Telegraph's daily correspondent Tarun Ganguly, Minister Jatin Chakraborty has said that why Usha Uthup stubbornly demands to sing at a government hall? Why doesn't she sing in the private theatre hall of Calcutta? Chakraborty said that he cannot allow Usha Uthup to conduct programmes in the halls under the government — Mahajati Sadan, Ravindra Sadan and University Institute.

When Telegraph correspondent Tarun Ganguly questioned Minister Jatin Chakraborty as to what is the ultimate reason for his displeasure with disco music, Jatin Chakraborty said that during the days of The Emergency in the country, the present government has encouraged disco-style music to diminish the culture of West Bengal. This was a serious conspiracy to hurt the dignified tradition of Ramakrishna Paramahamsa and Swami Vivekananda. This was a serious conspiracy to make the new generation of Bengal spineless and divert them from their moral values.

Justice Borooah, while detailing the case further said that Mrs Geeta Dey, assistant secretary of Vinodini Satya Goshthi, an institution in Calcutta, went to Mahajati Sadan on 18 May 1983, and in the absence of the secretary of Mahajati Sadan, she requested a staff member to allow Usha Uthup to perform at a charity show for the development of the Behala Cancer Hospital. But the official told Geeta Dey that Usha Uthup is prohibited from doing any programme there. Even N. Sarkar who was the chief of a cultural organization, Aroop, went to request the booking of Mahajati Sadan for Usha's show, but he also returned empty-handed.

N. Sarkar had also applied for a booking at Ravindra Sadan. But there too, he was told that the hall could not be given for an Usha Uthup show. Another cultural institution in Calcutta, Alaap, tried to book the same hall. But it was also denied a booking.

The judge also noted that on 6 July 1983, a signed petition by Chief Minister Jyoti Basu and West Bengal home secretary R.N. Sengupta was submitted to the court. It said that there will be no restriction on Usha Uthup to perform at the Netaji Indoor Stadium, Ravindra Sadan, Ahindra Manch and Shishir Manch. However, 'cabaret dance, snap dance and belly dance' should not be performed during her shows. The Justice, in his detailed verdict, shed light on the nature of pop music and wrote that it is important to understand what pop songs and disco songs are all about. On 2 August 1983, Justice Borooah noted that a successful, popular and profitable pop song is fully described in *The New Penguin Dictionary of Music* (1978). In short, it is a popular alternative to the classical music tradition. Citing Usha's affidavit in his judgment, he wrote that there is no such thing as 'disco music' in Western music. Hit tunes for pop songs are composed with many months of committed hard work. Quoting Usha's affidavit, the judge said that the petitioner never dances while singing a song. Nor does she allow anyone to dance on stage during her show. Hence, the allegation is wrong that the petitioner is a disco singer.

Justice P.C. Borooah made a very significant remark in the conclusion of his judgment:

> After reading the petitioner's affidavit, to be fully convinced, I took the trouble of listening to all the petitioner's songs that she has sung in English, Hindi and Bangla. I must frankly admit that I liked these songs. I did not find anything objectionable, vulgar and decadent while listening to all these songs. Many artists like Kamal Haasan from the South and Mithun Chakraborty from West Bengal gained considerable fame in terms of pop music and disco dancing. These two artists are no less than John Travolta, who became famous after the performance of the film Saturday Night Fever. Nazia Hassan became famous in India with her song, Disco Deewane. These facts reveal that even though pop and disco music are of foreign origin, they have settled in India. No minister or bureaucrat has the right to stop it. Freedom of speech and hearing is inseparable. These are two sides of the same coin.

Justice Borooah also mentioned in the judgment that the petitioner, Usha Uthup, has submitted her affidavit to the court and informed that the officials of Mahajati Sadan had banned her. But in the meantime, the hall was allotted to the Bangla and Hindi pop singer Meena Mukherjee and her team. Not only this, Amrik Singh Arora, who was a pop singer from Calcutta and also danced and sang songs, was given the hall for a programme at Mahajati Sadan on 3 July 1983. Tapas Bhattacharya did a similar programme in that hall. Therefore, this double standards of the government of West Bengal stood exposed. The judge noted: 'Minister Jatin Chakraborty has tarnished the reputation of his office with such activities. I hope by instructing him that in future he will refrain from such behaviour and will not be making nonsensical statements in the press.'

Usha felt deeply relieved after the final verdict. When she informed Appa over the phone, both Amma and Appa were extremely happy. Appa said, 'Usha, this is a big win. Now just do it. It is better to not get into any further conflict with the politicians.'

Indeed, the past four months were full of sleepless nights and restless days. Anjali and Sunny were very small. Usha was constantly afraid that what if her children were abducted from the school to harass her further. Regarding this fear, she also met with Chief Minister Jyoti Basu and West Bengal's chief of police. Jyoti Babu asked her to relax and asked if she wanted a security guard? But Usha refused, saying that the purpose of their meeting was not to get a security guard. But that she wanted to share her apprehensions as a precautionary measure. It was a strange coincidence during the case that Usha met Lily Chakraborty, wife of Jatin Chakraborty, at three or four shows. Some of Usha's close friends had told her that Jatin Chakraborty had taken action to ban her at the behest of his wife. Lily Chakraborty ran an organization and was active in social circles in Calcutta. When Usha met Lily at an event, she asked her, 'Why did Dada do this to me?'

Lily Chakraborty, without a pause, asked, 'Why don't you sing Rabindra Sangeet? Dada likes that music very much.'

'It's a promise. Now I will definitely sing a Rabindra Sangeet song in every show of mine,' Usha smilingly told Lily Chakraborty. However, in the meantime, the Calcutta High Court's decision came in favour of Usha. But she did not forget the promise made to Lily. So the day after the verdict, Usha went to see veteran singer Hemant Kumar. She requested Hemant Da to teach her Rabindra Sangeet and he happily agreed. The first Rabindra song that Usha learned from him was 'Ae Manihar Aamay Naa Naaj'. This song was written by Rabindranath Tagore when he was awarded the Nobel Prize. In this song, he says that the gemstone necklace doesn't suit him. And it will keep pinching him till he offers it to the Almighty. Usha also sang this Rabindra song in English—'Ae Manihar! Garland of Gems'. She gets overwhelmed even today when she sings this Rabindra song in her moment of achievement. When she received the Filmfare Award and the Padma Shri honour, the same Rabindra song resonated in her mind. When Usha immersed herself in Rabindra Sangeet, many songs soaked within her soul and life—'*O amar desher maati, tomar tate dhakai matha*', '*Se dine, du jane dule chinu bone*'. Usha also learnt many Rabindra songs from Suchitra Mitra, a notable practitioner of Rabindra Sangeet. One of the songs that Usha learnt is settled in her heart—'Gaan Guli Mor, Shaibaleri Dale . . .' Usha recalls that one Rabindra song which was very dear to her Appa was 'Oi Maloti Lata . . . Dole . . . Dole'.

Usha was also trained by Subhash Chaudhary, a teacher of Rabindra Sangeet for some time. Not only that, she passed the Rabindra music examination from Vishwa Bharati. In 1984, she released a Rabindra Sangeet album of hers—*Gaan Guli More!* Usha got the album released by Jatin Chakraborty.

Usha believes that she learned from every honour and setback in life. If not for the legal fight with Jatin Chakraborty, she would not have been so promptly oriented towards Rabindra Sangeet. After winning the case, Usha went to meet Jatin Chakraborty at his residence after returning from an overseas performance. She touched Jatin Babu's feet and said that both should forget what happened in the course of the legal battle. Jatin Chakraborty and his wife Lily were touched by Usha's humility. Jatin Babu used to smoke cigars, so Usha took cigars for him as a gift. She told him, 'Our love should prevail, Dada.' And Usha maintained this regard for him throughout his lifetime.

Jani and Usha had enrolled their son Sunny in Ooty's Lawrence School after much discussion. It was the same school where Jani had studied from ninth to the twelfth standard. A few months after the incident involving Jatin Chakraborty, Sunny had come to Calcutta on holiday. The verdict in the case had come. One evening, along with Sunny, Usha went to Kathleen, a cake shop located on Free School Street. Incidentally, Jatin Chakraborty also came there a few moments later. Usha whispered in Sunny's ears that she is going to greet Jatin Babu and she would like Sunny to come along and do the same. Teenager Sunny was angry that this man had harassed his Amma so much. So, he said to his Amma, 'Amma! I can't do this. I can't even think of bowing down to him.' Usha said, 'Sunny, please do it . . . for me.' The whole dialogue between mother and son took place within a few moments. On the insistence of his mother, Sunny touched Jatin Chakraborty's feet, but still angry rushed back and sat in the car. When Usha returned to the car with a cake after a few minutes of formal conversation with Jatin Chakraborty, she could see Sunny's face, blazing with anger.

'Why are you angry?' Usha asked.

'Why did you insist that I bow to that man?' Sunny sounded irritated.

'But tell me who won in that case? The defeated should be treated with more respect, son! This helps in healing his deep-rooted wound,' Usha told Sunny. And thus, Usha always maintained a respectable relationship with Jatin Chakraborty.

When his daughter living in Faridabad was murdered under mysterious circumstances, Usha immediately went to his house after hearing the news. Jatin Babu's eyes couldn't hide his tears. He said, 'Usha, we have done so many things, but you have forgotten everything and come as a daughter.' In later years, she became like a daughter to Jatin Babu's family. Whenever Usha came to know about health issues in Jatin Babu's family, she would stop everything and visit them. Every year during Durga Puja, Usha would send a dhoti–kurta set along with a saree for his wife. But Jatin Chakraborty was also one of a kind. From time to time, till the end, he would say, 'Usha, I am fond of you. But I don't like your pop music.' Usha would burst into laughter every time.

Jatin Chakraborty had to resign from his ministerial post in the Jyoti Basu government due to his arrogant nature. The Revolutionary Socialist Party (RSP) he belonged to was a constituent party in the Left Front government of West Bengal. Jatin was a senior leader and MLA from the RSP. He was a minister in Jyoti Basu's government on behalf of his party.

Jatin Chakraborty had directly accused Jyoti Basu of continuously ordering huge quantities of fluorescent tubes from the Bengal Lamps Works Limited to promote his son Chandan Basu's business interests. Jatin Chakraborty said that till 1979, the son of the chief minister was working in this company.

This was the first time that West Bengal saw a minister within the government directly accusing the chief minister. Jyoti Basu was terribly disturbed by what was happening. Ultimately, a decision was reached that either Jatin Chakraborty should express regret at his statement or resign from the ministry. Jatin Chakraborty preferred to quit. The day he resigned, Usha went to meet him and said, 'Dada, what did you do?'

'Usha, the court reprimanded me in your case. But no one will reprimand me for my resignation,' Jatin Chakraborty said with a smile.

17

Malligai Poo: The Jasmine Flowers

'Baati Nei . . . baati nae
Kolkata te baati nae
Gaaner Shohor
Praner Shohar
Shohor Onoopma
Aei nogori, Amar Kaache
Ruper Tilottama . . .'

This song was on Usha's popular album with Bengali tracks from 1993. Its music was by Rahul Dev Burman or Pancham Da, who died on 4 January 1994. Till 1980, the magic of Pancham Da ruled over Bollywood. His stars remained bright for nearly a decade and a half thereafter. The film *1942: A Love Story* was released on 15 April 1994, almost three and a half months after his passing. The film's music was composed by him. With its release, the songs of the film created an enormous buzz. It was the eternal magic of Pancham Da that left behind melodious echoes. There was a general perception that Pancham Da's last work was *1942: A Love Story*. But insiders knew that his last music was in Usha Uthup's album of Bangla songs, *Baati Nei*. This album is also the closest to Usha's soul to date. It contains exceptional songs like

'Prem Pore Jai Baba . . .', which even today twirls Usha's heart now and then.

Usha believes that Pancham Da lived in the embrace of music and not merely its discipline. He had a mystical formula, which became more intense while making melodies. He would wholeheartedly dwell freely in music, drown himself in the enchanting sounds, and appear with a rainbow tune. He was a serious listener. He had the unique skill of polishing a voice. Usha could not forget her experience from recording *Baati Nei*. Pancham Da wouldn't get tired of praising Usha enough by saying that 'Usha is a one-take singer', and Usha would smile and say, 'I have no other way, Dada! I am a live singer who doesn't get many chances.' But while recording the album, Pancham Da interrupted Usha, 'Oh Usha! Why are you singing with fear . . . chew on the words and sing boldly! *Baati Nei . . . baati nae . . .! Kolkata te baati nae/ Din dupure jyoti aache . . . ratti re baati nae . . .* Munch the words and sing daringly.'

Regarding the second song of the album, 'Preme Pore Jae Baba', Rahul Dev Burman again gave the same advice, chew and sing. After being urged repeatedly, Usha sang and when she heard the songs after the recording, her heart was flooded with happiness. But the apprehensions Usha had regarding a few songs in the album came true once the album was released. The newspapers in Calcutta carried headlines on the front page like, 'Usha Lampoons the Red Bastion'. It is noteworthy that in those days, there was a Left Front government in West Bengal and Jyoti Basu was the chief minister. Usha's song was on the electricity crisis in Calcutta as clearly as it was about the 'power' crisis in Calcutta, *Din dupure jyoti aache . . . ratti re baati nae . . .*

This news was highlighted in the newspapers for two consecutive days. Usha had a feeling that it would raise many eyebrows in the government. She was familiar with the Left's temperament. Since Usha was permanently residing in Calcutta, as a precautionary measure, she sought an appointment with Jyoti Basu. She was given time. Usha said to Jyoti Babu, 'Dada, before someone else says anything against my songs, I thought that I would meet with you and clear the air.'

'No problem. Because of that, your album is getting a lot of publicity.' Jyoti Babu deftly said, avoiding the topic, 'Art should never be banned. And Pancham has always been naughty,' he laughed.

Indeed, Rahul Dev Barman was always full of childish frolic, remembers Usha. He had amazing youthful qualities. He was a fan of fast cars and fine perfumes. The entire Burman family was very aristocratic and elegant. Usha has memories of Meera Dev Burman, Pancham Da's affectionate mother. Meera Dasgupta, who came to be known as Meera Dev Burman after becoming the wife of legendary music director Sachin Dev Burman, was a fine lyricist in Bengali films and was initiated into music by director and composer K.C. Dey (Manna Dey's uncle) and Bhishmadev Chattopadhyay. Meera also sang very well and contributed to many famous songs by her husband. Usha remembers how affectionately they used to meet. But after her only son, Rahul Dev Burman, passed away in 1994, Meera could not bear the shock and took to bed. So, Asha Bhosle, wife of Rahul Dev Burman, took the ninety-two-year-old Meera from her bungalow and admitted her in an old-age home called Sharan. But when this act was gravely condemned, she was brought back to her bungalow. In 2007, Meera passed away. Usha gets overwhelmed when she thinks about the Burman family. Her memorable songs 'One Two, Cha, Cha, Cha' and 'Shaan Se' are Rahul Dev Burman's gifts. When people heard the song 'Ek Do Cha, Cha, Cha', which was picturized on Aruna Irani in the film *Shalimar*, they said Asha Bhosle wouldn't have been able to do justice to this song. In the film *Shaan*, the song Usha sang, '*Doston se pyaar kiya, dushmano se badla liya . . . jo bhi kiya, humne kiya, shaan se . . .*' It became the theme song of the action thriller.

Usha got to work with veteran film music directors one after the other. Shankar–Jaikishan, R.D. Burman, Laxmikant–Pyarelal, Ilaiyaraaja, Anu Malik, Bappi Lahiri, Shankar Mahadevan, Salim–Sulaiman and A.R. Rahman being the primary ones among them. These music directors were well aware that Usha is a nightclub singer, so when a cinema song was in need of a Western mood, they would think of Usha. Initially, people would say that she only sings in English. It was because many of Usha's English songs had become popular. For instance, 'You Set My Heart on Fire', 'I Feel Love, Evergreen', 'I Would Like to Dance', 'Dance Little Lady, At Seventeen', and 'Going Out of My Head', etc., were her popular songs, which created her image as an English singer. But Usha was not limited to only English songs. Gradually, when most of the music directors were convinced that apart from Hindi and English, Usha has a good hold on Indian languages like Tamil, Telugu, Kannada, Malayalam and Konkani, they all began offering her songs. Usha sang for many south Indian music composers like Ilaiyaraaja, Britto Michael, Dharan, Sharath and K.V. Mahadevan. Usha also unfurled the magic of fusion in south Indian film songs. She says, 'I am a living example of fusion. I dress in pure traditional style, but I sing differently. This is fusion.' Usha smilingly concludes, 'Fusion is universal.' It's evident that she has always embraced this rare fusion-sense in her personality. Hence, her songs sung in Tamil films, 'Vegum, Vegum, Pogum, Pogum' (music: Illayaraaja), 'Life is the Flower' (music: Illayaraaja), 'Hello Love' (M. S. Viswanathan), 'Under the Mango Tree' (M. B. Srinivasan), 'Ketu Pattanam' (Illayaraaja) and 'Silai, Silai Than' (Illayaraaja) are as fresh in people's memory even today.

When Usha remembers Rahul Dev Burman for his free thought in music, she does not forget to remember Illayaraaja for his rigorous sense of discipline. Mani Ratnam's famous Tamil film *Anjali* has the music of Illayaraaja. When Usha was recording the song 'Vegum, Vegum, Pogum, Pogum' for this film, she was constantly alert, leaving no room for even a little mistake. Freedom, as with Pancham Da, wasn't possible with Illayaraaja. If he had his mind set on something particular for a song, he didn't like anything going otherwise. Not less or more. Yes, he used to allow freedom to the singer so that one can sing in their own distinctive style while relishing it, then he gave complete freedom. Illayaraaja's mastery of the idioms of Western music and Indian folk is rare. That is why Usha believes that if a singer sings a single song with Illayaraaja, then it is like life insurance for their music.

Even though the dynamic music director of Malayalam and Tamil films M.B. Sreenivasan is no longer in the world, even now Usha gets exhilarated remembering his dedication to music. Manamadurai Balakrishnan Sreenivasan, a Tamil Brahmin, was known as MBS in the south Indian film industry. He was one of the founding figures of the Indian People's Theatre Association (IPTA). He came to music direction with the encouragement of Bengali film director Nemai Ghosh. His first film was in Tamil, *Paadhai Theriyudhu Paar*. Famous Tamil lyricist Jayakanthan wrote the songs for this film. MBS also acted in a few Tamil films. Among them *Agraharathil Kazhutai* is notable. The free-spirited MBS married Kashmiri freedom fighter Dr Saifuddin Kichlu's daughter, Zahida Kichlu, after they fell in love. They had a son, Kabir. Unfortunately, none of the three are in the world now. MBS passed away on 9 March 1988, at the age of only sixty-two. Zahida died on 23 October 2002, and Kabir passed away on 4 April 2009.

It was MBS, under whose direction, Usha sang the first Tamil pop song in the film *Madana Malligai*. The song was called 'Malligai Poo' which became an evergreen hit. Its words went:

Mango tree
Pap pappappappa pap Pappappappa
Under a Mango tree

On the banks of the Kaveri
Moon beams peeping through
You gave me a garland of sweet Malligai poo,
Tender shoots of a golden tree
Reach out to the sun
To replace you in my life
O ho, ho, ho, ho, ho
There is none . . . there is none.
Pappa pappapappapa pappapapa papapa
Mango tree is in blossom.
The Mango tree is in fruit
Under the Mango tree for you
I wait with your garland of sweet Malligai poo . . .

Usha also sang several hit Malayalam songs, such as 'I Am in Love, Pitambara!', 'Oh Krishna', etc., under MBS's music direction. Usha also sang countless Malayalam hit songs for music directors M.S. Viswanathan, S.P. Venkatesh, L. Vaidyanathan, Tomin J. Thachankary, Shyam, Shailesh Narayanan, Alex Paul, G. Devarajan and Deepak Deb, among others.

Usha also has a long list of Telugu songs. The Telugu pop songs sung by her continue to charm listeners. The title song of the Telugu film *Race Gurram* directed by Surendra Reddy is sung by Usha:

Race gurram,race gurram
Hey, dhummu repe operation
Dhamu ape masu action
Demma repe natu faction
Race gurram,race gurram.

Usha has a heap of Kannada songs as well. The Kannada film *Kshana Kshana*, directed by Sunil Kumar Desai, was released in

2007. Music was given by R.P. Patnaik. Usha Uthup's title song rocked the film:

Dhin tarakatara, tum tanakatara Kshana kshana
Ariyada marama kalada dharma Kshana kshana
Kalawe sutaka kshana kshana Illelaru patak kshana kshana.

Kannada music director S.P. Chandrakant's 'Muttana Manninalli' is one of Usha's popular Kannada songs. Similarly, she has sung songs in many languages like Marathi, Bengali, Sindhi among others. She earned her place among music directors of all languages with her humility and simplicity. In the initial days, whenever she worked with any music director, she would say in advance that, 'I don't know *saregamapa*. I have no formal training in music. So, if I make any mistakes while singing, please let me know immediately. You will tell me which note is not right, and I will rectify it.' So the legendary music directors like Shankar–Jaikishan, Rahul Dev Burman and Laxmikant–Pyarelal used to say that Usha is the first and only singer who could say something like this with such honesty.

Usha was always certain that her final take was in the first five takes. More often than not in the first take. She could not stay comfortable after five takes. That was why Rahul Dev Burman used to say, 'Usha, you are a one-take singer.' Usha often noticed that if a line of a song was becoming prominent in the performance of her song, but the songwriter and composer preferred another line, she would stop and follow what they wanted. For example, according to Usha, the emphasis should have been upon the line *'Jalta hai dil'* in the song 'Tumhe Koi Aur Dekhe, Jalta Hai Dil', but from the point of view of the songwriter and composer, *'tumhe koi aur dekhe* needed more underlining.

Usha always agreed to what the songwriters and musicians wanted. Usha believes that learning from respected lyricists and musicians of different languages with humility not only educated her, but she received utmost affection and respect.

She remembers when she was recording the song 'Yeh Ye Maya' for Farhan Akhtar's film *Don 2*, how respectful the music director trio Shankar Mahadevan, Ehsaan Noorani and Loy Mendonsa were. In December 2011, when *Don 2* was released, its songs became tremendously popular. Loy also received much acclaim. Before becoming a music director, Loy Mendonsa was on the piano and keyboard for A.R. Rahman for a long time. It was in 1997 that Shankar, Ehsaan and Loy came together. They created more than fifty soundtracks in English, Hindi, Tamil, Telugu and Marathi languages. In music circles they are jocularly referred to as 'Amar Akbar Anthony'. For *Don 2*, Javed Akhtar wrote this song:

Na koi raat hai
Na koi din yahaan
Kya yeh andhera hai
Ki sirf hai dhuan
Aankhein dhoka khaati hain
Yeh kisko pata nahin
Jaane kya hai yahaan
Aur jaane yahaan kya nahin
Hai ye maya.
Heere jo lagte hai woh
Mumkin hai angaarein ho
Chingaari lagte hai jo
Ho sakta hai taare ho
Aankhein dhoka khaati hain
Yeh kisko pata nahin
Jaane kya hai yahaan
Aur jaane yahaan kya nahin
Hai ye maya . . .
Chehre hain sab ek se

Tu kaise pehchaanega
Dushman hai ya dost hain
Tu kaise yeh jaanega
Aankhein dhoka khaati hain
Yeh kisko pata nahin
Jaane kya hai yahaan
Aur jaane yahaan kya nahin
Hai ye maya hai ye maya
Hai ye maya . . .

When this song written by Javed Akhtar came to Shankar–Ehsaan–Loy, they decided first that this theme song, blazing with the shrill strategies of Don, should be sung by a powerful male singer with a heavy voice. Two-three rough cuts were recorded as well. But it wasn't working out. Finally, Shankar, Ehsaan and Loy got in touch with Usha Uthup. She agreed and the recording took place. It was a magical recording. Film director Farhan Akhtar happily tweeted the following: 'Recorded a song with Usha Uthup for *Don 2*! What a voice and what amazing energy and attitude! A Rockstar in a Kanjeevaram saree.'

Usha knew him as A.S. Dilip, when he used to play the keyboards for Illayaraaja. Later he changed his name to A.R. Rahman and became famous as the Mozart of Madras. He composed the music for Ramgopal Varma's *Dawood* and Usha sang the title song for it.

Usha believes that the way A.R. Rahman created a unique fusion of Indian classical music, electronica and the traditional orchestra of the country was rare. Usha remembers when Rahman had especially written a song for her, 'Tu Bole Glass Aadha Khali', for the film *Jaane Tu . . . Ya Jaane Na*, and for some reason, when Usha couldn't find time to record it, Rahman sang the song himself instead.

Alokesh 'Bappi' Lahiri is one musician of Bollywood whose name Usha takes most affectionately. Many of her famous songs have been composed by Bappi. In the 1980s, when Bappi came on the scene with his exciting urban disco music, it had a direct impact on music directors like Rahul Dev Burman. Usha's voice suited Bappi's compositions. All the songs sung by Usha for the films *Pyara Dushman*, *Vardaat* and *Disco Dancer* were super hits. All these songs were embellished with music by Bappi Lahiri. The track 'Koi Yahan Nache, Nache' from the film *Disco Dancer*; 'Hari Om Hari' from *Pyara Dushman*; 'Rambha Ho' from the film *Armaan*; and two songs of *Vardaat*, 'Main Hoon Tera, Naa Tu Hai Meri' and 'Tu Mujhe Jaan Se Bhi Pyara Hai', were all hits because of their happy colours and celebratory fervour. Two songs of *Vardaat* were duets sung by Usha and Bappi. It seemed like Bappi's thin voice was getting lost in Usha's heavier voice. So despite these songs being hits, Usha decided that she will never sing in a duet because it is difficult for the other voice to sustain with hers. The peculiarity of the duet hits from *Vardaat* was that it was difficult to distinguish between the male and female voices. *Vardaat* did not succeed at the box office, but Usha engraved its songs in the people's mind by singing them at countless stage shows.

The song, 'Hari Om Hari' in the film *Pyara Dushman* was so powerfully brilliant that Usha's vocals with picturization featuring Kalpana Iyer became imperative for other songs. Bappi Lahiri had used the tune of the English song, 'One Way Ticket' by Neil Sedaka and made popular by the British disco band, Eruption. But, those were not the days of the Internet when people could match the tunes of both songs. After this, Kalpana Iyer, who danced to Usha's song 'Rambha Ho' in the film *Armaan*, became eminently unforgettable. The film was released in 1981, and 'Rambha Ho' is still an evergreen hit. It is clear that Usha's powerful songs had put Kalpana Iyer in the ranks of Bollywood's sensual actresses and dancers like Helen, Bindu and Aruna Irani. Composed by Bappi Lahiri and propelled by' Usha's voice, 'Rambha Ho' was shot with Kalpana Iyer dancing at Goa's famous carnival.

Bappi Lahiri provided a provocative tune to 'Rambha Ho', which he took from the album *Cuba* by the French group The Gibson Brothers. The album was released in 1979 and two years later in 1981, Bappi Lahiri presented 'Rambha Ho' on the lines of 'Que Sera Mi Vida', a super-hit song from the same album. The meaning of 'Sera Mi Vida' is 'that will be my life', originally written by Nelly Byl and Jean Kluger. Usha had sung a cover of this original song a few times even before the recording of 'Rambha Ho'. So when lyricist Indeevar wrote the song 'Rambha Ho' and Bappi Lahiri said that this song should be sung in the style of The Gibson Brothers, Usha did not need much rehearsal for it. Today, despite many decades that having passed, the depth of this song may remain unknown to many. The first line of this song, '*Rambha ho, rambha ho*', is actually about the incomparable beauty, Rambha, born out of the Samudra Manthan (churning of the ocean of milk) as stated in the Bhagavata Purana. It says that if one stays young, misery and illness stay away and all wishes come true. Indeevar also created the magic of 'Rambha Ho' in Hindi, and there was a parallel to it, 'Que Sera Mi Vida' by The Gibson Brothers:

> *If you should go, go, go*
> *Que sera mi vida*
> *How am I gonna live without your love*
> *If ever you should go?*
> *Que sera mi vida*
> *How am I gonna find my way alone*
> *If ever you should go?*
> *How can I know what I would do*
> *If I was really losing you when it isn't true?*
> *(When it isn't true)*
> *How can I know how I'd react*
> *Before I have to face the fact of a broken heart?*
> *If you should go, go, go*

Que sera mi vida
How am I gonna live without your love
If ever you should go?
Que sera mi vida
How am I gonna find my way alone
If ever you should go?
How can I see you miles away
I know too well you gonna stay
Ev'ry night and day, ev'ry night and day
You never know just what you've got
You only feel it means a lot
When it's gone and lost
If you should go, go, go
Que sera mi vida
How am I gonna live without your love
If ever you should go?
Que sera mi vida
How am I gonna find my way alone
If ever you should go?
So if you really wanna see
The way my life is gonna be
If you're leavin' me, if you're leavin' me
Just slip away and close the door
And make your mind at least before
Seven weeks or more
If you should go, go, go
If you should go, go, go
Que sera mi vida
How am I gonna live without your love
If ever you should go?
Que sera mi vida
How am I gonna find my way alone
If ever you should go?

Que sera mi vida
How am I gonna live without your love
If ever you should go?

However, while Usha sang and created magic with *Rambha Ho* on the lines of *Que Sera Mi Vida* by The Gibson Brothers, simultaneously, she sang another delightful song by American actress and singer Doris Day called 'Que, Sera, Sera' in its original form. This song is also very close to Usha's heart. Doris Day got international acclaim with this track. Its music was given by Bernard Harmon. However, initially, Doris Day herself didn't consider this song as a significant one. She always avoided the song with a smile saying that it was a children's song. In fact, in the suspense thriller film *The Man Who Knew Too Much*, Doris sang it as a lullaby to put a little boy to sleep. Doris who passed away at the age of ninety-seven on 13 May 2019 always kept this song in the second place till her last years. But it had its own global magic. In 1956, soon after its release, the Tamil film *Aravalli* had a super hit Tamil song with the same tune. It was a duet. Nine years after the Tamil film, Vijay Bhatt Movies made a film in Telugu, *Thodu Nida*, in which N.T. Rama Rao was the hero. In the film, Bhanumathi sang the entire song 'Que Sera, Sera' without changing a single word. To this day, Usha irrevocably sings this song passionately during her stage shows:

When I was just a little girl
I asked my mother, what will I be
Will I be pretty
Will I be rich
Here's what she said to me
Que sera, sera
Whatever will be, will be
The future's not ours to see

Que sera, sera
What will be, will be
When I grew up and fell in love
I asked my sweetheart, what lies ahead
Will we have rainbows
Day after day
Here's what my sweetheart said
Que sera, sera
Whatever will be, will be
The future's not ours to see
Que sera, sera
What will be, will be
Now I have children of my own
They ask their mother, what will I be
Will I be handsome
Will I be rich
I tell them tenderly
Que sera, sera
Whatever will be, will be
The future's not ours to see
Que sera, sera
What will be, will be . . .

Usha knows that there is a special selective audience that likes this song by Doris Day. Like 'Matilda', which is a peculiar favourite for some. But sung on the lines of The Gibson Brothers' 'Que Sera Mi Vida', her evergreen song, 'Rambha Ho' is loved by all. Usha recalls the days at Mehboob Studio when the echo machine, Roland 601 was used for the first time during the recording of 'Rambha Ho'. In this song, the magic of the resonance of *Ho . . . Ho . . .* was possible due to this machine. Because the echo machine was being used in the recording of the song, the sound engineer Black Cyril gave it all. It was Black Cyril who first used an echo machine in a song. Bappi Lahiri also got noticed as the music director for the track, which is why in 2008, when the film *Slumdog Millionaire* was released, there were accusations that A.R. Rahman had made the song 'Jai Ho' on the lines of 'Rambha Ho'.

Things would have been strained between Bappi and Rahman but Usha along with some common friends handled the situation. Usha is grateful to Bappi Lahiri for many songs. It is Bappi who made Usha sing for a heroine for the first time. The film *Locket* was released in 1986 and its director was Ramesh Ahuja. It had Jeetendra and Rekha in the lead roles. Usha sang a song for the character that Rekha played, 'Aaa main gul badan'. In 1990, Bappi also gave Usha an opportunity to sing for Sridevi in the film *Nakabandi*. The song was written by Anjaan: *Nakabandi nakabandi / Aaka maka na ka maka / Dhoom dhoom chaka chaka / Nakabandi nakabandi / Are you ready are you ready / Nakabandi nakabandi . . .*

Usha also sang for Shabana Azmi in the film *Godmother*. Bollywood has a tendency to recreate all kinds of successes. Be it a film, or a song. Years after the glorious success of 'Rambha Ho' there were several songs reflecting its mood, spirit and thought. In the film *Shirin Farhad Ki Toh Nikal Padi*, released in August 2012, there was a song by Usha called 'Rambha Mein Samba'. The song was penned by Faraz Ali and composed by Jeet Ganguly. There were many songs in this film including those by Shreya Ghoshal, Neeraj Sridhar, among others. But neither the film nor the songs created any stir. Whatever little bit was heard was Usha's song:

> *Rambha mein Samba*
> *Rasta hain lamba*
> *Chahat mein fir bhi tum ek U-turn le lo na.*

The glory of 'Rambha Ho' remains intact. In recent years, Usha sang for the film *Revolver Rani* that released in 2014, and subsequently in 2016, she sang for two films—*Kafiron Ki Namaz* and *Rock On 2*. Advaita Nemlekar had composed the music for the film *Kafiron Ki Namaz* directed by Ram Ramesh Sharma, released digitally in April 2016. The song sung by Usha in the film, '*Ye raat Monalisa jaise sangin hai / aadhi khushi, aadhi ghameen hai*', is full of excitement and joy.

The Hindi film *Rock On 2*, directed by Shujaat Saudagar, was released on 11 November 2016. The song sung by Usha was written by Javed Akhtar and Kit Shangpliang, who is from the North-east. The song, originally based on a popular Khasi folk tune, had music by Shankar, Ehsaan and Loy. The same trio that gave the music of *Don 2*. Usha sang this song with a band from Shillong, Summersault. In the Khasi language, the song she sung, titled, 'Hoi Kiw', means 'Let's go'.

The gusto of Khasi folk music and Usha's joy made this song of *Rock On 2*, a memorable one:

Hoi kiw . . .
Hoi kiw, hoi kiw, hoi kiw
Ka dei ka Dorbar Shnong
Ha leh, ka dei ka Dorbar Bah,
Hoi kiw, hoi kiw, hoi kiw . . .
Adhoorey rastey, tootey pul Thakey-thakey kadam
Ghadi-ghadi hain zulmo aur ghadi-ghadi sitam,
Mita do yeh andherey aur mita do sarey gum
Chalo-chalo ki derey manzilon pe daaley hum
Hoi kiw, hoi kiw, hoi kiw . . .

After this song from *Rock On 2*, Usha sang for a few Hindi films and a Goan film as well. However, some of these are yet to be released. In 2019, Usha's song 'Lucifer Anthem' in the Malayalam film *Lucifer* became a success. The song was composed by Deepak Dev and Usha's vocal flair is exhibited in this political thriller released globally. The film, written by Murali Gopi and directed by Prithviraj Sukumaran, stars Malayalam superstar Mohan Lal and actress Manju Warrier. But above all, there is Usha's 'Lucifer Anthem':

> *Every day is an endless search*
> *For this thing called love*
> *Keeps on playing hide and seek*
> *Like lightning from above*
> *Behind the cloud there in the sky*
> *You are the one*
> *Then I realize my love*
> *You have the sun*
> *Are you the truth or . . .*
> *Just all illusion.*
> *Are you for real or . . .*
> *Just a mirage*
> *I look for you*
> *Wait for you*
> *Live for you*
> *Die for you*
> *But they gonna*
> *Get you for sure*
> *You are the greatest one forever*
> *Oh Fallen angel . . .*
> *Love you to life forever*
> *Oh Lucifer . . .*

In her five-decade-long career, Usha has worked with music directors in diverse languages and received boundless affection from them. When Usha remembers them all, she feels that she is standing in a mango forest. Bustling with joy and cheer. Her own voice starts to resonate in her subconscious:

Under a mango tree
On the banks of Kaveri
Moon beams peeping through
You gave me a garland of sweet Malligai poo, Malligai poo . . .

18

Duet with the World

'Music has kept the whole world close to each other for ages.' Usha, who frequently says this, has not only supported cultural exchanges and artistes frequently travelling to each other's countries, but has also worked effectively towards it. She believes that artistes across the world have a soulful affinity towards India. Had it not been for this, veteran American singer Frank Sinatra would not have shown his fondness for India by singing 'Indian Summer' during the 1960s. Usha gets overwhelmed by singing this song by her childhood favourite singer, Sinatra:

> *Summer! You old Indian summer,*
> *You're the tear that comes after June times laughter.*
> *You see so many dreams that don't come true*
> *Dreams we fashioned when summertime was new.*
> *You are here to watch over*
> *Some heart that is broken,*
> *By a word that somebody left unspoken.*
> *You're the ghost of a romance in June going astray,*
> *Fading too soon, that's why I say,*
> *'Farewell to you, Indian summer.'*
> *You are here to watch over*

A heart that is broken,
By a word that somebody left unspoken.
You're the ghost of a romance in June going astray,
Fading too soon, that's why I say,
'Farewell to you, Indian summer,'
You old Indian summer.

Many generations have passed, and even today, Frank Sinatra continues to resonate among the music lovers of India, just like decades ago. The famous violinist of America, Yehudi Menuhin, had a deep attachment with India. This is the reason why in 1966, he and India's pioneering sitarist Pandit Ravi Shankar recorded the album *West Meets East* in the UK for their singular duo of violin and sitar and released it in 1967. It won the Grammy Award. Even today, the fusion of both the great artistes is a unique example of the finest form of chamber music. Usha has an endless list of those who liked India. She remembers English singers Chris Martin and Ed Sheeran. Likewise, Spanish singer Enrique Iglesias and Canadian singer Justin Bieber. All of them have performed in India. Usha recalls American singing sensation Michael Jackson, popularly known as the King of Pop coming to Mumbai for a concert in 1996.

Usha believes that any genre of music or art is a collective act. She asks, 'Will the world be transformed by my music alone? Can we claim our heritage without Noor Jehan and Mehdi Hassan's voice? Can we be complete without Abida Parveen of Pakistan and Runa Laila of Bangladesh? Is there anyone who can replace Ghulam Ali in our memory? Never.' Usha believes that her story is incomplete without them.

This is the global unity of art, a gleaming knot of eternal worldly brotherhood. Gentle, but strong. Usha remembers the affection of Kenya's Prime Minister, Jomo Kenyatta, in 1978 when he honoured her with the honorary citizenship of Kenya. Indian performers have always been celebrated by the whole world. She cites famous artists of Indian origin spread across the world, of whom the countrymen are not even aware of. They are all part of us. For instance, how can people forget the famous director Richard Attenborough's film *Gandhi*, which was released in 1982?

Sir Ben Kingsley played the role of Gandhi in the biopic. He lived the character so well on the silver screen that his role became an unforgettable one. But to date, most Indians do not know that England-born Ben Kingsley is actually from a Gujarati family of Indian origin and his real name is Krishna Pandit Bhanji. His father Rahimtulla Harji Bhanji, of Indian origin, was born in Kenya and was a doctor by profession. He married Anna Lina Marie, a British actress. Krishna Pandit Bhanji, who later became famous as Ben Kingsley, is their son. Ben Kingsley did countless memorable films in his cine career of fifty years, including *House of Sand and Fog*, *Hugo*, *Iron Man* and *The Jungle Book* apart from *Gandhi*. These days, Ben lives in his home in south-eastern England.

But what is one Ben Kingsley? How many Indians know about the famous American television actor Eric Avari, that he was born in Darjeeling, West Bengal, and is basically a Parsi? His real name is Nariman Eruch Avari. He has done many popular films like *The Beast*, *The Mummy* and *Home Alone*. Similarly, there is English–American actress Gabrielle Anwar, who lives in Florida and has done several international films. Her father, Tariq Anwar, is of Indian origin. Usha fondly remembers the British-born Canadian actress, Hannah Simon. She is the daughter of an Indian father and an English mother. Her popular films are *Sati Shaves Her Head* and *Killing Gunther*, among others.

Similarly, M. Night Shyamalan of Tamil and Malayali parentage, whose original name is Manoj Nelliattu Shyamalan, is an iconic American filmmaker and actor. Shyamalan's most memorable film, which has won the Padma Shri and the Nebula

Award, is *Praying with Anger* made in 1992. This is an iconic film based on his memories of India. A parallel story is that of American actress, Janina Gaonkar. Her father, P.V. Ganesh Gaonkar, is an engineer by profession and her mother's name is Mohra Gaonkar. Mohra is half Indian and half Dutch. P. Ganesh Gaonkar is originally from Bombay. Usha cites British actress Jessica Clarke who is a mixture of Indian, Irish and Nigerian blood. Similar is the case with American actress Anita Devi, popularly known as Annette Mahendru. Her father is of Indian origin, and her mother is from Russia.

Usha believes that this universal family of artistes is in her veins—from Yehudi Menuhin to Noor Jehan and Ben Kingsley. There is no Usha without them. Usha favours the idea that not only artistes of Indian origin settled abroad, but artistes from all over the world should travel with absolute joy to each other's countries. Society and governments also have to be aware of this. She says, 'This organic fusion is needed even more today in this era of globalization.' And with a smile, she says, 'So I always say that I am a complete example of fusion.' After a mild pause, an emotional Usha adds, 'This whole life . . . This whole world is a form of mixed music.'

When Usha had gone to perform at the United Nations, she was overjoyed with pride seeing India's tricolour among the national flags of other countries. Her eyes filled with happy tears. She had a feeling that we are an important part of this cosmic universe. Seeing the Indian flag fluttering amid countless other national flags made Usha realize at a deeper level that all these countries of the world are sibling nations born from the belly of Mother Earth. This is the unique familial bonding of the world. Many veterans of the world, including Kofi Annan, were present that evening to listen to Usha's show.

Usha was anxious while going to perform at the United Nations. Many questions were coming to her mind about what kind of audience will be there. But after finishing the show, she came to the conclusion that from Calcutta to the United Nations, the sentiments and emotions inhabiting the human souls are alike.

An interesting incident took place in the United Nations auditorium. The alarm started ringing during the security check before entering. Security requested Usha to remove her silver bangles. But despite removing them, the alarm didn't stop. The security then requested her to remove the necklace and watch. Even after that, the sound of the alarm continued. In those days, Shashi Tharoor was in the United Nations. Shashi and Usha go a long way back. Shashi's mother, Lily Tharoor, and Usha's elder sister, Indira, were close friends. Shashi also got worried seeing Usha stuck in security check. It was found that the alarm did not stop due to Usha's zari-embroidered saree. Wherever the show happens around the world, Usha always appears on the stage in a saree. In Usha's words, 'The saree is truly a global garment. It has many avatars. It is not just a garment but an identity and our language. It is actually the garment of a woman's soul.' She says smilingly, 'If Mother Earth ever appeared in a human form, she would come in a saree.'

19

Stage Craft

There is lot that goes on behind curtain calls, lights, sound check, mike levels. The audience, while leaving the auditorium or an open-air show, gives credit to the artistes who have performed with all their spirited energy on the adorned stage in the rain of lights. The performers and their team's compositions on stage also receive full recognition and remuneration. But the people behind and around the stage, who remain alert as eagles for all the technical nuances ranging from stage-decor to lights, sound and electricity, and those who maintain the vanity van at the venue along with managing the availability of temporary toilets for the artists—they remain lost in the darkness of neglect. There are many small errands to be run by those behind and around the stage. For instance, there may be a sudden need for a steaming iron for clothes at the venue, everyone in the team including the artistes, have to be provided tea or coffee. There are many similar chores to be taken care of.

While working for the stars on the stage, these 'non-stars' of the team may also put their lives to risk from say, an electric shock or while climbing up to set the lights at a height. They could fall and be disabled for life. Even to dazzle the audience with the glare of lights and special effects could involve grave risks. But the crew makes it happen time and time again.

For long, Usha's heart ached for her neglected colleagues with low incomes. She felt something should be done for the welfare and honour of those who live for the convenience and glory of the stars in the limelight. She kept remembering all these colleagues, who executed small tasks and now, because of old age, they aren't able to work any more. She missed them more now than when they were young and active. Therefore, in the year 2011, Usha envisaged the creation of an institution called Stage Craft in Calcutta for these neglected colleagues. For the initial discussion on its establishment, honourable personalities of Calcutta's music world like Mahua Lahiri, owner of Asha Audio, Gautam Jain, owner of Real Reel event company, Anil Kuriakose, the famous online editor in electronic media and Shiladitya Chaudhary, owner of the PR company Sagittarius were called.

This meeting led to the setting up of the Stage Craft Foundation. It was decided that workers who contribute significantly behind and around the stage every year be given not only respect but also financial assistance. Famous Bengali film actor Prosenjit also extended his hand of cooperation after hearing about this initiative. Gradually, the caravan of people associated with Calcutta cinema and cultural campaigns grew.

Since Usha had initiated this campaign, its credibility was irrefutable. Due to Usha, the cinema giants of south India also joined it. The media also appreciated this meaningful campaign, so it also extended support. From the finest cabaret dancer of her times, Shefali, who was struggling financially, to the legendary Salim Jokerwala who trained comedians, Stage Craft honoured these charismatic people, but also provided financial support.

Usha's initiative became an inspiration for others. Gradually, many institutions across the country joined Stage Craft. However, raising funds for the non-stars is almost like cycling uphill on a mountain. But Stage Craft is Usha's mission. It is her dream that the organization lives on even after her.

20

Actress Usha

During her childhood, Usha was a matchless mimic. She used to display her skill at imitating others mostly at Pathan Aunty's house. Then Pathan Aunty, doubling with laughter, would say, 'She is a copycat monkey.' Just as Usha hadn't imagined as a child that music would be her life, similarly she didn't know that at some point in time she would be acting in films. But in the invisible womb of life, there was a lot awaiting her in the future, acting included.

In 1970, Usha got the opportunity to appear on the silver screen for the first time. That year, she sang two songs in the film, *Bombay Talkie*, a Merchant Ivory production, directed by James Ivory—'Hariom Tatasat' and 'Good Times and Bad Times'. In the film, she was presented as herself, the singer Usha Iyer. Similarly in the film *Bombay to Goa*, which came out in 1971, she was seen singing 'Rain' on-screen as Usha Iyer. She was twenty-three at that time. After this she appeared with actress P. V. Bhanumati in a Tamil film singing 'Wanga Sambandhi Wanga'. Four years later, in 1975, she appeared in the Tamil film *Melnatu Maruagal*. In it too, she was featured as singer Usha Uthup. The director of this film was A.P. Nagarajan and composers were Illayaraaja and Kunnakudi Vaidyanathan. The film starred Kamal Haasan, Shiv

Kumar, French actress Lawrence Pourtale, Jayasudha, Poornam
Vishwanathan and Usha Uthup.

The film stars Shiv Kumar as the elder brother, whose wife's
role is played by the French actress Lawrence Pourtale. Kamal
Haasan plays the younger brother. Actress Jayasudha plays the role
of Kamal Haasan's wife. The film revolves around two brothers
and their wives. The elder brother is married to a foreigner, who
is an admirer of Tamil culture and traditions, while the younger
brother's wife, despite being Tamil, prefers the Western lifestyle.
Haasan's name in this film is Raja. Lawrence Pourtale plays
Meera. Jayasudha plays the role of Raja's wife, Sudha. Usha has
come on screen in her original identity, of a pop singer. She is seen
singing this lovely song:

> *Love is beautiful for all mankind*
> *Living for love is reason 'n' rhyme*
> *There is so much for us to do*
> *Why don't you smile and sing along too*
> *Life is a flower*
> *Love is a treasure*
> *Youth it's glamour*
> *Where is the pleasure?*
> *Come along hand in hand*
> *Sing along with me*
> *Life is merry and bright*
> *As you can see*
> *Love is beautiful . . .*

It is a great honour for a singer to be shown on the screen with
their real name and identity. In 1976, the Tamil thriller *Oorukku
Ujjhaipavan* (Worker for the Country), directed by M. Krishnan
Nair, was released. The hero was played by M.G. Ramachandran
and the heroine was Vanisri. Venniradai Nirmala was in a

supporting role in the film. The music was by M.S. Viswanathan. The film was actually a remake of the 1970 Kannada film *Baalu Belagithu*. It was also made in Hindi under the title *Humshakal*. Usha was shown singing the song 'It's Easy to Fool You'. In this duet song, S.P. Balasubrahmanyam joined her:

It's easy to fool you,
To twist and turn you.
Catch me if you can,
Come try . . . oh my man.

After a long time an old wish came true in 2006 when Usha appeared in the Malayalam film *Pothan Vava* as the mother of superstar Mammootty. It was a touching role. In this film, she didn't feature as a pop singer, rather she came on screen as an actress. A few years later, the popular Tamil romantic comedy *Manamdhan Ambu* (Cupid's Arrow) was released. The film had veteran actors like Kamal Haasan, R. Madhavan, Trisha and Sangeet in the lead roles. The story was by Kamal Haasan and it was directed by K.S. Ravi Kumar. Usha played the role of Madhavan's mother. After this Tamil film, she again appeared in a Malayalam film, *Chattakari*, in 2012. It was a poignant romantic film directed by Santosh Sethumadhavan. The film focused on the story of an Anglo-Indian girl who is in love with a Hindu boy. Once the boy learns that his girlfriend has become pregnant, he leaves her and walks away. The girl struggles with her circumstances. The film had the same script as that of the much-talked-about Hindi film *Julie*.

However, in addition to these films from south India, Usha played roles in films in other languages such as Bengali and Hindi. In the Hindi film *Saat Khoon Maaf* directed by Vishal Bhardwaj, she played Priyanka Chopra's governess. However, in this film she also sang the famous song 'Darling! Aankhon Se Aakhein Chaar

Karne Do'. Usha was also in the film *Rock On 2*. Then she played
the lead role in a short Bengali film *Maa* and appeared again on
the big screen as her real self, Usha Uthup, in a short Bengali film
titled *Bow Barracks Forever*. Similarly, in another short Bengali
film, she played the role of an elderly Davy Aunty, a middle-aged
Anglo–Indian woman struggling with loneliness, yet full of life.

In this way, Usha appeared in films across languages. Even
Lata Mangeshkar didn't get as many opportunities to appear on
the silver screen as her real self. While she acted in her father
Hridaynath Mangeshkar's musical plays from the age of five, it
was Master Vinayak who gave her a small role in the Marathi
film *Pahili Manglagaur*. Lata also sang the song 'Nataly Chaitrachi
Navalai' in this film. In 1945, Lata and Asha had small roles in
Vinayak's first Hindi film *Badi Maa*. In it, Lata Mangeshkar
also sang a prayer song 'Mata Tere Chaon Mein'. After Master
Vinayak passed away in 1948, music director Ghulam Haider
nurtured Lata and Asha completely as singers. On the other hand,
Usha Uthup got several opportunities to appear in many films,
both as a character actress as well as in her identity as a singer.

In 2019, Usha played the role of Akshara Hassan's grandmother
in *Achham Madam Nanam Payirappu*, a Tamil film written by Raja
Ramamurthy. In it, Akshara is a girl who is learning Carnatic
music.

After watching this interesting selection of films, the audience
gets the sense that if Usha had pursued a full-fledged acting career,
she would have been a success in that too. But then who would
have rowed the boat of joy in the sea of rhythm with her solid
voice!

21

Usha and Her Running Train

'Aao bachcho khel dikhaayein
Chhuk-chhuk karati rel chalaayein
Aage peeche, peeche aage
Line se lekin koi na bhaage
Saari sidhi line me chalna
Aankhein dono miche rakhna
Band aankhon se dekha jaaye
Aankh khule to kuchh na paaye
Aao bachcho rel chalaayein!

Dharampur–Brahmapur, Brahmapur–Dharampur, Mangalore–
Bangalore, Bangalore–Mangalore, Mandwa–Khandwa,
Khandwa–Mandwa,
Raipur - Jaipur, Jaipur–Raipur, Talegaon–Malegaon, Malegaon–
Talegaon,
Nellore–Vellore, Vellore–Nellore, Sholapur–Kolhapur, Kolhapur–
Sholapur, Kukkal–Dindigal, Dindigal–Kukkal,
Machilipatnam–Bimblipatnam, Bimblipatnam–Machilipatnam,
Ongole–Nargol, Nargol–Ongole,
Koregaon–Goregaon, Goregaon–Koregaon, Ahmedabad–Madaabaad,
Madaabaad–Ahmedabad, Shautpur–Jodhpur, Jodhpur–Shautpur,

Chhuk-chhuk-chhuk-chhuk
Beech wali station hole
Ruk-ruk, ruk-ruk rail gaadi . . .'

In 1968, a film titled *Aashirwad* was made under the direction of Hrishikesh Mukherjee. It was produced by N.C. Sippy. The music was by Vasant Desai and in the lead role was Bollywood veteran and everybody's beloved Dada Muni, Ashok Kumar. The way Ashok Kumar performed the children's poem 'Rail Gaadi' by the famous poet Harindranath Chattopadhyay was so memorable that the audience of that era hasn't forgotten it till now.

Even today, Usha listens to this lovely poem by Harindranath Chattopadhyay. While listening to this children's song, Usha feels she is on a train journey from Bombay to Madras with Appa–Amma and all her siblings during the holidays. When this film came out in 1968, a playful Usha would narrate this poem in Ashok Kumar's style for everyone's benefit.

Usha used to meet Dada Muni on several occasions in Bombay, but that evening Usha's happiness was beyond belief when she came to know that Harindranath Chattopadhyay was coming to her show to listen to her. After the show was over, Usha invited him on stage and took his blessings. What Harindranath Chattopadhyay said that day still echoes in Usha's ears. He said, 'This girl's voice has deep joy. She will always bloom and thrive and the quietened sorrow that resides in the depths of her soul will take her ahead.'

Usha remembers that after his comments, she couldn't hold back her tears on the stage. There were four or five such occasions in her early days in Bombay when Harindranath Chattopadhyay came to listen to her during her shows. He was a prominent personality and poet of that era noted for his writing in Bengali and Hindi, especially poems for children. He also had a similar place in theatre and cinema. He played unforgettable roles in several films. His powerful role of Dadaji in Hrishikesh Mukherjee's *Bawarchi* became memorable. Born in Hyderabad, Harindranath Chattopadhyay considered his real elder sister—the Nightingale of India, Sarojini Naidu—as the ideal of his life. It is noteworthy that Sarojini Naidu was also a sentimental poetess. Like his elder sister, Harindranath was also interested in active politics in the early phase of his life. This is the reason that Harindranath won the election for the first Lok Sabha of the country from the Vijayawada parliamentary constituency as an independent candidate supported by the Communist Party. From 1952 to 1957, his contribution as a member of the Lok Sabha was significant.

Harindranath Chattopadhyay married Kamaladevi, who played a role in the revival of Indian handicrafts. She, a resident of Mangalore, was first married at the age of fourteen. But after two years, she was widowed. Harindranath Chattopadhyay married the child widow Kamala and presented a model for society to follow. In later years, Tejaswini Kamala became known as the cultural ambassador of India. Ram Chattopadhyay was the only son of Harindranath and Kamaladevi Chattopadhyay, who introduced colour in Bollywood films.

Usha is proud of the fact that in later years she got constant affection from Harindranath. His compositions reside in Usha's heart. Even today, she quotes one of his poems *The Curd Seller*, while communicating with the audience during her stage shows. Before reciting the lines of the poem, she says that the value of everything has increased but human life has become cheaper. She narrates 'The Curd Seller' in her inimitable style:

Come taste these curds
Come taste these curds
They are white as snow
They are white as birds
Come taste these curds

They say the price of everything, is really going high
The only price that is going down today, is human life
Come taste these curds . . .

Harindranath Chattopadhyay's poem *Rail Gaadi* covers the whole of India, from the north to the south. Children circle around the Indian subcontinent on that train. They enjoy the diversity of the country. Given the prevailing circumstances in India, Usha also created her own 'Peace Train'. It was her desire to present *Ekta Express: The Peace Train* on stage. This desire became even more powerful when she saw the communal, ethnic and provincial tensions flaring up in the country.

Usha envisaged that they present a train sequence on stage, which travels all over India from Kashmir to Kanyakumari. In this high voltage show, she wanted to present songs in all the languages of the country. One song each in every language. She approached many people to make this project a reality. Finally, Eric Osario, a gentleman from Mangalore, extended his hand of cooperation. He talked to the chairman of the Bank of Maharashtra, Ellen C.A. Pereria who agreed to provide support, following which preparations for the show began. The entire stage was built like a railway station with the continuous echo of the train running on the lateral side of the stage. Projections of some mood shots made one believe that it was a real train journey. Usha also made a wonderful combination of sound and light. Finally, in the year 2009, Usha presented her *Kashmir to Kanyakumari Ekta Express* at the St Aloysius College Centenary Ground in Mangalore, the main port city of Karnataka.

Usha sang songs in nineteen languages, including Kashmiri, Assamese, Hindi, Tamil, Telugu, Kannada and Marathi. At the start, the soft redolence of 'Raghupati Raghav Rajaram' followed by the continuous flow of songs in different languages was like softly falling rain for three and a half hours. There was a large map of India on both the sides of the stage and wherever 'the peace train' stopped, a bulb lit up to indicate the station. The train started from Kashmir even as a Kashmiri poet recited a poem in his language. This was followed by Usha's song in the Kashmiri language. When the train arrived in Guwahati and left, a poem was recited in Assamese before Usha's song in the same language. This was the pattern for the collective rendition of songs in nineteen languages. In the final phase of the Peace Train Show, Usha sang in the Tulu language spoken in Karnataka and parts of Kerala. The audience was absolutely ecstatic.

Yekka Saka . . . Yekka Saka, Yekka Saka . . . Yekka Saka
Yekka Sakkala Batterittela
Akka Pandudu, Leppunakulu Batterittela
Akka Pandudu, Leppunakulu
Yekka Saka . . . Yekka Saka, Yekka Sakkala . . .

This Tulu song is drenched with the sweet feeling of love at first sight. During her Peace Train/Ekta Express performance, Usha singing songs in various languages looked no less than the famous magician P.C. Sorcar. Indeed, her Peace Train Show was a wonderful musical concept. She did not leave out anything amid the rain of songs —from her popular Hindi tracks such as 'Dum Maro Dum', 'Shaan Se' and 'Rambha Ho' to Dr Rajkumar's Kannada song 'Huttidare Kannada Naddinalli Huttabeku' and Goan musician Chris Perry's famous song 'Novaro Mujo Porchugala Thavan'. And by the time the train reached the last station, Kanyakumari, it was the turn of 'Sare Jahan Se Achcha' and finally the national anthem.

The way Indian Railways connects India from Kashmir to Kanyakumari, Usha, with a rosary of songs in different languages, made a garland of unity through the Peace Train. As a singer, she lit up the lamp of Indian spirit and unity for the world to see.

22

Magic of the Shoe

'As I was a-walking the other day,
I peeped in a window just over the way
And old and bent and feeble too,
There sat an old cobbler a-making a shoe
With a rack-a-tac-tac and a rack-a-tack-too,
This is the way he makes a shoe.
With a bright little awl, he makes a hole,
Right through the upper and then through the sole.
He puts in a peg, he puts in two,
And a ha-ha-ha-ha and he hammers it through.'

Usha loves this poem on cobblers. She has had an attachment to them since her childhood. When she was in school and had to take money from her Appa beyond her regular pocket money, she would wake up early in the morning and start polishing his shoes. Seeing Usha hard at work, Appa would smile and say to Usha's Amma, 'Min, if nothing else, Usha will definitely make a good cobbler.' That way at an early age, Usha learnt to earn a little extra through polishing, ironing and stitching clothes. It was said that she was a talented tailor and washerwoman too!

Usha's love for shoes still remains. In 1969, she suffered partial paralysis in her left leg. Even then, with the calipers in her feet, she wore a leather shoe specially designed for her. To this day, a small part of that problem persists in her left leg. When her feet issue got worse while constantly standing during the shows, her daughter Anjali said, 'Amma, you should also wear sneakers for the shows. That will bring relief to your feet.'

How strange it would feel to stand on the stage wearing sneakers. Usha was in a disarray but suddenly the sleeping artist from Sir JJ School of Art within her woke up and a unique idea flashed in her mind. If the sneaker was decorated, then it could look good and bring relief to her feet. Usha thought that if the jagged pieces of old Kanjeevaram sarees were cut and pasted on her shoes, the sneakers would look royal. This would require the services of a cobbler. Usha asked her driver, Lakhinder, to look for one.

Lakhinder was from the Muzaffarpur district of Bihar and a trusted employee for years. After a long search, Lakhinder found a cobbler. Coincidentally, he also belonged to Bihar. They talked and Usha explained to the cobbler how to redesign the shoes by pasting pieces of her Kanjeevaram saree on an old pair of sneakers. But the cobbler who went home due to a family problem did not return. So, Lakhinder started looking for another cobbler. This time too, he got two cobbler brothers from Bihar—Mishri Das and Sushil Das.

It was a blessing for the brothers to meet Usha. They were from Judi village of Pakdi Barama block in Nawada district of Bihar and were working as cobblers in Calcutta for the past two and a half decades. After understanding the design from Usha, the duo started reinventing the old sneakers with cuttings from a Kanjeevaram saree. Mishri and Sushil took two days to work on a pair of shoes and charged Rs 500 for it. Usha liked their work. She began wearing the 'designer' shoes regularly on stage. Thanks to this, the trouble she faced while standing for long hours was almost gone. After shows, intrigued women started asking her about her shoes and where she bought them? Usha started telling everyone about Mishri and Sushil and how these two brothers helped her imagination come true with the shoes.

This is how Mishri and Sushil started getting orders for 'designer' shoes. But Usha did not stop there. She was a fighter from the very beginning. To increase Mishri and Sushil's popularity, she took them along by air to the famous INK 2018 event in Hyderabad, which was a platform for the exchange of cutting-edge ideas and inspiring stories. When Usha took the stage with both of them, people warmly welcomed and celebrated Mishri and Sushil. While on the stage, Mishri and Sushil were crafting 'designer' shoes and Usha was singing:

Ye joote Calcutta wale,
Dekho saree hai Madrasi.
Ye choodi hai Hyderabadi,
Aur ye dil hai Hindustani.

Mishri and Sushil were overwhelmed by the show. They never imagined that Usha Didi would take them from the narrow lanes of Beltalla (Bhawanipur) in Calcutta and put them centre stage.

But Usha was not satisfied with doing this much. To champion the welfare of Mishri and Sushil, she started a campaign for the upliftment of the cobblers of Calcutta. For this, she took an appointment with the President of India, Ramnath Kovind, in the last week of April 2019. The memorandum she submitted to the President is worth reading:

In-service,

His Excellency, Honourable President of India, Rashtrapati Bhavan, New Delhi

Subject: A humble appeal regarding the protection of the negligible cobbler community of Calcutta.

Respected Your Excellency,

First of all my heartfelt gratitude that you have graciously given your precious time to meet at the Rashtrapati Bhavan.

I want to draw your attention to the pitiful condition of the extremely negligible number of cobblers of West Bengal.

You are familiar with the fact that the Chamars or the tanner community is a caste group found in the Indian subcontinent, which is kept at the bottom level of the society even after so many decades of the country's independence.

The number of tanners is only 1.25 per cent in the whole of West Bengal. The condition of this community here is extremely pathetic. In Uttar Pradesh, where these tanners constitute 16 per cent of the population, and 11 per cent each in Punjab and Haryana. Due to their significant population in the provinces like Uttar Pradesh and Punjab, the respective governments also cannot ignore them.

Honourable Mayawatiji who hails from this community got the opportunity to become the Chief Minister of Uttar Pradesh four times. But due to the population of only 1.25 per cent in West Bengal, neither the government nor the society cares about the deplorable condition of this community.

The pain and plight of this community saddened me and I decided to do something for them in my capacity. I started the process of getting the old shoes recycled through the cobblers of Calcutta Mishri Das and Sushil Das among others and selling them in the designer-shoe market. Of course, it is a small beginning but I hope that in future it will give them satisfactory economic benefit. To make the country familiar with the art of these tanners, I also took them along with me to my programmes outside the city.

Your Excellency!

You are kindly requested that please give proper instructions to the government that their agencies should support this art of shoe recycling of the poor tanners like Mishri Das and Sushil Das of Calcutta. In their regular monitoring, the government agencies should encourage them as much as possible. This will give a new ray of hope to the struggling tanner community of the country. I hope that you will consider my plea kindly.

Regards,
Yours faithfully,
Usha Uthup

23

Those Unforgettable Faces of Power

Usha, who always maintained a distance from politicians, was forced to collide with West Bengal's Leftist minister Jatin Chakraborty and as per her nature, she finally turned that bitterness into a loving relationship with the Chakraborty family. But it is true that she always liked to witness politicians from afar. During her childhood days, she had a chance to see Prime Minister Jawaharlal Nehru because Appa was on duty during Nehruji's visit to Bombay. When all of Usha's siblings insisted that they wanted to see the Prime Minister of the country, Appa arranged for them to be taken along. Another proud moment for Usha was when her brother Shamu received a certificate from Pandit Nehru for being an excellent NCC cadet. Pandit Nehru shook hands with Shamu after patting his back. When Shamu, a teenager, returned home after shaking hands with the prime minister, Usha immediately shook hands with her brother since he had shaken hands with the PM just a short while ago.

As a child, Usha used to wonder if like Shamu Bhaiya, she would ever get an opportunity to shake hands with the prime minister of the country? Years later, when Usha gained name and fame and a time was decided for her to meet Prime Minister Indira Gandhi, she was excited like a little girl. In fact, Usha had sent a letter to the prime minister's office stating that she wanted to present a new album of her songs, *Beautiful Sunday*, to Indira Gandhi. In response, one day, Usha got a call from Mrs Gandhi's aide R.K. Dhawan that the prime minister had approved the time requested by her. A week before Usha was supposed to meet the PM she could not sleep. She kept practising in her mind what she would say when she meets Indiraji and what would she say before leaving? Usha discussed this at length with her father-in-law, Brig. C.C. Uthup. It is noteworthy that after retiring from the army, Brig. Uthup was the managing director of the Modern Bakery in Delhi. After much thought, Usha finalized what she would say to the prime minister.

It was the first week of January when Usha left for the prime minister's residence along with her father-in-law in his ambassador car. She was nervous and quiet all the way. It was morning and extremely cold in Delhi. The temperature was around 9 degrees Celsius. Usha was dressed in a silk saree for the meeting. When they reached the guest room of the prime minister's residence, Mr Dhawan received them. A few moments later Mrs Gandhi came in. Indiraji affectionately shook hands with Usha and Brig. Uthup and asked them to be seated. Usha recalls the moment how her seven-day rehearsal came to nought, as she had forgotten everything she had thought of saying to Indiraji. Usha was simply mesmerized by Mrs Gandhi's personality. When Indiraji initiated the conversation, Usha became her normal self. Indiraji asked with a surprised smile, 'Usha, the temperature in Delhi has dropped to 9 degrees. Where is your shawl?' Before Usha could say anything, Indiraji called a staff member and said, 'Bring a wonderful shawl for Usha.'

An emotional and teary Usha said, 'Madam, you are very sweet.'

Indiraji smiled. 'Usha, would you like to give me your new music album?'

'Of course! I have come to present you the same. But as soon as I met you, I also forgot why I came here.' Usha was comfortable by now.

'I heard you at the Hotel Ashok and Hotel Akbar. Both my sons also like your songs very much,' Indiraji said affectionately. Then during tea, when Brig. Uthup said that he used to be in the Sikh Regiment, Indiraji quipped, 'I remembered! I have met you before once, Brigadier.' Those unforgettable fifteen minutes with Indiraji were like a three-hour-film that, according to Usha, whizzed by in just a few seconds.

A few meetings with Rajiv Gandhi also remain memorable for Usha. The first time Usha met him was at the Hotel Oberoi in Delhi. He hadn't entered politics at that time. That evening Rajiv Gandhi had come along with his dear friend Amitabh Bachchan. Usha was performing. Amitabh had once been friends with Jani in Calcutta, so Usha was acquainted with him.

During the song, Amitabh and Rajiv Gandhi sent to her a song-request note, on which was written 'Matilda'. Usha fulfilled their request.

'Matilda' has always been a lucky song for her. After this, Usha met Rajiv on several occasions. In 1976, Mrs Gandhi sent Usha to the Indian Food Festival held in Hong Kong. Rajiv Gandhi was also there with his wife Sonia Gandhi to attend the festival. When Usha was rehearsing for her evening show at Hong Kong's Hilton Hotel's famous nightclub Eagle's Nest, Rajiv and Sonia reached there. It was 10 a.m. After the rehearsal was over, Usha went straight to this beautiful couple. Rajiv Gandhi smiled, 'Both of us had just come to hear you.'

'But listening to just the rehearsals will not do. You come to our show in the evening.' Usha said.

'Me? In the night show?' Rajiv Gandhi said, laughing. 'Usha, political vultures will gather during the evening show. I will feel choked.'

Then there was no meeting with Rajiv Gandhi for many years. Finally, they met when he was the prime minister. Usha's meeting with him was arranged by Mani Shankar Aiyar. Usha had met Mani Shankar at a show in Shimla. He said he would fix the time of her meeting with the PM. Actually, Usha had discussed some of her plans with Mani Shankar, and he had said that it would only take a functional shape after meeting the PM. Mani Shankar Aiyar fixed an appointment with Rajiv Gandhi. Usha arrived at the prime minister's residence at 10 Janpath in Delhi, on time.

Rajiv Gandhi came to the meeting room and the next few moments were spent reminiscing about old times when he had heard 'Matilda' with Amitabh Bachchan in Delhi's Hotel Oberoi by making a special request to Usha. Sonia Gandhi also joined them during tea. Rajiv Gandhi said, 'Both of my children love your songs too.' Rajiv Gandhi called Priyanka and got her to meet Usha. Priyanka told Usha her list of favourite songs by her.

Usha told Rajiv Gandhi about her plan. Just like World Tale, a globally acclaimed pop music show in Germany, why not bring together Indian artists and do a good pop music programme on Doordarshan for the entire country. This would appeal to the younger generation and make pop music popular. Rajiv Gandhi really liked Usha's suggestion, and he immediately instructed the director-general of Doordarshan to act. It was following this meeting that in 1985–1986 the popular music programme *Pop Time* was started on Doordarshan.

The concept of the event was that six renowned singers would showcase talent. Each would be given two to three episodes to anchor. Each episode would feature four to five new pop singers. Usha set an entire panel for *Pop Time* based on this concept. She involved Sharon Prabhakar, Parvati Khan, Preity Sagar, Elisha Chinoy, Gurdas Mann and Louis Banks, besides herself. This show was appreciated all over the country. The programme proved to be a milestone for Indian pop.

Usha's meetings with political stalwarts are countless. Be it West Bengal chief minister Jyoti Basu, Mamata Banerjee to Tamil Nadu chief minister J. Jayalalithaa. Usha remembers Jayalalithaa's command over various languages—Hindi, English, Kannada and obviously, Tamil. Usha recalls how alert Jayalalithaa was regarding the pronunciation of different languages. She had been a classmate of Usha's brother Shyamsunder's wife, Padma. Usha knew Jayalalithaa since she was an actress on the Tamil silver screen. The superstar of Tamil cinema and Tamil Nadu's chief minister, M.G. Ramachandran was her godfather.

M.G. Ramachandran in his lifetime had declared Jayalalithaa as his political successor. But as soon as he passed away, heavy political mobilization had begun against Jayalalithaa. By cracking that labyrinth, Jayalalithaa finally managed to become the chief minister of Tamil Nadu. When she became the CM for the first time, Usha went to Madras especially to congratulate her. Usha's arrival made Jayalalithaa immensely happy. They both talked for a long time. She inquired about the well-being of her family members, some of whom she knew closely. With Usha, she also shared her experiences of how difficult it is for a woman to manage the balance of power.

In the past decades, Usha also got the opportunity to meet the presidents of the country. In 2011, she received the Padma Shri award from President Pratibha Patil. But meeting A.P.J. Abdul Kalam is forever etched in Usha's consciousness. Dr Kalam wanted to record his self-written prayer song 'Peace Prayer' in Usha's voice. It all happened in 2015 through an organization called the Foundation for Unity of Religion and Enlightened Citizenship (FUREC) with which Usha was associated. It is through this institution that Usha's first meeting with Dr Kalam was scheduled. There were two more meetings with him related to the recording of his prayer. When Usha presented it to Dr Kalam, he became very emotional. He is no more, but every word of the 'Peace Prayer' written by him is eternal in Usha's voice:

> *Oh Almighty, create thoughts and actions in the minds of the people*
> *of our nation, so that they may live united. May they live united*
> *Oh Almighty, this is my prayer*
> *Oh Almighty, help them choose the right path, bless all the people of*
> *our nation with strength of character and of righteousness*
> *Oh Almighty, this is my prayer*
> *Guide the people to be tolerant of different points of view and*
> *transform enmity and hatred into love and harmony*
> *Bless the people to work and persevere, our country to transform into*
> *a prosperous and peaceful nation of the world*
> *Oh Almighty, help religious leaders to strengthen people of our nation*
> *to combat divisive forces. Forces that divide.*
> *Oh Almighty, this is my prayer*
> *Oh Almighty, help us to believe the nation is bigger than the*
> *individual. Let's spread love and peace throughout the universe*
> *Oh, Almighty, this is my prayer . . .*

24

Many Flaws, Many Fears

During her childhood years, Zakia Pathan, Usha's favourite Pathan Aunty, would get furious whenever she saw anyone leaving salt on the plate or wasting even a grain of it. She used to say, 'The amount of salt a man wastes in his life, after death he has to carry each grain of salt on his eyelids. So if your plate has some leftover salt, then put it in water and clean the utensils thoroughly, but do not waste salt.' Usha still fears wasting salt. She cannot bear the shortage of four things in her house—water, salt, milk and incense sticks. The wastage of these four things is also unacceptable to her.

Usha, who always tells music directors about her shortcomings, expects them to also point out any error or lack of any element in her vocal delivery. Even today, from time to time, she introspects on her shortcomings and fears.

Usha believes that the biggest shortcoming that has remained with her is that she cannot say no to anyone immediately. She trusts every relationship blindly, till the other person betrays her trust and leaves. Usha says that although she looks very powerful from the outside, she is quite fragile within. She was always afraid of the dark. That is the reason why she cannot sleep in her room with the lights turned off. Whenever she travels for shows and stays at a hotel, she keeps the television and lights on. By leaving the television on, she feels reassured that she isn't alone in the room. Whenever there was a power cut at home, Anjali, her daughter, would say, 'Amma, don't be afraid. I will just light a candle.' While travelling by air, Usha always fears an accident. However, due to busy work schedules, she has to fly.

She gave up learning to drive years ago. Once, while learning to drive in the compound of her home in Cochin, she suddenly felt that something was wrong. She tried to stop the car with her foot by leaving the steering and opening the car door. The trainer sitting next to her stopped the car. But after that, Usha vowed that she would never drive again.

She is also afraid of any expanse of water, and doctors also scare her. 'I respect the doctors a lot. But my hands and feet start to swell when I go to them. I don't know what they will say,' Usha says, smiling like a little girl.

Usha has a natural attachment to people. But a sea of faces also has its own peculiarities. Usha had to go through some strange experiences during her foreign trips, which she has not been able to forget till now. It was in the 1980s when Usha went to do a show in Nairobi, the capital of Kenya. She was accompanied by her dear friend Anita Sukul. After finishing the show, Usha and Anita Sukul came out of the International Casino in Nairobi. They were going to the hotel next to the casino, where Usha was staying. Usha and Anita were laughing and talking to each other when all of a sudden, a young Korean man suddenly leaped at Usha like a leopard, and she collapsed. By that time a crowd of people had gathered and the young Korean was subdued. Usha was rushed to the hospital. Her ribs were injured, so the doctor plastered them. This, however, did not deter Usha from wearing a saree that covered the plaster and perform the very next day in Nairobi. However, from that day on, she remains fully alert around anyone who is behaving in an unusual manner.

Usha is also afraid of getting inside an elevator or on an escalator. Even today, Usha feels shaken remembering an incident that happened during a trip to America. Usha had a series of concerts in the US. There were many consecutive shows and Usha stayed with her team at the prestigious New Yorker hotel in New York. Usha used to return to the hotel in New York with her team late at night after concerts. The team had figured that it was better to stay at one hotel in New York and go to different places for concerts and come back to base late at night rather than stay at different hotels.

In America, their shows were on weekends when everyone has a holiday. Therefore, there was a break of five days between Usha's shows. The arrangements at the New Yorker hotel were very good. Usha's room was on the twenty-sixth floor. One morning, Usha and her music team decided that they would go out for lunch. Everybody agreed to gather in the lobby of the hotel at 11 a.m. Usha had told her friends that her daughter Anjali's friend ran a restaurant called the Kathi Factory in New York. So everyone could go there.

Usha got down from the lift and came to the lobby at the scheduled time. She suddenly realized that she had left the address of The Kathi Factory in her room. So, she went up on the elevator to fetch the address from her room on the twenty-sixth floor. Little did she know that an accident awaited her in the lift. It suddenly stopped on the tenth floor. Usha was alone in the lift. She pressed several up and down buttons. But the lift did not budge. Usha also pushed the emergency button of the lift in panic. But this also proved to be ineffective. An unsettled Usha began trying to contact her colleagues on her mobile phone, but in vain.

Luckily, Usha had the hotel's key card for her room. On it, the hotel's address and phone number were printed. Usha called the number from her mobile phone. The girl at the reception told Usha that the hotel manager was aware that the elevator was stuck for ten minutes. She said that the process of fixing it had already begun.

The receptionist hung up. By now Usha was suffocating in the lift and she felt there was a lack of oxygen. She thought she would die in the next one or two minutes. While Usha was struggling to breathe in the elevator, a call came on her mobile. It was a female voice, 'I am calling from the management of this hotel. What work do you do?'

'I am a singer.' Usha somehow finished her sentence.

'By the time the elevator door opens, can you sing a song for me?' asked the lady from the hotel management team.

'Here I am dying, and you are asking me to sing a song!' Usha was almost in tears.

'Please listen to me. Anything, sing any song,' the woman pleaded.

'Okay.' Usha began. She sang two songs: 'Side by Side' and 'Rain'. She was on the last line of the second song when there was a loud sound at the lift door. The next moment she saw that one side of the lift had been cut. The hotel attendants were now putting a strong bridge between the cut side and the lift beside it on the right, which too had been cut open. The attendants then requested Usha to move to the other elevator. Usha was in a terrible state of panic, but with the constant encouragement of the hotel staff, she stepped on the bridge and courageously entered the second lift. When she came down, the hotel lobby was packed with a restless crowd of people. Usha was given first aid to relax her. When she became comfortable, the girl from the hotel management came to see her. She smiled and said, 'I asked you to sing to get your mind off the danger.'

However, since that incident, Usha is still afraid to get into an elevator alone. She tells all her well-wishers that they must keep their mobiles with them while going in a lift so that in case of any problem, they can call and alert someone about the crisis.

'Life is too short. Why should we lose it in hating instead of loving?' Usha, who always walks with this philosophy of life, finds it difficult to share those who are close to her with others. She feels that it's one of her biggest flaws. She always struggles with herself to be free of this sentiment.

'I keep getting flustered trying to read between the lines. If Jani or Sunny or any of my family members are not talking to me, then I start speculating in my mind whether I have done something wrong. It is possible that they are silent for some other reason which has nothing to do with me. However, I have gained a little control over this very sensitive disease of mine to understand the inner world of others,' Usha says with a smile.

25

The Only Matchstick

After the death of one of her sons, Tyaagaraj aka Babu, Amma would sometimes say with misty eyes, 'Usha, if you have only a rupee and a son, then one feels scared. If that goes, you have nothing left.' Amma left the world five years after Appa passed away. But she was very emotional about her only surviving son, Shyamsundar Sami. Amma used to say, 'Usha, he is the only matchstick in the Sami family's matchbox.'

Shyamsundar Sami began his career with the Western India Match Company. It was an international matchstick firm based in Sweden. Shyamsundar Sami hasn't forgotten the experience of making delicate matchsticks from the wood of the semal and poplar trees. During his job in the company, he lived in Patna for nearly three years and saw each and every corner of Bihar. In later years, Shamu worked with Wimco company and retired as its CEO. Shamu lives with his wife, Padma, in Bombay these days. Padma and Usha are of the same age. Padma and Shamu's was a love marriage—both knew each other since childhood.

They played together. The two were actually close relatives. Shamu's relatives have often said about Shamu, 'If the end of the marriage line and the thumb have an archipelago at the root, then the person will be married to a close relative.' Shamu remembers how the iconic Carnatic singer M.S. Subbulakshmi came and sang at the Jhoola ceremony at his wedding. Actually, Padma's father was M.S. Subbulakshmi's family doctor. Padma was Shamu's maternal grandfather Hallasya K. Nadhan's second wife Swarnambal's elder sister Balambika's granddaughter. It is worth recalling that Balambika was the wife of Hallasya K. Nadhan's elder brother, V.S. Sundaresh Iyer. Padma's father, Dr V.S. Subrahmanyam, and mother, Kamla, were an inseparable part of the family. Padma's father was a noted ENT physician and mother Kamla was a scholar who translated the Ramayana, Mahabharata and Shrimad Bhagwat from Sanskrit into English. Padma says, 'My father and Usha's mother were first cousins.' She adds further, 'We were all fifteen cousins.'

Padma would wait for the day when Usha and all her brothers and sisters would come to Madras during the holidays. Padma remembers, 'Usha was skilled in tailoring. I learnt the art of sewing from her. And music was the universal knot that tied our entire family. Shamu was a lover of classical music from the beginning. He always loved listening to Kishori Amonkar, M.S. Subbulakshmi and Bhimsen Joshi. Shamu is also skilled in playing a number of musical instruments.'

Padma adds with a smile, 'Of course, Shamu is a classical music fan. But whenever Usha comes over, Shamu doesn't desist from asking her to sing songs from two or three of his favourite films. These songs are "Kasmein Vaade, Pyaar Wafaa", "Chingari Koi Bhadke" and "Ek Chatur Naar". Every time Usha says at the outset, "Please, Shamu Bhaiya! Don't ask for those same old three songs." But Shamu never gives up without listening to those three songs. Shamu says in absolute delight, "All my sisters have been singing. But Usha is different. She sings as if flowers of worship are offered one after the other. Usha has her own special signature."'

Padma recalls that Shamu used to be enchanted whenever he sang duets with Uma, his other sister. Shamu has a unique affection for Uma's son, Adi. Padma says, 'Uncle and nephew often have something to do.' Shamu was interested in flying since school days. During his student life, he was in the air wing of the NCC. Padma laughs and adds, 'Just recently, Shamu and Adi have made a model plane together. They guide it with a remote control.'

26

The Blossoming Family Tree of Madras

The giant old Nagalinga, also known as the cannonball tree, stands on one side of the entrance to the large premises of Shanti. It turns red from the root to the crest with its ruddy pink flowers during the rainy season. Usha always loved the Nagalinga tree. It is now more than six decades, but Usha feels it sprouted just the other day. There used to be many exotic trees bejewelled with enticing beehives at Usha's maternal grandparents' house in Madras. There were countless birds and butterflies too.

Shanti was a like a bounteous orchard with the Marina Beach also close by. No one knew when she would run off to the beach with her maternal cousins while playing at Shanti. But everyone knew that if Usha and her cousins weren't at Shanti, then surely they could be found on the beach.

Shanti and the sea still exist, and whenever Usha visits Madras she never misses an opportunity to visit these two places. Her aunt and maternal uncle still live in Shanti.

Shanti is situated on Dr Radhakrishnan Salai's seventh lane. At the mouth of this lane, former president Dr Sarvepalli Radhakrishnan's residence is situated in all its heritage and glory. But what do the birds of Madras have to do with these historical details? They are only fond of the branches of the Nagalinga tree.

And they love the deep pink flowers that bloom on it. When one places the Nagalinga flower on the palm and looks closely at it, it seems that Lord Shiva is sitting inside and the Nagaraja with its infinite hoods is waving over him. The flowers of the Nagalinga tree are very beautiful, tender and fragrant. They are also called Shivalingi and Kailashpati.

Shanti is truly a house of melody. When a flock of fluttering birds gather and sing on the branches of the Nagalinga, every fragment of this large scenic house seems to quiver with joy. There is another old wild tree at the other corner of the entrance. It resembles Jatayu, the divine bird from the Ramayana. Flowers do not bloom on it, but it is a royal tree, rich and green. According to Nirmala Chandar, Usha's loving aunt Papu Ma who lives in a flat in Shanti, several Gulmohar trees are also present on the premises since the last five to ten years. The Nagalinga tree was planted at the main gate by her father, Hallasya. Papu Ma not only offers Nagalinga flowers to all the gods in her daily worship but, in the end, she also worships the Nagalinga flower by offering another flower to it. Papu Ma believes that Lord Shiva along with his Nagaraja resides in it.

Shanti no longer has its earlier grandeur. In Papu Ma's memory, the first small house built here looked dilapidated but remained safe. Later, her father, Usha's maternal grandfather, Hallasya K. Nadhan, built a big house there with eight to nine rooms. He also built a floor above it. In those days, his elder brother V.S. Sundaresh Iyer lived next door to Shanti. His house too was no less beautiful and was called Gitalaya.

In the 1990s, the residents of Shanti and Gitalaya decided that the two premises should be merged into two blocks. In 1992, both sections were ready. Papu Ma's husband, V.V. Chandar, had a big role in the reconstruction. Now, the huge complex has two sections—Shanti and Gitalaya. Indeed, Hallasya K. Nadhan's family continues to fulfil his dream of living together as a joint family, the foundation of which he had laid. Previously some family members lived in Vidya Colony near Shanti. But now there is no one there. The only remaining among the relatives are V.S. Shankar and his wife, the famous veena player Vidya Shankar. They live in the Gitalaya section.

The descendants of Hallasya K. Nadhan live in Shanti. His daughter, Papu Ma, his son and Usha's maternal uncle, V.H. Ram, aka Peri Ambi, live there. Usha's Kripakar Mamu passed away, but in a flat at Shanti, his son V.K. Ashok lives. In another flat lives Usha's other maternal uncle Chinn Ambi as in V.H. Balkrishnan with his wife. Papu Ma's daughter and son-in-law, Anuradha and Nagendra also live in a flat there. Papu Ma's husband V.V. Chandar passed away a few years ago, but she never experienced any loneliness due to the presence of her daughter and son-in-law. Papu Ma is the guardian of all the members at Shanti. An emotional Papu Ma says, 'My father's heartfelt wish was that his family would always be together, so it is with his blessing that all of us siblings live together.'

Papu Ma's happiness doubled and quadrupled over the years as her grandson, Anuradha's son Rishabh, also came to live with his Russian wife Shasha at Shanti. Rishabh studied in Russia. Over there, he married the lovely Shasha. Both Rishabh and Shasha are ardent music lovers. Rishabh plays the piano and Shasha plays the cello. She loves Madras and Shanti's intensely intimate atmosphere.

Whenever Usha visits Madras, she goes to Shanti. She feels fulfilled meeting her maternal family members who have boundless love for each other. Papu Ma cherishes memories of Usha as a child. Papu Ma remembers that whenever she visited her elder sister Minnie Sami in Bombay, Usha would not leave her alone for a moment. When Usha learnt that Papu Ma was going back to Madras, she wouldn't stop crying. Papu Ma would only leave for the station after consoling Usha. Papu Ma recalls an incident when Usha was only five or six years old. Papu Ma was returning to Madras after meeting her Minnie Di. After crying a lot, Usha secretly wrapped a toffee in a silver-coloured paper and put it in her fist and said, 'Papu Ma, always keep it carefully. Nothing will happen to you.' Papu Mama kept the toffee safe all these years. A couple of years ago, when Usha was in some trouble, Papu Ma gave that toffee to her wrapped in silver foil and said, 'Usha, now you keep it carefully. Nothing will ever happen to you!' Holding that toffee in her palm, Usha's eyes became moist thinking how Papu Ma had securely kept her token of love for six decades.

Usha's maternal uncle Peri Ambi aka V.H. Ram and his wife, Vasanti, also remember Usha with similar affection. Vasanti and Papu Ma's relationship also has another dimension apart from being sisters-in-law. Vasanti is also the cousin of late V. Chandar, Papu Ma's husband. Papu Ma's relationship with Peri Ambi and Vasanti is wonderfully multi-layered. Peri Ambi beamingly says, 'In this way, both Nirmala Chandar and Vasanti are each other's sister-in-law.' Peri Ambi, who has worked in Delhi for thirty-four years is now writing books while living at Shanti. Two of his books, *The Earth Is Flat* and *Glimpses of Reality*, were much acclaimed.

Another one of Usha's beloved maternal uncles, Chinn Ambi, that is, V.H. Balakrishna, and his wife, Sumati, get overwhelmed at the mention of Usha. Unfortunately, Chinn Ambi's eyesight is almost gone. But the music has kept his soul illuminated. His music collection has the rarest records. Despite his poor eyesight, he knows where a record is placed. Chinn Ambi listens to at least one of Usha's songs every day. If a visitor comes over to Shanti, Chinn Ambi says with an authoritative requesting tone, 'Would it be appropriate that you go away from Usha's maternal home without listening to one of her songs?' Obviously, who can resist such a request?

Chinn Ambi has several stories from Usha's childhood to her initial struggling days. He still remembers her evening shows at Hotel Savera in Madras where Usha used to sing. One evening Usha was not feeling too well before a show. She vomited once or twice. The hotel's manager also noticed that she was under the weather. But he said that many people had booked tickets to listen to Usha. In such a situation, a cancellation would affect the credibility of the hotel. Eventually, Usha somehow came on the stage. Chinn Ambi remembers that the show that evening was better than Usha's previous ones.

Hotel Savera is still there in Chennai. However, it no longer retains its old glory. With the changing times, Savera has also taken on a new avatar. Its original owner, Shyam Sundar Reddy, is no longer in business. He came to Madras in 1968 from the Gudur region of Andhra Pradesh and laid the foundation of the hotel with his brothers. Hotel Savera has been a symbol of the united spirit of Andhra Pradesh and Tamil Nadu in Madras from the beginning and continues to abide by the same spirit. There were hardly any political stalwarts and cine stars of their time who wouldn't have enjoyed the hospitality of Savera. There were two two-star hotels in Madras since the late 1960s. One was Connemara, now run by the Taj Hotels group, and the other was Savera, owned by the Reddy family.

In August 2012, when the founder of Savera, Shyam Sundar Reddy, passed away, his son Vijay Kumar Reddy took over the management. When Vijay Reddy passed away at a young age in March 2019, Vijay's graceful and efficient wife, Nina Reddy, took over the reins. In the good old days when Usha used to sing at the hotel's nightclub Golden Bowl, it had a high ceiling and was furnished like a film set. From Raj Kapoor to Kamal Haasan, who didn't visit this magnetic place when they were in Madras? Nina had heard about those golden times from her husband and her father-in-law. Those were the days when the evenings at the

Golden Bowl would dance to the beat of Usha's songs. Usha always had a soft corner for Nina.

Whenever she comes to Madras, she meets her. Says Nina, 'Savera and Ushaji are synonymous with each other. She is the golden flag of the Savera.' In 1998, however, the Golden Bowl was renamed Malgudi in memory of the illustrious writer R.K. Narayan. But the golden glow of the Golden Bowl is indelible in the minds of the people of Madras. Many times, R.K. Narayan was present there just to listen to Usha. Nina Reddy's friend Shailaja Chetlur is also a friend of Usha's. Shailaja is associated with film production. She says, 'These days, even in Madras, girls who wear traditional clothes are jokingly called "Mallipoo babe". But to this day, Ushaji makes an appearance on the international stage with the essence of the Mallipoo look.'

Nawab Asif Ali, a descendant of the nawab of Arcot, is a dedicated music lover. He has a fine command over the piano. Once a year, Asif Ali organizes the Nawab of Arcot Evening in Madras. In 2016, Usha illuminated this evening. Nawab Asif says, 'Usha lives in the breath of Madras. Listeners feel that time stops when they listen to Usha's songs. Madras has a special right over her.'

The people of Madras have endearing stories to narrate about Usha. She too has a bouquet of stories for Madras. It is said that one learns by listening to facts. One believes by hearing the truth. But one always remembers hearing a tale. Usha is also a narrator, a wonderful storyteller!

This is where the couple Vishwanath and Shobha come in. Originally from Palakkad, Kerala, Vishwanath was born and brought up in Bombay. His wife, Shobha, was also from Palakkad. Shobha and Vishwanath married for love. Instead of Malayalam, both mostly speak Tamil. The couple lived in the US for seven years and both were in the field of teaching. Their son Kaushik was born in the US. When he was three, Shobha began teaching him with the help of audiobooks. The couple noticed that children learn quickly in this way. The audiobook concept inspired Shobha and Vishwanath to consider returning to India and starting an audiobooks venture, keeping in mind the Indian narrative. Therefore, in 1993, Shobha and Vishwanath returned to India and made Madras their base. After detailed research, they found that the children's magazines *Chandamama* and *Amar Chitra Katha* played an important role in laying the foundation of children's knowledge in different languages. After this study, the couple set up the Karadi Tales company in 1996. In Tamil, Malayalam and Kannada, Karadi means a bear. Just as Chiku rabbit narrates stories to children in the children's magazine *Champak*, the children's friend, a bear, narrates interesting stories in Karadi Tales.

Shobha and Vishwanath's venture was successful and a hit with children. From Girish Karnad to Usha Uthup, Naseeruddin Shah, Nandita Das, Vidya Balan and Sanjay Dutt, they all lent their voices to the Karadi Tales. The basic objective of the Karadi Tales was to give children joy and knowledge without entangling them in formal learning. Usha Uthup narrated most of the stories in Hindi and English. Vishwanath says, 'Most of the stories in Karadi Tales are essentially music along with storytelling. Ushaji has the ability to present music and narrate stories in different languages. The Karadi rhymes are immensely popular among children. There are twenty rhymes made for children so far by Karadi Tales, and all of them are in the voice of Ushaji. The kids love her presentations like Eyes on the Peacock's Tail, Magic Vessels, and A Curly Tale. Karadi Tales also organizes Usha's special show for kids from time to time, *The Bakbak Show*.'

According to Vishwanath, there have already been two dozen Bakbak Shows in the country so far. Vishwanath says with a smile, 'Ushaji has her own magic with children. Once they grow up, these children will also hear her popular songs like "Rambha Ho" and "Shaan Se".'

Among the stories presented that are full of joy, there is also the beautifully enchanting Nagalinga tree from the premises of Shanti, with glistening blue waves of the Marina Beach and fragrant ruddy pink flowers. There are also butterflies, birds and a honeycomb of bees. There is a reason why the people of Madras are so proud of Usha.

27

Loving Friends

Nitin Bose is a memorable name in Hindi and Bengali cinema. He was associated with the New Theatres from the 1930s to early 1940s. Hindi and Bengali films were made under the New Theaters banner. Nitin Bose directed many notable films. The Bengali film *Bhagya Chakra*, directed by him in 1935, was a film that used playback songs for the first time. The playback singers included Parul Ghosh, Suprabha Sarkar and K.C. Dey. This new experiment in music and songs in later years paved the golden path for playback singers in Indian cinema. *Bhagya Chakra* was remade in Hindi as *Dhoop Chhaon* with playback singers in it.

Later, when Nitin Bose had differences with New Theatres' founder, B.N. Sarkar, Nitin moved to Bombay from Calcutta and directed several classic films for Bombay Talkies and Filmistaan. *Ganga Jamuna*, starring Dilip Kumar and Vyjayanthimala, was his most successful film. He was awarded the Dadasaheb Phalke Lifetime Achievement Award in 1977 for his remarkable contribution to cinema. In later years, Nitin Bose came to live permanently with his wife Shanti Bose in Calcutta.

Nitin Bose and his wife's immense affection is treasured by Usha. He never considered her any less than his daughters, Rina and Neeta. Although Nitin Bose's elder daughter Rina Banerjee is older than Usha, the two have been thick friends for the past fifty-one years. Usha's circle of acquaintances is vast but her world of friends is limited. She is simply Usha among friends and nothing else. Rina Banerjee is one of her old friends. Rina often says, 'Usha has enriched me in many ways. She has illuminated my inner glory.' Rina's father passed away in 1986 at the age of eighty-nine and her mother, Shanti Bose, at the age of about 100. Rina recalls that if her mother did not see Usha for a couple of weeks, she would get irritated, 'O Rina! *Amaar Usha kothaay*? (Where is my Usha?)' And Usha was no less! Sometimes she would say to Mrs Bose, 'O Ma! *Tomar baro meye khoob badmash!* (Your elder daughter is really naughty).' In response, Shanti Bose would smile and say, '*Aami jani* . . . (I know . . . I know, Usha).' Rina remembers there wasn't a festival when Usha did not bring clothes for Ma and Baba.

Recalling her first meeting with Usha, Rina Banerjee says, 'That was the January or February of 1969. There were many residential flats for executives of big companies on D.L. Khan Road, Calcutta. Among them was a Minto Park Syndicate Building in which a family friend of ours, Ramamurthy, lived. In those days, Usha's elder sister Indira and her husband, Chinu, lived in Taratala Road in Calcutta. All of us, that is me, my husband Sunil, Indira and Chinu, and Jani Uthup were all Ramamurthy's friends. That day, all of us were invited to lunch by Ramamurthy. On reaching there, we saw a girl in her early twenties dressed in a black saree and blouse with white flowers in her hair sitting on the couch. She had a bowl full of pickles in her hand. That typical Madrasi girl looked a bit eccentric at first glance. Someone introduced her, saying, "This is Usha Iyer. She will be singing in Trincas for a couple of weeks from this evening." I was surprised to hear that and wondered what this girl would be singing? With the same eagerness, I went to Trincas and was amazed after hearing Usha. Usha really enchanted us with her songs.'

After that, Rina became a friend forever. It seemed God had arranged this long-lasting friendship. When Rina first met Usha, she was not married to Jani Chako Uthup. But after Usha's marriage to Jani, Rina and Usha's friendship rose to greater heights. Rina smiles, 'In fact, we were tea wives.' Rina's husband, Sunil Kumar Banerjee, worked in a tea company just like Jani. Sunil was earlier posted at the Tea Research Centre in Jorhat. When Jani was transferred to Cochin for a few years after his marriage to Usha, Sunil Banerjee was also posted in Cochin with James Finlay & Co. In Cochin, Rina and Usha's house was absolutely face-to-face. Often their evenings were spent together. There was a regular exchange of dishes between both houses. Usha knew that Rina loved *kappa* (boiled and seasoned tapioca) and fish curry. So whenever she used to make it in her home, she used to send it to Rina. This friendship of five decades steadily deepened over time. Rina and Sunil have two daughters, Arunika and Devika.

Their younger daughter Devika has unfortunately been battling cancer for some time. It is Usha who reaches Rina's home at Mandavil Garden in Gariahat and gives her solace. Through Rina Banerjee, Usha got another dear friend, Savita Chawla. For the past twenty-two years, Savita had been running a boutique in her house with a team of skilled workers. Initially, it was called Mayuri Creations, and Savita had two Marwari friends on board. After a short interval, they left but Savita continued with her work. Rina Banerjee used to get her suits and blouses stitched at Savita's outfit. Usha found Savita through Rina. One afternoon Savita was surprised to see Usha at the door of her house on Circus Avenue. Savita still remembers that afternoon in 2000. Her only daughter Sheetal was engaged a few days earlier, and she was busy preparing for the wedding.

'That Sunday has been imprinted in my mind to this day,' says Savita. However, when she opened the door that day, she couldn't believe her eyes for a moment when she saw Usha Uthup standing before her. She hadn't ever imagined that she would be meeting her favourite singer in this fashion. In a blink, many memories flashed through Savita's mind that day. Recollections from years ago. Savita's maternal grandmother lived near Nariman Point, Bombay. And her parents also lived in Bombay. During the holidays, Savita used to come to Nani's house to have fun. Sometimes she would stay with her grandmother for months. On those evenings, Savita's aunts would say, 'C'mon Savita, let's go to Talk of the Town to listen to Usha Iyer.' This was how, during her youth, Savita heard Usha many times and became a fan. She noticed how beautifully Usha communicated with her audience while singing.

After a few years, Savita permanently moved to Calcutta after marrying Raj Chawla who was from the city. Raj's work was related to the supply of water purification chemicals. Sometime later, Savita came to know from the newspapers and some family friends that Usha had also settled in Calcutta. But Savita never thought that she would meet Usha. Then a series of interactions unfolded and before they knew, Savita was making suits and blouses for Usha and they began meeting daily. When in Calcutta, Usha used to reach Savita's place almost every morning at eight. Then they would chat on various subjects for a couple of hours, ranging from fashion and cinema to politics, sports and whatnot. Savita would be fascinated by Usha's never-ending treasure of engrossing tales.

Savita recalls that a few years ago a flyover was being built near her house and the entire road was dug up. Usha would cross the broken road and come to her boutique on the first floor, despite the discomfort to her feet. If Savita mentioned her interesting meetings with Usha, people were not ready to believe her. People were used to watching Usha in a saree and whenever Savita told them she stitches suits for her, they would be surprised. Savita Chawla recalls that during the early days, Usha came in the mornings always wearing a white or a black suit. No other colour. One day Savita's daughter Sheetal told Usha, 'Aunty, you will look great in suits in other colours too.' Sheetal then designed some suits for Usha in different colours. However, she knew that Usha never liked light pink, purple or light blue. She liked green and a few other shades.

Like her mother, Sheetal also loves her Usha Aunty. Sheetal's only teenage daughter Simran also eagerly awaits her arrival. When Simran was born in 2003, Savita renamed her boutique after her granddaughter as the Simran Boutique.

Sheetal, along with her husband, Gautam Khanna, helps her mother in running the boutique. It has a staff of fifteen. Whenever Usha comes to Simran Boutique, she greets all the tailors. She says to the head tailor Alimuddin, 'Alimuddin Bhai, if you spoil my clothes, I will beat you a lot.' And every time, Alimuddin smiles and replies, 'You just say that. When have you ever done that?'

According to Sheetal, 'Everyone waits for Usha Aunty to visit.' Like her mother, Sheetal also has many captivating stories about Usha. She remembers once when one of the clients got a bold and revealing blouse stitched for herself and had come to fetch it. Coincidentally, Usha also reached the boutique at the same time. Seeing the revealing blouse, Usha out of curiosity asked the woman if she could wear the blouse and show it to her. The woman was ready, but she said, 'You sing one of your songs for me and I will wear the blouse ten times for you.' Usha didn't disappoint. She sang for her.

Usha, who has been on the sewing machine since childhood, always designs her own clothes. Savita smiles and says, 'She is a design in herself.' Savita's daughter Sheetal adds, 'No matter how much fashion comes into the world, Usha Aunty's saree, bangles, bindi and jewellery will remain in her own style. For the tailoring of her suit, she always sketches the design for our Masterji explaining how the pleats of the salwar should fall . . .'

After a pause, Sheetal adds, 'Every time Aunty instructs Masterji that the stitching of the suit should be absolutely like a Mughal salwar, not an *ain salwar*.'

The 'ain salwar' has an interesting story behind it. As a child, Usha used to see that Pathan Aunty would get really angry when a salwar's pleat wasn't right, and both the legs of the salwar would go in different directions. Pathan Aunty would then say to her daughter Jamila, 'This is now an "ain salwar".' Usha got a sense of finesse when it came to salwar-suit sets from Pathan Aunty and Jamila. During the IPL match in Calcutta, Jamila was happy to see Usha in a dark purple suit on TV. She called Usha from Bangalore and said, 'It was great to see you in a purple suit during the match. Usha laughed and asked Jamila, 'I hope it wasn't an ain salwar?'. 'Oh no. Perfect salwar,' Jamila said with a loud laugh. In fact, in the IPL match, actors Shah Rukh Khan and Juhi Chawla's team wore deep purple dress. Personally, purple is not Usha's favourite colour. But during the match, Usha was seen in a dark purple outfit in the visitors' gallery.

Preserving things is an old hobby for Usha. Like old friendships, old memories, old jewellery, old shoes and old tattered clothes too. Savita Chawla recalls how on Usha's insistence, she had made quilts for her with her Kanjeevaram sarees damaged during the floods in Calcutta. In fact, Usha's many Kanjeevaram sarees kept in the lower rack of the shelves were damaged in the floods. But Usha was determined to give new life to them. Savita laughs and says, 'Sarees can also make a quilt, I never imagined that. But under the guidance of my dear friend, I got the quilts stitched and couldn't stop looking at those magnificent creations.' Even today, from time to time, Usha persuades Savita to get quilts made out of her old Kanjeevaram sarees.

Dilip Raja and Nandita Raja, directors of the Kanishka brand, located at Gariahat, Calcutta, also have a fascinating role in enriching Usha's wardrobe. Dilip, who is from Madhya Pradesh, makes beautiful sarees with block prints with his pretty Bengali wife, Nandita. On a few occasions when Usha saw Nandita during events in Calcutta, she was instantly attracted to the block print sarees. Initially, Usha was under the impression that the Kanishka sarees were expensive. But when she got well-acquainted with Nandita and Dileep, she realized that her perception was wrong regarding the prices. This is how she became an admirer of Kanishka sarees. Once Usha was making a video called 'Kolkata, Kolkata', when something came to her mind and she requested Dilip and Nandita to block-print the words of the song 'Aha! Tumi Koto Sundari Kolkata' from the video on a saree. In this way, Nandita and Dileep got the entire song's lyrics prepared into wooden block prints.

When that saree was ready, it became the talk of the town. Usha also requested Dilip and Nandita to print the same song on shirt fabric for her music team. Usha designed shirts with the same cloth for all musicians! That video gained immense popularity and set a trend. Later, Usha requested Dilip and Nandita to print the words of another song, '*Jo kuch bhi ho jaaye, hum ye kahenge! Hum ek the, hum ek hain, hum ek rahenge*', printed on a saree. Following that, she also got the song, 'Bombay Meri Hai' in Hindi and Marathi and a Malayalam song, 'Ente Keralam Ethra Sundaram', printed on a saree. This was how Usha got many sarees made by Dilip and Nandita, with songs in several languages. When Usha is mentioned, Dileep and Nandita are overwhelmed, 'She is an unbelievable source of endless energy. We have been friends for forty years now. She is a constant companion to her friends and the chlorophyll for her listeners. No matter how glum someone is, they come alive when they meet her.'

Usha also has a 'baby friend', Anita Sukul, in her short and sweet list of friends. Anita and her husband Sanjib Sukul are her family friends for the past five decades. When Usha lovingly calls Anita, 'Baby Anita', Anita merrily pretends to be irritated. Their

friendship is filled with the warmth of unending love. Anita is
originally from Kutch in Gujarat. But when her grandfather
came to Calcutta for business, he never went back. Anita's
father, Dharam Singh Suraiya, carried on his ancestral business
in Calcutta. Anita remembers that she was only twelve when she
went with her father to see a show by Indira and Usha at the Kala
Mandir in Calcutta. It was a two-and-a-half-hour musical show,
but after watching it, a young Anita concluded that while Indira
was the focus of the show, the vibe was from Usha's voice.

From that day onwards, Anita was in such awe of Usha's songs
that she dared to go alone to Trincas in the evenings to listen to her.
Anita's house was located on Russell Street, near Park Street. She
told the family driver that he would be paid overtime for dropping
her at Trincas and bringing her back. Dharam Singh Suraiya used
to laugh at this craze of his daughter. Usha was also very fond of
seeing baby Anita at the front table every evening at Trincas. And
after the show, the warmth with which Anita would meet her was
precious to Usha. Thus, Anita became friends with Usha who was
almost ten years older than her, a friendship that was appreciated
by all. Such was the friendship between the two that when Anita
went to see the film *Yaadon Ki Baaraat* with school friends at the
Light House cinema on her birthday, Usha was also invited. Anita
recalls that in those days when Usha used to get some leisure time,
both of them would go to see a film together. She has lost count
of how many times they have seen films together at the Basusree
cinema in south Calcutta.

When Usha started living in Calcutta permanently after her
marriage to Jani, Baby Anita started coming to her house more
often. Anita would reach the Queen's Mansion flat, where Usha's
lived, in the morning on a holiday and return home after dinner
late in the evening. However, Anita was afraid of Jani's serious and
quiet personality, so she would eat and drink without uttering a
word during dinner. But in the family friendship of so many years,

Anita has blended so effortlessly with Usha's family that now, sometimes, she also converses boldly with Jani Bhaisaheb. She smiles, 'I am not a baby anymore. Now I speak in Jani Bhaisaheb's presence.'

Anita says that she has learned the essentials of life from her 'big friend' Usha, like packing luggage for trips, travelling vigilantly, and taking care of the kitchen on special occasions. At the same time, Usha also believes that she takes Baby Anita's opinion on most of her important decisions.

Like Rina and Anita, Usha's other companion is her school friend Roshan Irani. Roshan has been living in Pune for a long time. Usha and Roshan used to study together in Bombay's Convent of Jesus and Mary. Roshan's father owned a large chips company—Golden Wafers. Roshan's family was affluent and seeing the lifestyle at Roshan's house, Usha understood for the first time how rich people live. But Roshan remained untouched by all the wealth. Usha and she would exchange their tiffins. And whenever Usha went to Roshan's house, her mother would treat her with great love. Roshan's younger brother Boman Irani was a beautiful child, like a bunny. Later, he became active in the theatre circuit and earned a good name in films too. When Boman grew up, Usha told him that he should concentrate on Hindi theatre and cinema.

As a child, Roshan also used to visit Usha. Usha's elder brother Shamu believed that Roshan came to meet Usha for two reasons. One, she is attracted to her brother Babu and secondly, the urge to drink rasam brought her there. Usha used to get annoyed with this joke. She did not like anyone making fun of her friend. Roshan married Hosi Irani who has his own business. They have two daughters. So Usha always consults Roshan on any issue related to her daughter, Anjali. Roshan has been her confidante on every personal and family matter. But Usha has been regularly miffed with Roshan on one particular issue. Whenever she told her about any fight with Jani, Roshan would side with Jani saying, 'It's your fault Usha. You make a mountain out of a molehill.'

Usha's list of precious friendships include three couples—Arundhati Pal Chaudhary (nickname, Tutulia) and her husband Apu Pal Chaudhary; Sheela Janaki Ram, a native of Thanjavur, Tamil Nadu, and her husband Ashok Janakiram, who have been living in Calcutta for a long time; and Supriya Chattopadhyay (Usha's 'Ladli Koyalia') and her husband, Arup Chattopadhyay. Tutulia's husband, Apu, runs a petrol pump. Sheela's husband is in the shipping business. Sheela runs an organization called Arsh Vidyanidhi in Calcutta for the education of orphans. Supriya's husband is an expert in ceramics.

Recalling her first meeting with Usha, Sheela says, 'We grew up listening to Didi's songs. But once on the occasion of the Pongal festival, the meeting with her at the Stadel Restaurant in Calcutta finally turned into a friendship in a moment. Later, we used to see each other during our morning walk at the Calcutta Cricket and Football Club. We used to greet each other and go our own ways. But one day she said, 'There is a puja in the house. We will love you to join us.' I went to her house. I was fascinated to see how intently she worships. I liked how she blends her Tamil culture with her personal life so wonderfully.' Usha's friend Tutulia is exultant when she speaks of Usha: 'Guys! She is our Mother Teresa.' Tutulia's husband, Apu Pal Chaudhary, adds with a chuckle, 'I am an alcoholic, and Usha Di is a workaholic.'

It is now a daily routine that these friends meet during their morning walk. Then they head to the Azad Hind Chai dhaba located on a roadside corner in Ballygunge and carry on their discussions on a wide range of subjects—from politics, fashion to cuisine. Usha says, 'After every morning, I wait for the next morning.' Among similar priceless friends, there is Sukanya of the ladies' parlour Highlights, and her two exclusive allies, Jhumku and Boudi. When Usha reaches Highlights to wear the maangtika in her hair, not only Sukanya, Jhumku and Boudi but the other girls, Pinky, Pooja, Shukla and Jaya also get excited. Usha remembers their birthdays and visits Highlights with a cake and celebrates the day with great warmth. She finds excuses for celebration at every instance. This is the reason why Usha is an eternal celebration not only for her family and friends, but also for her vast audience.

28

Umbuka

There is an old Christian cemetery near Khan Market on Prithviraj Road in Delhi. Rani's grave is over there. The striking white marble stone epitaph says:

In ever loving memory of our Rani Mol
Born February 14, 1953
Died July 6, 1963
The light of your life will ever shine in ours!
Mummy Daddy Janiba, Aniba and Chhoti! Inserted by Her Parents
Brigadier and Mrs C.C. Uthup.

In the desolate, hot summer afternoons this graveyard remains lost and solemnly silent amid parched trees. On rainy days, there is an unseen sereneness amid the trees soaked in greenery. During the harsh winters of Delhi, it seems as if the broken white feathers of the fairies who died are hidden in the words on the epitaphs.

Was Rani Mol, who was buried at the age of ten in this graveyard, a fairy?

'Yes, she was a fairy. My little angel!' Says Usha with great love and affection. In Malayalam, *mol* means a little girl or a daughter.

Rani Mol was a cute little girl. Jani Chako, Uthup's younger sister, who said goodbye to the world at the age of ten. After her treatment in Delhi, when Rani passed away and was buried in this graveyard near Khan Market, Usha was not known in the family. Usha arrived in the Uthup family seven to eight years after Rani's demise. Of course, Usha had never seen Rani, but saw many lovely pictures of Rani. She came to know from Jani that Rani was buried in this graveyard in Delhi.

So, when Usha went to Delhi for the first time after her marriage to Jani, she came to this graveyard to meet her youngest sister-in-law, Rani Mol. She went there with a bouquet of tulips and red roses. After reaching Rani's grave, she felt that a happy little girl came running and embraced her. That day and today, for the last four decades, Usha has not returned from Delhi without offering flowers at Rani Mol's grave. She believes that whenever she comes to Delhi, Rani waits for her. It happened only once or twice that she went to Delhi and returned without meeting Rani, and she felt that Rani was sad. So she never let down Rani's love.

Every time she goes to the cemetery, Usha requests the caretaker to never let Rani's grave be covered with dust. Usha also keeps the phone number of the caretaker and checks with him from time to time. She is the only member of the Uthup family who visits Rani's grave so often. She especially sends flowers on 14 February and 6 July, Rani's birth and death anniversaries.

This is Usha. She also maintains relationships with those whom she has never met and will not ever meet. Be it a small celebration at her in-laws or her maternal side of the family, Usha takes time out in the midst of several engagements. Her father-in-law, Brig. C.C. Uthup, is no longer in the world but she never forgets to visit the family home in Kottayam to see her mother-in-law, Thangamma, on her birthday. She is over ninety now, but knows that on her birthday Usha will come to Kottayam from across the seven seas. Recalling the early days, Usha and her mother-in-law jokingly remember how at one point Thangamma protested against the marriage of her son Jani to Usha who was from a non-Christian family. Thangamma fondly remembers how easily Usha from a traditional Tamil Brahmin family got settled so effortlessly in a Christian family.

Usha was a vegetarian since her childhood. Non-vegetarian food was prohibited at her home. But as her in-laws were Christian, Usha graciously learnt to cook a range of non-vegetarian dishes. Initially, when she cooked meat and fish for her husband and children and no one appreciated it, she felt dejected. But one day a friend sensed her unhappiness and said, 'Usha, when you do your show, you give love to people through your songs. Give love to the people through your kitchen too. Remember that you are a giver . . .'

When all the family members gather, even today Usha prepares payasam for everyone. Her Chimooz Aunty Chicken Curry is a permanent favourite among her family members. They get excited when she brings together the chicken pieces, onion, garlic, ginger, red chilli and turmeric on low heat in her kitchen. Usha's grandchildren, Riyad and Ayesha, especially like the payasam and chicken made by their Umbuka's hands. Ayesha and Riyad call Usha Umbuka. And she, in turn, is totally dedicated to them.

When Usha's children, Anjali and Sunny, were in school, Usha used to prepare their lunch box herself, despite there being a nanny in the house, and Jani's as well when he was leaving for office. Usha's interest in the kitchen developed by looking at Madras Patti Ma and her Amma. How engrossed they used to be while preparing food! Usha was not familiar with north Indian dishes like paneer and rajma. But after coming to Calcutta, she learned how to cook both these dishes. Usha's first day with Rajma was very difficult because she did not know that she had to soak it in water the night before. When the rajma was uncooked despite being on the fire for two hours, an upset Usha called the cook at

Trincas and asked for the rajma recipe. Usha believes that cooking is the foremost art in the world.

Usha remembers that no matter how great a party Appa would return from, he would say to Amma, 'Min, it was nothing like your food.'

Usha learnt through her family the essence of how the word kitchen originated from the word 'rasa'. Usha learnt the strength of family love at her home while growing up. She has always kept her family above everything else. During early interviews, when journalists asked her how she balanced her family life and her profession, Usha replied, 'I don't allow one to interfere with the other. I keep both in two separate watertight compartments. I don't allow one to flow into the other.'

Usha says today that she had been lying for a long time, because it is not easy, if not impossible, for a woman engaged in public life to keep family and profession separate. She remembers that after returning from a show, she would find many of the household chores not done. She often had a clash with Jani over this. And Jani was also one of a kind—extremely headstrong. Usha recalls that when she got into a clash with Jani over essential household chores, she used to go and sit on a bench outside hoping that he might come to appease her. But when no one came to pacify her, she would quietly go inside and resume the housework. Then Jani would simply glance at her and get busy reading something. Usha finally decided that she would make true the lie she had been telling about balancing the family and profession in her interviews.

She never talks about music among the family members. When a new song has to be sung by her, she has a habit of sitting in her room along with a notebook and writing the song many times to internalize it. Soak in it and make it her own. If she has to listen to a tune in the house, she hears it softly after closing the door of her room. She listens to the melody and music like a prayer, during which no intrusion is allowed. If Jani is watching a cricket, tennis or football match on the television, Usha does her work by sitting in another room. In this way, the clash between family and profession is almost nil now. Once you understand that you cannot change your personal life in your own way, then there is no problem. Coming to this realization brought her great relief. Usha admits that if her husband and children had not supported her, she would not have been able to do so much work.

Since stage shows are the focal point of her music, she is away for more than fifteen days every month. While in Calcutta, there was no day when Usha wasn't busy with a programme or a show. There was Studio Vibrations' work as well. Usha believes that she is able to do all this by cutting down on family time. Therefore, she always makes sure that she is there for each member of the family (this extends from sisters, brothers to her mother-in-law and sister-in-law) in happiness, sorrow and in times of need. Her family members also believe that Usha may not be able to give regular time due to her busy schedule but she will be the first family member to reach on important occasions.

On 4 April 2018, after battling cancer for a long time, when Usha's elder sister Dr Uma Pocha passed away in Bombay, Usha cancelled all her programmes and reached Bombay. But what is significant here is that there was no such month during Uma Di's illness when Usha had not gone to meet her in Bombay. She also commemorates Uma Di's memorial day with the same warmth and reverence.

Usha's true copy is her daughter Anjali. Like her mother, a family lover and a great friend. She lives permanently in Cochin with her husband, John Kurien. She is a popular radio jockey at the Malayalam Manorama's radio station Radio Mango. On hearing the voice of Anjali Uthup Kurian on the radio, one would wonder if that is Usha. It is the same voice, the same style, the same warmth, the same carefree attitude and the same happiness.

Anjali's favourite line is, 'Let go, let God.' On occasions, when Usha is busy and if Anjali is in Calcutta, Usha hands over her mobile phone to Anjali. Interestingly, Anjali then becomes Usha Uthup. She talks on the phone and callers get convinced that Usha Uthup is on the line.

Anjali was named by her maternal grandmother, Meenambal aka Minnie Sami. Minnie had said to Usha, 'She is God's Anjali. Full of smiles and melody.' Anjali always excelled in studies as well as extracurricular activities. She studied English literature at the Loreto Convent and St Xavier's College after completing her schooling from the La Martiniere School in Calcutta.

A travel and music lover, Anjali's first love has undoubtedly been music, like Usha. Whenever Minnie Sami came to Calcutta, she would find that Anjali woke up with a song, played one while studying and slept while listening to a song. Minnie Sami used to wonder how one can concentrate during studies while listening to a song so loudly. But Anjali is Anjali. Anjali has been like Usha when it comes to friendship. Amit Ghosh from Calcutta was settled in the Anglo–Indian village of McCluskieganj in Jharkhand (then, undivided Bihar). During his stay in Germany, Amit Ghosh married a German girl, Ilona. Amit and Ilona had a daughter, Rebecca, who used to study with Anjali at the La Martiniere School. She was in the school hostel because her parents were based in McCluskieganj. Rebecca didn't seem to like the hostel even for a single moment. She cried incessantly. Anjali would be deeply saddened seeing Rebecca's plight.

So, one day, she asked Usha, 'Amma, can I keep a friend of mine with me at home?' Usha agreed but said that Rebecca's parents' permission had to be taken. When Amit and Ilona came to Calcutta and Rebecca told them about Anjali's proposal, they loved it. Then, Rebecca stayed at Usha's house as her daughter for as long as she lived in Calcutta. Rebecca is now settled in the US with her husband. But Anjali and Rebecca are still close.

Some time ago when Rebecca's father Amit Ghosh passed away, Rebecca came to Calcutta from America for the funeral and Anjali came to Calcutta to be with her. She stayed with Rebecca until the entire funeral proceedings were completed.

Rebecca recounts all the episodes from her schooldays with affection. She recalls how Anjali used to get two dozen dosas made by her Amma for her school friends. Even today, Anjali is the same. When she arrives at a party, she shines like her Amma. Anjali says, 'Amma is the model of my life. She is skilled in many ways. Remarkably hard-working and extremely generous. There is no match to her courage.' An overwhelmed Anjali adds, 'Whether sewing, cooking or painting, there is no one like Amma. From childhood to college, whenever I asked for a new suit, Amma would take me along and buy fabric of my choice and stitch an elegant dress for me overnight. When my children were baptized, it was Amma who made clothes for them on that special occasion and what fine and beautiful embroidery she did on them.' Anjali recalls that when return gifts had to be given at Christmas, Amma would buy jute bags from Gariahat and stay up all night painting them. She would write the names of each recipient in artistic style on the bags, making them a unique gift. No one could buy something like that in the market.

Anjali is also an ardent admirer of her mother's cooking. According to her, Usha can make sixteen types of dishes. And every dish is unique in itself. Anjali laughs saying that her Amma doesn't know counting. 'If we ask for one garment, she will bring a dozen. When asked for a cake, she would bring ten cakes.' Anjali says that her Amma celebrates all kinds of festivals—from Durga Puja to Christmas and Eid. She is always there for her friends and colleagues. Anjali smiles, 'So I tell Amma that you are doormat. Amma, who is afraid of the dark, of climbing alone in the elevator is equally daring. Once when Sunny and I were still in school, we suddenly felt the floor of the house getting increasingly hot. We ran and told Amma. She is a police officer's daughter, so without any delay, she went to the flat just below ours. It was locked since the family had gone out. A fire had broken inside. The fire brigade arrived by then. They broke down the door and entered. Amma also went in with them and helped the fire brigade team till the end in extinguishing the fire.'

Anjali's husband John is serious and quiet by nature. Whereas Anjali is carefree and nonchalant! Their married life's balance is based on simply being there for each other. The union of Anjali and John was perhaps uniquely created by God. Jani Uthup did his schooling in Ooty, which is next to Coonoor. Since childhood, Jani was in awe of the natural aura and beauty of Coonoor in the Nilgiri hills. Immediately after Anjali's birth, Jani was transferred to Coonoor for three months. He was overjoyed. Even today Jani's love for Coonoor hasn't changed. He decided to celebrate his fiftieth birthday on 4 September in Coonoor. It was a sweet coincidence that John was also invited on the occasion.

Like Jani, John also hails from Kottayam. Anjali and John Kurien's first meeting on Jani's birthday proved to be love at first sight. In 1996, both of them got married in Cochin. Earlier John was with R.P. Goenka's Harrisons and Malayalam Tea Company. Later he quit his job and started his own business. Regarding his mother-in-law, John says, 'She is my friend more than a mother-in-law.'

Anjali and John have a daughter, Ayesha, and a son, Riyad. Ayesha was born on 11 March 2000, and Riyad on 14 February 2004. Usha has boundless love for her granddaughter and grandson. Ayesha, who studies at the Symbiosis College in Pune, has taken to music, like her grandmother and mother. In 2014, when Usha, Anjali and Ayesha performed together at a programme by Ink in Cochin, this song performed by three generations became etched in people's memory. Ayesha's voice is different from her grandmother and mother, but she is as dedicated as her grandmother to music. Everyone in the family knows that Ayesha will take forward Studio Vibrations' legacy.

Ayesha's younger brother Riyad is slightly different from and more easy-going than his sister. Riyad is schooling in Cochin, and despite the pressure of studies, whenever his beloved Umbuka reaches Cochin, his heart is full of joy. Going to Calcutta is also like a celebration for Riyad because of his dearest Umbuka's love, pampering and bearing his every tantrum. Riyad is his Umbuka's 'Master Valentino' as his birthday falls on Valentine's Day, 14 February. So his Umbuka is his 'Valentine Girl'.

Riyad is very possessive about his grandmother and does not like her attention to be distracted when he is with her. So, when they go out to a market, a restaurant or a movie theatre, he makes sure that no one makes eye contact with his Umbuka. He knows that once that happens, people will start to gather around Usha for photographs and autographs. Riyad doesn't like that. So, he constantly whispers to her, 'Eyes down, Umbuka, eyes down . . .'

Riyad's obedient Umbuka immediately looked down, obeying his command. Still, people don't stop milling around her when they see her. Riyad's innocent helplessness is worth watching. Usha's fans, eager to get autographs and photographs with her, don't budge until their wishes are met.

'It is God's grace to become a grandmother,' says Usha. When Anjali was about to become a mother, Usha was happy to imagine how she would take Anjali's child in her arms and walk around. Years later, Usha recalls the mild impact of partial paralysis in one of her feet that affects her to date. When Ayesha was born, lost in happiness, she did not realize for many months that she had any problem with her feet.

Tiredness and discomfort are anyway not in Usha's dictionary. No matter how tired she is and if someone asks her if she is exhausted, then her quick response is, 'Not exactly.' This quality of his mother amazes Sunny. According to him, 'I have never heard the word "jet lag" from Amma's mouth, despite her long travels abroad. Once she arrived in Calcutta from America at six in the morning. Her show was in Durgapur that evening. She wore her clothes at the airport. They were ordered from home. She went straight from the airport to Durgapur and reached home in the middle of the night after performing there.'

Reserved by nature, Sunny is obviously very proud of his Amma. In 1997, selected veterans were awarded the Lifetime Achievement Award. The event took place at the Rajiv Gandhi Indoor Stadium in Delhi. Rockstars Bon Jovi and Peter Andre among other international celebrities were present. Sunny remembers that after being honoured, Amma said that she would like to meet the audience. Sunny feared that amid these international rockstars, how much attention the audience would pay to his Amma. But there was no end to Sunny's happiness when he saw the enthusiasm and respect for his mother. That evening when Usha started singing 'Fever', one of her favourite songs, the entire stadium resonated with applause.

An introverted Sunny loves his Amma with all his life, because she stands for everything he desires. Sunny is confident that if ten of his friends come home without informing, Amma will not let them all go without a meal. Sunny says, 'Amma is very soft inside. But she can shake up the Himalayas.'

Usha regrets that her son Sunny hasn't got married yet. Sunny, a year younger than Anjali, is employed with a tea company in Calcutta. Thinking about Sunny's single life, Usha's heart sinks. In the silence of her room in Calcutta's Ballygunge, she wells up thinking what will happen to Sunny after her? Who will take care of him? Suddenly, Riyad's face appears. Whenever the slightest disheartening expression appears on Usha's face, a worried Riyad puts his arms around her and says, 'Change your dialogue, Umbuka . . . Please change your dialogue.'

29

An Invisible World

Strange Life of Ivan Osokin is a book that is eternally embedded in Usha's heart. P.D. Ouspensky's novel was published in Russian in 1915. In 1947, it got an English translation. Usha must have bought countless copies to gift to her loved ones. Moscow-born Pyotr Dimainovich Ouspensky was a writer along with being a mathematician. A disciple of the thinker and mystic Gurdjieff, Ouspensky's protagonist Ivan Osokin wishes to correct his mistakes after the relentless failed struggles of his life. But when he is given an opportunity to relive his past, he goes on to commit the same errors he wished to rectify. This character is actually a living symbol of Nietzsche's theory of eternal recurrence.

Usha often wondered if her life resembled that of Ivan Osokin. Was she, like Ivan Osokin, a victim of eternal recurrence? There was a strange tremor in her mind—a divine occurrence. She remembered that since childhood, she felt an invisible world unfold within her. Recurrence! Recurrence! Usha had also told Amma many times as a child that she felt whatever she is experiencing in the present had taken place already. And this continued till today. Was she reliving her past life again, exactly? She felt that she might never be able to solve this inner conflict.

Life's meteoric circle often startles. In 2015 Usha was invited as the chief guest at a doctors' conference held in Cochin. It was a few months after her return from the event in the last week of June 2015 when one afternoon a courier arrived at her address in Calcutta. On opening the packet, Usha found a book by a well-known doctor Philip G. Thomas from Cochin. Dr Thomas had written a complimentary note on the opening page of the book: 'To Usha Uthup, Anjali and Ayesha. With compliments and many thanks for the wonderful music over the years and continuing still.' After glancing through the pages, Usha tried to remember if she had met Dr Thomas at the doctors' conference in Cochin? But she couldn't remember anything.

She thought perhaps Anjali, living in Cochin, knew him. That was why Dr Thomas had also mentioned Anjali and her daughter Ayesha. Usha, out of curiosity, called Anjali immediately. She confirmed that she knows Dr Thomas. Anjali also said that Dr Thomas is a renowned kidney and liver specialist. Usha asked Anjali to meet the doctor and thank him for the book.

In July 2015, everyone from Sunny's office in Calcutta underwent an annual medical checkup. Usha remembers that after returning from the studio in the evening, she was watching TV in her room when Sunny walked in after returning home from work. There was a deep uneasiness on his face. While sitting down, he said, 'Amma! There is bad news for you.'

'What bad news?' Usha's voice trembled.

'The doctor has said that my kidney is failing. My creatinine has reached 8.60, Amma. The doctor has suggested that I must start dialysis soon.' Sunny's voice was downcast. Usha felt her brain becoming increasingly numb. It did not take long for her to understand that the dark storm of sadness had entered her house. Sunny was just forty-two. '

She wondered what would happen now. Distressed, she called Subir Dutt, her family doctor in Calcutta. Dr Dutt gave an appointment for the coming day. He too confirmed that Sunny suffered from kidney failure. After this unfortunate news, Jani, Anjali, John—the entire family was in shock. Ultimately, Sunny decided that he will undergo all further treatment in Cochin. Usha went to Cochin in the second week of July with Sunny. Anjali, who was already there, had figured out an appointment with the doctor at the hospital. On reaching Cochin, Sunny's dialysis began. A restless Usha was eager to do anything for her son. When Sunny's condition stabilized a little during the ongoing dialysis, Usha visited the Tirupati Balaji temple. Along with the prayer for Sunny's long and healthy life, she also made an offering of her long, beautiful hair that touched her waist. The magnificent tresses always adorned with a garland of Malligai Poo, fragrant white jasmine flowers, were gone.

Seeing Amma's chopped hair, Sunny's eyes were flooded with tears. A few months passed while Sunny underwent dialysis in Cochin. In 2016, he underwent a kidney transplant in Cochin, which was conducted by none other than Dr Philip G. Thomas. On the day of the transplant, Usha kept getting flashes from two months ago when Dr Thomas's novel *Transplant Story* had arrived by courier at her Calcutta address. And now, her son had to undergo a transplant. Would Osokin's invisible world play out in her life too? She pleaded with God that it should not happen. But while pleading, she repeatedly felt as if Ivan Osokin was on her side constantly hitting his head and crying bitterly. Perhaps his request to be saved from the recurrence was again going unheard.

Sunny had chickenpox after the kidney transplant. One morning, Anjali came out of his hospital room crying, 'The chicken pox has also erupted on the transplant stitches and the stitches are almost open, Amma.' Usha felt as if she was going to sink into an eternal abyss. Oh, invisible world! Now what? The doctors handled the situation somehow. In the midst of this long course of treatment, Usha, concealing her tears, performed shows from time to time as it was not easy to bear the cost of a kidney transplant. After a long time, Usha came back to Calcutta with Sunny. It felt like everything would be back on track. But exactly one year later, Sunny's condition deteriorated.

Doctors conducted a thorough investigation and came to the conclusion that Sunny's body was rejecting the transplanted kidney. Nothing could have been more brutal for Usha other than this news. The doctors said that another 'kidney transplant would make no sense. Sunny would have to survive on dialysis.' This information was the last nail on Usha's desolate and distressed mind. To end this grief, Sunny's elder sister Anjali started the Sunny Foundation to help kidney patients across the country.

Usha wondered, 'What does the invisible world not want? A gloomy house in complete numbness, and from nowhere the pure throbbing of the zealous music that resonates?' She felt everything was mysterious, with countless strange delusions. She tried not to let her sadness spill in Sunny's presence. He remembered how Amma always had one hack for all kinds of aches, from feet to stomach or head, 'Go! Wash your face, you will be fine.'

In her mind, Usha could sense the erupting tides of despair within. The smell of the earth swirling in the midst of a grave life. Usha teared up over and over again. She tried to convince herself that everything would be all right. She remembered Amma even as she washed her face repeatedly before going to a show. She would come slowly on to the stage bathed in light and with the announcement, 'Our great and the greatest, Padmashri Usha Uthup.' Then would come the relentless applause, the mic covered with the corner of her saree, and with her evergreen familiar smile she would ask the audience, 'So, ready to rock?'

The very next moment, Usha would feel as if she had entered the Almighty's mystical chant house: 'I Believe in Music, I Believe in Love . . .' Her mantra would enliven the atmosphere. She now started each show with that line. It became her life mantra, which gave salvation to the soul. She felt it was music and love that channels life in her and grinds her sorrow with great rhythm. Usha was always aware of how a perplexed mind can survive with the courage of art. As the musicians on stage progressed towards her next song, she sang a song for herself that would be ever enduring:

> *Somebody told me,*
> *He said the waves of this vast and great sea,*
> *Will one day take me holding me by my hand,*
> *To a lovely beach with shining sand,*
> *Hidden in the rays of the sun*
> *Hidden in the light of the sun.*
> *Nobody knows*
> *how I exist or how I have even survived*
> *Sometimes I get up in the middle of the night,*
> *I hear voices singing together so bright . . .*
> *My God, he knows me well by now.*
> *I am standing right at his doorstep*
> *Dreaming the same dream every day . . .*
> *Take my soul along with you*
> *As you would do a friend*
> *To a place where the sun weaves a collage . . .*
> *Woven with colours of love . . .*

Today, as Usha sees it, the boat of joy is rowing steadily in the river of rhythm. Waving the little flag of the celebration of the inner self amid the mysterious and unknown murk. The sail of the boat keeps shuddering. It's strange! The sky itself appears to be dissolving in the sky. And the earth immerses itself into the earth. The unbending question prevails: What does the invisible world want? The suffering of the world sleeps restfully in Usha's songs. There are teardrops. Still they rejoice! There is joy in the earthly world! Oh, the invisible world! The God of recurrences! Hail! Hail! Hail!

Appendix

Usha Uthup has sung numerous songs in Hindi, Bengali, Marathi, Rajasthani, Oria, Assamese, Punjabi, Bhojpuri, Gujarati, Malayalam, Tamil, Telugu, Kannada, Konkani, Dogri, Khasi and English, as well as in French, Swahili, German, Italian, Spanish, Nepali, Russian and the languages spoken in Sri Lanka and South Africa. Here's a list of some of her albums and songs.

Albums

1. *Usha Uthup in Devotional Mood* (Gathani Records, 1987)

2. *Jai Kali, Jai Calcuttawali* (T-Series, 1989; Bangla)

- 'Ilish Macher Paturi'
- 'Jai Kali, Jai Kali'
- 'A B C D Podte Pari'
- 'Misjidete Achhe Bhogoban'
- 'Aaj Shono Boli'
- 'Taxi-Taxi'
- 'Shudhu Saatpake'
- 'Jodi Prithvita Hoto'

- 'Chokhe Chhilo Swapno'
- 'Iraq-Iran Noi'

3. *Aha! Tumi Koto Sundari Kolkata* (Hindustan Records, 1990; Bangla)

- 'Aha! Tumi Koto Sundari Kolkata'
- 'Mone Theek Aache Toh'
- 'Besh Chilam'
- 'Ichandani Raate'
- 'Jeevan Te Nesha Legechhe'
- 'Ashtapato Noshti Vash'
- 'Prem Roye Dhorede Aami'
- 'Book Bhore Jodi Hasha Jeto Chinlona Keu Chinlona'

4. *Garo Modern Songs* (Modil Records, 1991)
5. *Usha Lohori* (DG Records, 1991; Bangla)
   Lyrics: Nirmal Dasgupta
   Music: Subrata Das

- 'Nach-Nach'
- 'Aam Aabar Aisi Chhoni Kakere O Go Saathi'
- 'Kaino Aei Khoon Jhorono'
- 'Kato Jaay Din Baaki'
- 'Hatha Ashaar Moto'
- 'Tumi Aishe Jokhon Dadaale'
- 'Ki Darun Jhoodwa Hawa'

6. *Didi* (Gathani Records; Bangla)

- 'Didi'
- 'Mukhei Tore Takka'
- 'O Gunodhar Mantri Moshai'

- 'Soojo Tomake Pronam'
- 'O Ma Ganga'
- 'Prithivir Teen Bhaag Jol'
- 'Ai Shudhu Prarthana'
- 'Teen Shau Bochhor Pare'

7. *Happy-Happy New Year* (Gathani Records,1994; Bangla)

- 'Happy-Happy New Year'
- 'Ghumata Saurale'
- 'Bodo Loker Khayal'
- 'Vyasata Amar Bhai'
- 'Chamcha Re Chamcha Re'
- 'Aaj Kato Din Maake Dekhini'
- 'Hakuna Matata'
- 'Bodhu Shobai Hoi Na'

8. *Bhalo Theko Tomra Shobai* (Gathani Records, 1994; Bangla)

- 'Aaye Swapno Sajai'
- 'Aaye Shwapnon Sajai'
- 'Jani Na Aachena'
- 'Mone Koto Ki Likhe Jaaye'
- 'Kothai Harano Jaye'
- 'Neel Swapnare Isharai'
- 'Aisho Aao Ekbaar'
- 'Aishe Chhe Khushir Plavon'

9. *Jackpot* (Sagarika Records, 1994)

- 'Aajekar Din Boshe Thakbe'
- 'Ai Khane Tadatadi'
- 'Sritir Album'

- 'Bideshi Mallar Chiro Nobin Kolkata'
- 'Jaa Kichhu Achhe'
- 'E Manina Manina'
- 'Aik Poloke'

10. *Hindi Tagore Songs* (Gathani Records, 1996)
11. *Mega Mix* (T-Series, 1997; Hindi Songs)
12. *Kolkata-Kolkata* (Super Cassette Industries, 1997; Bangla)

- 'Kolkata'
- 'Aami Sri Sri'
- 'Aam Kolkatar Roshogulla'
- 'Ek Din Dal Bendhe'
- 'Hoyto Tomar Jonno'
- 'Shono Kono Ek Din'
- 'Ke Jaane Kau Ghanta'
- 'Ki Naame Deke'
- 'Jeebone Ki Paabna'
- 'Aakash Aeto Meghala'

13. *Chand Bodoni* (Polygram India, 1999; Bangla)

- 'Bado Locker Beeti Low'
- 'Gehile Ki Asiben'
- 'Thakile Dobakhana'
- 'Bankura Matike'
- 'Bhalo Koira'
- 'Sohag Chand Bodoni'
- 'O Raja Re Tui'
- 'Illishmachh Re'
- 'Sanjhe Phote'
- 'Alla Megh De'

14. *Tumi Je Garbo Amadere* (HMV, 2001; Bangla)

- 'Aamar Ghar, Barir Naam'
- 'Aami Shilpi'
- 'Janogon'
- 'Ae Duniya Sacha'
- 'Shyam Bina'
- 'Aage Jaan Le'
- 'Bado Bipake'
- 'Ektai Desh Amadere'
- 'Oligoli-Oligoli'
- 'Kaal Ke Hobe'
- 'O Mamoni'
- 'Tumi Je Garbo Amader'

15. *Nazrul Geeti* (Gathani Records, 2003)
16. *Tera Mera Pyaar Jawan* (Concord Records, 2003)
    Music: R.D. Burman
17. *Kolkata* (Concord Records, 2003)
    Music: R.D. Burman
18. *Dinaguli More – Tagore Songs* (Gathani Records, 2003)
19. *Ishtishaner Railgadita* (Universal Records, 2005)
20. *London–Paris–America* (Ariane Cassettes, 2008; Bangla)

- 'London–Paris–America'
- 'Aadhar Periye'
- 'Ghatona Jodi Kichhu Na Ghate'
- 'Aei Duniyay Bekaar Ami'
- 'Sundari Go'
- 'Gobheer Nishithe'
- 'Ektu-Ektu Kore'
- 'Pratham Dekhte'

Hindi Film Songs

1. 'Jogan Pritam Ki' (from the film *Devi*; 1970)
2. 'Hare Rama, Hare Krishna' (*Hare Rama, Hare Krishna*, 1971)
3. 'One Two, Cha Cha Cha' (*Shalimar*, 1978)
4. 'Shaan Se . . .' (*Shaan*, 1980)
5. 'Doston Se Pyaar Kiya' (*Shaan*, 1980)
6. 'Hari Om Hari' (*Pyara Dushman*, 1980)
7. 'Tu Mujhe Jaan Se Pyara Hai' (*Wardat*, 1981)
8. 'Rambha Ho' (*Armaan*, 1981)
9. 'Koi Yaahan Nache Nache' (*Disco Dancer*, 1982)
10. 'Naaka Bandi' (*Naaka Bandi*, 1990)
11. 'Uri . . . Uri Baba' (*Dushman Devta*, 1991)
12. 'Daud' (*Daud*, 1997)
13. 'Raja Ki Kahani' (*Godmother*, 1999)
14. 'Vande Mataram' (*Kabhi Khushi Kabhie Gham*, 2001)
15. 'Din Hai Na Ye Raat' (*Bhoot*, 2003)
16. 'Kabhi Pa Liya, Toh Kabhi Kho Diya' (*Joggers' Park*, 2003)
17. 'Teri Meri Merry Christmas' (*Bow Barracks Forever*, 2004)
18. 'Wicket Bacha' (*Hattrick*, 2007)
19. 'Darling' (*Saat Khoon Maaf*, 2011)
20. 'Hai Ye Maya' (*Don 2*, 2011)
21. 'Ami Sotti Bolchi' (*Kahaani*, 2012)
22. 'Samba in Ramba' (*Shirin Farhad Ki Toh Nikal Padi*, 2012)
23. 'Hoi Kiev' (*Rock On 2*, 2016)
24. 'Ye Raat Mona Lisa' (*Kaafiron Ki Namaaz*, 2016

Tamil/Telugu Film Songs

1. 'Love Is Beautiful' (Tamil film *Melanatu Marumangal*, 1975)
2. 'Vegum-Vegum, Pogum-Pogum' (Tamil film *Anjali, Sal*, 1991)
3. 'Keecharalu' (Telugu film *Keechuralu*, 1991)

4. 'Race Gurram' (Telugu film *Race Gurram*, 2014)
5. 'Dirty Picture' (Telugu film *Thikka*, 2016)

English Albums

1. *Celebrate Christmas with Usha*

- 'Feliz Navidad'
- 'When a Child Is Born'
- 'White Christmas'
- 'Joy to the World'
- 'Blue Christmas'
- 'Christmas Polka'
- 'Silver Bells'
- 'Oh Come! All Ye Faithful'
- 'Jingle Bells'
- 'The First Noel'
- 'Mary's Boy Child'
- 'Silent Night'

2. *Mary's Boy Child*

- 'Long Time Ago'
- 'Heaven Achieved Is Born'
- 'White Christmas'
- 'Joy to the World'
- 'Blue Christmas'
- 'Old Christmas Card'
- 'Oh! Christmas Tree!'
- 'Christmas'
- 'Oh Come! All Ye Faithful'
- 'Felish Navidad'
- 'Silver Bells'

3. *Mary's Boy Child (Long Time Ago)*

- 'The First Noel'
- 'Old Lang Sign'
- 'Jingle Bells'
- 'Silent Night'
- 'Hark the Herald Angels Sing'
- 'Sing Along with Usha'
- 'Sing-A-Long with Usha'

4. *In the Mood*

- 'Labamba'
- 'Lemon Tree'
- 'Island in the Sun'
- 'Shame and Scandal'
- 'Cha . . . Cha Medley'
- 'O Mari . . . Mari'
- 'Autumn Leaves'
- 'Candy La Missy'
- 'Afro Medley'
- 'Yellow Bird Medley'

5. *Down Memory Lane*

- 'Jambalaya'
- 'Beautiful Sunday'
- 'Rain'
- 'Love Story'
- 'Hotel California'
- 'Bye . . . Bye . . . Brown Eyes'
- 'Sunny'
- 'When You Smile'

- 'Killing Me Softly'
- 'I Believe in Music'
- 'Come Down Jesus'
- 'You Have Got a Friend'
- 'We Will Meet Again'

6. *Garland of Gems*

- 'I Have Come to You' (in Bangla, 'Baro Asha Kore')
- 'For You Life Has Just Begun' (in Bengali, 'Tomar Holo Shuru')
- 'Ye Banks and Brace' (in Bangla, 'Phule-Phule, Dhole-Dhole')
- 'Oh My Lord, My Weariness' (in Bangla, 'Clanty Amar')
- 'Drink to Me Only' (in Bangla, 'Katobaro Bebhichinu')
- 'If There Is No One Answering' ('Jadi Tor Dak Shune Keuna')
- 'Old Lang Syne' (in Bengali, 'Purano Shei Diner Katha')
- 'I Am Not Worthy' (in Bengali, 'A Monihar Aamay')

Songs That Often Featured in Shows

1. 'I Will Survive'
2. 'Big Spender'
3. 'My Hearts Belongs to Daddy'
4. 'Mother Teresa'
5. 'Windmills of Your Mind'
6. 'Twilight Zone'
7. 'Night Moves'
8. 'You Only Live Twice'
9. 'Scotch and Soda'
10. 'One Note Samba'
11. 'Carnival Song'
12. 'Diamonds Are Forever'
13. 'Certain Smile'

14. 'God Made'
15. 'A Hard Day's Night'
16. 'Malaika'
17. 'We Will Meet Again'
18. 'Rock Your Baby'
19. 'Broadway'
20. 'Seasons in the Sun'
21. 'Stand By Me'
22. 'Come Together'
23. 'Can't Buy Me Love'
24. 'Bridge over Troubled Waters'
25. 'Kung Fu Fighting'
26. 'Rock You Baby'
27. 'Going Out of My Head'
28. 'I Will Be Your Audience'
29. 'Sing a Song'
30. 'Spinning Wheels'
31. 'The Way a Woman Loves'
32. 'The Way We Were'
33. 'Feel Like Making Love'
34. 'Rasputin'
35. 'Mamamia'
36. 'Brown Girl'
37. 'Babylon'
38. 'Shadow of Your Smile'
39. 'Love Me and Leave Me'
40. 'Taste of Honey'
41. 'You Only Live Twice'
42. 'Anando-Anando'
43. 'If'
44. 'Tears in Heaven'
45. 'Viva Spania'
46. 'Sway'

Malayalam Film Songs

1. 'Love is Just Around' (*Chattakari*)
2. 'I Am in Love' (*Kanyakumari*)
3. 'Pitambara . . . O Krishna' (*Sivatandavam*)
4. 'Where There Is' (*Rendu Penkuttigal*)
5. 'Oh My Darling' (*Oru Sumangaliyude Katha*)
6. 'Chalo-Chalo' (*Janam*)
7. 'Najani Ratriye' (*Daivatinde Vigartigal*)
8. 'Nanthyar Vilakkum' (*Daivatinde Vigartigal*)
9. 'Jinchik-Chikacha' (*Kalamariyil Kalyan Yogam*)
10. 'Ellaroom Chollanam' (*Ezhunilappanthal*)
11. 'Siddharth' (*Siddharth*)
12. 'Manassilore' (*Rapid Action Force*)
13. 'Melam Gutti' (*Rapid Action Force*)
14. 'Vaave' (*Pothen Vava*)
15. 'Allolam A. Andigallu' (*Ideal Couple*)
16. 'Vidhiyunnu Kodhiyunu' (*Bombay March 12*)
17. 'Amburane' (*Lucifer*)
18. 'L Anthem' (*Lucifer*)

Video Albums

1. 'Aila'
2. 'Kolkata-Kolkata'
3. 'Tsunami' (in Bangla, Hindi and Tamil)
4. 'Drink to Me'
5. 'Doordarshan – Pop Time'
6. 'I Believe in Music'
7. 'Chhota-Chhota'
8. 'White Winged'
9. 'Windmills of Mind'
10. 'Jambalaya'

11. 'Bombay Meri Hai'
12. 'Care of Kolkata'
13. 'Didi'
14. 'Habibi'
15. 'Night Names'
16. 'Prakrit'
17. 'Poshto'
18. 'Ranna-Vanna'
19. 'Shoes in a Saree'
20. 'Bachhor-Bachhor Marthe Ashur'
21. 'Skyfall'
22. 'Aalote-Aalote'
23. 'World Cup Goli Cricket'
24. 'One Day'

Songs in Other Languages

1. 'Era Bini Tu' (Fiji)
2. 'Pankhira' (Gujarati)
3. 'Dhagalalagali' (Marathi)
4. 'Lily Merlin' (German)
5. 'Tulips from Amsterdam' (English)
6. 'Tikjala' (Russian)
7. 'Kandy Lamisi'
8. 'Kannoni'
9. 'Longa Vachcha' (Punjabi)
10. 'Kali Teri' (Punjabi)
11. 'Anjan Ki Siti' (Marwari)
12. 'Unchi Atariya' (Bhojpuri)
13. 'Tuk Dekhi Mur Ga' (Assamese)
14. 'Kali Pagga' (Dogri)